BATTLING TERRORISM

In memory of my late father R. Jackson Nyamuya Maogoto Sr. His guiding philosophy – always dream with your eyes open; your dreams will come true – is a source of inspiration. Thanks are due to him for instilling in me the doctrine that the search to know constitutes one of the highest values in human society. This book is dedicated to Helena Anne Anolak, a fine, young lady with a heart of gold and endless faith in humanity. Her moral and emotional support was as valuable as the time I spent writing this book.

Battling Terrorism

Legal Perspectives on the Use of Force and
the War on Terror

JACKSON NYAMUYA MAOGOTO
University of Newcastle, Australia

ASHGATE

Published by
Ashgate Publishing Limited
Gower House
Croft Road
Aldershot
Hampshire GU11 3HR
England

Ashgate Publishing Company
Suite 420
101 Cherry Street
Burlington, VT 05401-4405
USA

Ashgate website: http://www.ashgate.com

British Library Cataloguing in Publication Data
Maogoto, Jackson Nyamuya, 1975-
   Battling terrorism : legal perspectives on the use of force
   and the war on terror
   1. Intervention (International law) 2. Terrorism - Prevention
   3. War on Terrorism, 2001-
   I. Title
   341.5'84

Library of Congress Cataloging-in-Publication Data
Maogoto, Jackson Nyamuya, 1975-
   Battling terrorism : legal perspectives on the use of force and the war on terror /
by Jackson Nyamuya Maogoto.
      p. cm.
   Includes bibliographical references and index.
   ISBN 0-7546-4407-3
   1. War (International law) 2. War on Terrorism, 2001--Law and legislation--United
States. 3. Terrorism--Prevention--International
cooperation. I. Title.

   KZ6374.M36 2005
   345'.02--dc22

                                                                                2005005530
ISBN 0 7546 4407 3

Printed and bound in Great Britain by TJ International Ltd, Padstow, Cornwall.

Contents

Acknowledgements

I wish to acknowledge the support of my mother Mary S. G. Maogoto, the person who first taught me how to read and write. I acknowledge the support of my siblings (Richard, Edwin and Lillian). I wish to also make warm mention of my mentor Professor Tim McCormack, Director, Asia-Pacific Centre for Military Law (University of Melbourne). The values of hard work and rigorous intellectual curiosity that he instilled in me as a postgraduate student continue to motivate me in seeking new intellectual horizons.

I acknowledge the material support of the University of Newcastle and in particular the financial support extended in the form of an Early Career Research Grant. Thanks too to the School of Law, especially the support, guidance and inspiration of the Dean, Professor Ted Wright, Deputy Dean, Katherine Lindsay and Professor Frank Bates.

Last and by no means least, a special word of gratitude to Ashgate Publishing Ltd who made this project possible. I am indebted to the team at Ashgate for their generous professional advice and enlightening guidance which made a daunting task much easier.

Introduction

At the beginning of the 20th century and particularly during the era of the League of Nations, the freedom to resort to war became more and more restricted. The right of self-defence gained in significance, displacing the expansive right of self-preservation. This development first culminated in the conclusion of the Kellogg-Briand Pact in 1928.[1] The general prohibition of war laid down in Article I of the Pact was subject only to the reservation of the right of self-defence.[2] Consequently, it was solely in the exercise of the right of self-defence that use of military force could still be lawful. The failure of the League to enforce the constraints on the waging of warfare, however, paved the way for sovereign excesses leading to the outbreak of World War II. The end of World War II saw the birth of the United Nations and another effort to put in place an international security regime to guarantee peace.

When the UN Charter was drafted in 1945, the right of self-defence was the only included exception (reserved to state discretion) to the general prohibition of the use of force. Previously, in addition to self-defence, customary international law had accepted reprisal, retaliation and retribution as legitimate responses by states whose interests had been injured.[3] Under the UN Charter,[4] unilateral acts of force not characterized as self-defence, regardless of motive, were made illegal. Individual or collective self-defence became the cornerstone relating to use of force and since then has been invoked with regard to almost every use of external military force.

The volatile Cold War era that ushered in the UN era saw to it that any use of external military force by states was almost always pegged on the right of self-defence in response to an attack rather than in anticipation. The dangers of a recognition of pre-emptive or anticipatory self-defence were easily understood. In addition, condemnation was almost always certain whenever any attempts were made to base use of force on any of the earlier acceptable forms of self-help recognized in customary international law.

The UN Charter, while seeming to present a neat and tidy regime on the use of force, nonetheless reflects the drafters singular focus on creating a political system to govern conflicts between states.[5] They did not contemplate the existence of international terrorists nor '... fully anticipate the existence, tenacity and technology of modern day terrorism'.[6] The UN Charter simply does not directly address the subtler modes in which terrorists began to operate in the post-World War II period.[7]

Against a background of wars by proxy in the Cold War era fuelled by divisive bipolar politics, terrorist violence was undergoing transformation and escalating precipitously. As national liberation movements increasingly attained their goal of self-determination, terrorism motivated by religious and ideological motivations took centre stage and frequently led to acts of violence with higher levels of fatalities than the relatively more targeted incidents of violence perpetrated by many secular liberation movements. The confluence of terrorists and state sponsorship was transforming ordinary groups, with otherwise limited capabilities, into more powerful and menacing opponents, converting them from weak and financially impoverished groups into formidable, well-endowed terrorist organizations with ability to attract recruits and sustain their struggle.[8]

States generally initiate a legal response as their first reaction to international terrorist activities. Until recently, the law enforcement approach predominated counter-terrorism responses. Legal mechanisms such as extradition and prosecution are primary examples of legal responses used by states against international terrorists. This approach considers terrorist events as purely criminal acts to be addressed by the domestic criminal justice system and its components. Equally important, a law enforcement response to terrorist acts *ensures due process* and is a more precise instrument in meting out *individualized justice*. Despite the clear-cut positives that the domestic legal enforcement framework offers, it was proving to be an inadequate and insufficient mechanism for deterring terrorist attacks especially in the face of rising capabilities of transnational terrorist entities with the capacity to launch devastating attacks.

In the 1980s international terrorism was coming of age and maturing with the marriage of state-sponsored terrorism and religious extremism. In addition, the world was awash with sophisticated weaponry available to terrorists everywhere, including plastic explosives and hand-held, precision-guided surface-to-air missiles. Amidst a background of rising deadliness of terrorists with easy access to a range of low-tech and high-tech weapons, states (notably Israel and the US) began to suggest that terrorist acts might be approached from a conflict management perspective, rather than exclusively from a law enforcement viewpoint. This stance was premised on the notion that if it is desired to wage war against terrorism, then terrorists must be seen, not as criminals, but as persons jeopardizing national security. The belief is that only the use of armed force will result in the degree of decisive action that will minimize the likelihood that offenders will go unpunished. Isolating terrorist groups and states supporting terrorism seemed the urgent (though not new) primary goal of international cooperation aiming at pressuring countries to make measures unilaterally or multilaterally to deprive terrorist groups of mobility, safe havens and sources of income.

It was increasingly clear that modern terrorists were successfully choosing technology to exploit the vulnerabilities of modern societies. With citizens tending to live, work and travel in close proximity, providing concentrated targets, modern societies are particularly susceptible to massive attacks and weapons of mass destruction (WMDs).[9] This fact was not lost on perpetrators of terrorism as witnessed by its growing capabilities and lethalness throughout the Cold War era.[10]

In the early years of the UN, the use of military force as a counter-terrorism measure was debated almost entirely in terms of Israeli counter-terror practice. This is not surprising considering that a Palestinian group (the militant Popular Front for the Liberation of Palestine) was responsible for the incident that is considered to mark the beginning of the current era of international terrorism when it hijacked an Israeli El Al commercial flight on 22 July 1968.[11]

Israel opted for a mixture of retaliatory and anticipatory defence actions. Frequently, it resorted with success to pre-emptive destruction of enemy military assets premised on 'anticipatory self-defence'. Although the right of self-defence against an actual armed attack is clear, the use of force to retaliate for past attacks or to deter future attacks was (and still is) controversial. Many emphasized that Israel's defiance of the United Nations and UN war-decision law destroyed respect for the United Nations and international law. However, United Nations debates emphasizing the illegality of the pre-emptive character of the Israeli actions suffered from a tendency to mix *jus ad bellum* with *jus in bello*, thus preventing development of any meaningful discourse. Part of the reason for the stifled legal and political discourse regarding use of military force in counter-terrorism is of course the very nature of the Arab-Israeli conflict, shrouded as it was (and is) in notions of just cause and just means, creating a headache in the process of distinguishing lawful insurgency from terrorism on the one hand and legitimate military reaction to terrorism or insurgency on the other hand. Many thorny questions in relation to the Arab-Israeli conflict served to split the international community, since the use of military force was against an uncertain mosaic of a war of national liberation and a war against terrorism.[12]

The debate on the use of military force assumed renewed discussion and a different dimension shorn of all the complexities of the Arab-Israeli conflict with the US attack on Libya on 14 April 1986. The United States (whose interests and citizens were and are a primary target of terrorists) replaced Israel in the classic confrontation between the Security Council's restrictive view of counter-terror self-defence and the concomitant permissive view of war of national liberation terrorism, as well as the long-held Israeli view of the efficacy of counter-terror self-defence and deterrence. The United States had reached the conclusion that counter-terror self-defence and deterrence warranted preventive/retaliatory attacks. The United States stance was of particular interest as it was unencumbered by the political and legal complexities of Israel, involved in a war against terror, suppression of resistance and obligations of an occupying power all on one tapestry.

The US stance of 'passive, reactive and patient defence response'[13] to terrorism of the early 1970s which lasted to the spring of 1984 had shifted to a 'no compromise' and very proactive approach encapsulated in the Reagan and Shultz Doctrines.[14] The Reagan and Shultz Doctrines were part of the growing attempt in the 1980s to find new avenues within the international framework on the use of force to combat the increasing number and lethality of international terrorist acts.[15] Existing domestic and international mechanisms had proven to be spectacularly ineffective in dealing with the terrorist threat. Despite hundreds of terrorist attacks international terrorists continued to elude justice. Attempts to have terrorists captured and extradited often failed and the trend then and now is much the same. Unilateral military actions which had been outlawed by the UN Charter became a preferred but controversial response. Depriving terrorist groups of mobility and safe havens became the urgent primary goal of unilateral action.

With the end of the Cold War, a new era of hot peace was seemingly in the making. One thing remained constant and fixed – the justification for external use of military force by states (excepting UN authorized missions) remained pegged on self-defence. However, the atmosphere of great optimism, a hope for reduced international tension and a greater chance for world peace masked the fact that most of the world's problems were not simply by-products of global politics, a view that seemed to prevail during the political bipolarization of the Cold War era. In particular, terrorism was gradually undergoing a transformation into a separate, generic policy issue. The development of terrorism as a transnational enterprise would soon make it more than ever a separate unit of policy concern not simply for states, but the international community. In view of the fact that terrorist groups may have reach and sophistication that is global, there is little doubt that international terrorism presents a threat that traditional theories for the use of military force are inadequate to deal with, and that were not contemplated at the time of the UN Charter.[16]

Though terrorism has always been high on the international agenda, it was the 11 September 2001 (hereinafter 'September 11') attacks that brought the issue of terrorism and the international regime on the use of force into a new, urgent and sustained debate. The tragic events of September 11 prompted the international community to examine international terrorism anew. The magnitude of the acts went beyond terrorism as it was known and statements from various capitals around the world pointed to a need to develop new strategies to confront a new reality. The US response (with the active support of the international community) was to launch a broad assault on Al-Qaeda and its host government, the Taliban regime of Afghanistan. The attacks of September 11, the American response and the international community's approval of the military action represent a new paradigm in the international law relating to the use of force. Previously acts of terrorism were seen as criminal acts, carried out by private, non-governmental entities. In contrast, the September 11 attacks were being regarded as an act of war. This marked a turning point in the long-standing premise in international law that force, aggression and armed attacks are instruments of relations between states. Terrorism was no longer merely a serious threat to peace and stability to be combated through domestic and international penal mechanisms; use of force was now seen as an attractive and satisfying countermeasure in managing terrorism.

September 11 generated a new dimension in legal and political discourse. The attacks generated the momentum for the international legal system to co-opt military response to counter terrorism within the regime of lawful force contained in the UN Charter. With the US at the forefront, many of the strict requirements of the *Nicaragua Case*, which considered the issue of state responsibility in light of international norms on the use of force, are now being challenged as well as the requirement that self-defence can only be in response to, not in anticipation of, an armed attack. These developments seem to infuse Article 51 of the UN Charter with a new focus. However, what appeared to be an emerging development in the use of force was soon trapped in murky waters. Support for the US (and any new discourse on the use of terrorism) fizzled away when the US chose to squander the legal and moral capital it had gained in the action against Afghanistan by invading Iraq on a mish-mash of justifications that were generally met with international scepticism and subsequently discredited.

Despite the US's misadvised adventure into Iraq, terrorism and in particular counter-terrorism measures now occupy central ground on the international agenda. Because of the nature of threats posed by international terrorism, it is claimed that a proper understanding of the right of self-defence should now extend to authorizing pre-emptive attacks against potential aggressors, cutting them off before they are able to launch strikes that might be devastating in their scale and scope. This guiding principle (reminiscent of the Cold War era Reagan and Shultz Doctrines) is being worked up as a central tenet of the United States' strategic posture – the 'Bush Doctrine'.[17] The fullest exposition was given by President George Bush Jr in a speech at West Point on 1 June 2002. Warning that the United States faced 'a threat with no precedent' through the proliferation of weapons of mass destruction and the emergence of global terrorism, President Bush said that the traditional strategies of deterrence and containment were no longer sufficient.[18] Deterrence meant nothing 'against shadowy terrorist networks with no nation or citizens to defend' and containment could not work 'when unbalanced dictators with weapons of mass destruction can deliver those weapons on missiles or secretly provide them to terrorist allies'.[19] Under these circumstances, he concluded, 'If we wait for threats to fully materialize, we will have waited too long.'[20] US administration officials have stressed that the kind of pre-emptive actions that are envisaged by this doctrine are not exclusively military; nevertheless it clearly allows for armed strikes as a last resort. Although Iraq is the most obvious case in which a policy of pre-emptive self-defence was invoked, the doctrine is intended to have wider application.

Recognizing the inapplicability of the right to self-defence in its classic formulation to its 'war on terror', the Bush administration attempts to strike new legal ground with the strategy of 'offensive defense'. This term is, however, misleading as it implies an attack in the shadow of an imminent and unavoidable threat from another and sidesteps the real logic underlying the doctrine – strike now because the threat, while distant, may be harder to eliminate in the future.[21] Professor George E. Bisharat identifies the fundamental problem of this approach: 'There is no such doctrine currently accepted in international law and the suggestion that there should be due to the unique challenges of the "war on terror," has generally been met with consternation.'[22] A future in which individual states act unilaterally to prevent perceived incipient threats or to retaliate against terrorist attacks across the globe is one that would decentralize the use of war and lead to anarchic, piecemeal, random, and unilateral enforcement of the desirable shared goal of stamping out terrorism.

September 11 presents a challenge for international law. Use of military force as a countermeasure against terrorism can no longer be dismissed as a heavy-handed response. There is a need to address legitimate states' concerns or risk letting states establish new practices in a vacuum. Professor Philip Bobbitt identifies the challenge of creating a new legal regime for the post-Cold War era, in which the international community now faces undeterrable threats.[23] Bobbitt notes two distinct temptations; to spiral into 'a chaos of self-help' or, alternatively, to 'use the discredited multilateral institutions of the nation-state as a way of frustrating action in order to control the acts of its strongest member, the United States'.[24]

If one accepts that some right of pre-emptive self-defence might exist under international law, the next question is how far it extends. The Bush Doctrine seeks to 'effectively clos[e] down dangerous regimes before they become imminent threats' and thus represents a usurpation of the Security Council's role in global affairs. With states like Iraq, though, Professor Benvenisti argues that the conventional rules still apply.[25] It is essential to the international system to have a clear principle that 'no single country has the capacity to make a judgment over the intentions of another country'.[26]

Professor Thomas Franck, in support of Benvenisti's position, argues that it is inherently undesirable for the United States or any other country to take pre-emptive action unilaterally.[27] He characterizes the difficulty posed by anticipatory self-defence as that of finding a reasonable middle ground between the *reductio ad absurdum* of two extremes:

> If you insisted that a small country wait for a neighbour to attack it with nuclear weapons before responding…everybody would just say the law is an ass. On the other hand, if you have a law which says that any country that feels threatened is free to attack any country from which it feels the threat is emanating, then you don't have a law at all.[28]

Extending this point to a general principle, Franck says that when you have a rule in international law that has to be interpreted reasonably (as with the right of self-defence), the process by which it is interpreted becomes more important than the substance of the rule itself. It could not simply be interpreted by a single country, with no attempt to persuade other countries of the necessity of its actions. 'If the process [of interpreting the rule] is an entirely unilateral one, in which the strong do as they will, and the weak have to accept it, then we're right back to the Peloponnesian wars …'[29]

This book has as its central aim an examination of the use of military force to counter terrorism. It is premised on the central theme that the right to self-defence is visibly enrolled in a process of change, and evaluates this within the framework of the uncertainty and indeterminacy of state practice and the legal framework on the use of force articulated in the UN Charter. What is the status of pre-emptive self-defence and other forms of self-help in international law, and how do they apply towards rogue states? Is the use of lethal and non-lethal military force an acceptable trend in the fight against state-sponsored terrorism? These are important questions which the book will grapple with.

Chapter 1 of the book covers the international regime on the use of force. The chapter addresses the development relating to the use of force in international law. It tackles the League of Nations and the United Nations regimes on the use of force to lay ground for the subsequent chapters which discuss the use of military force to counter terrorism through the prism of international law. Threaded through the chapter too is the steady rise of terrorism and its ascendancy to the international agenda. Chapter 2 focuses on developing a working definition of terrorism as well as offering a *tour de horizon* of the range of countermeasures that states have from time to time used in countering terrorism. This falls in two broad approaches – law enforcement and conflict management.

Chapter 3 commences the discussion on the use of force and terrorism, actively focusing on the Cold War era. The chapter notes the UN's chequered history in dealing with terrorism and the resulting moves by states (particularly the US and Israel) to seek to circumvent the provisions of the UN Charter or to stretch them in seeking to co-opt the use of military force as a valid countermeasure against terrorism. It notes the uncertainty of these arguments based on the fact that they are anchored in unclear terms, with the use of force in self-defence often intertwined with the concepts of reprisal and retaliation. While the chapter will make reference to relevant major incidents involving Israel, the book will not seek to undertake a systematic look at Israel and terrorism, considering that the Arab-Israeli conflict presents a difficult tapestry of war against terror and war in the cause of national liberation that has spawned thousands of hostile acts in one form or another.

Chapters 4 and 5 of the book move to the post Cold War era, in particular focusing on post-September 11. Chapter 4 explores the notion of anticipatory self-defence that is encapsulated in the Bush Doctrine – a strong echo of the right of self-preservation and its collorary, anticipatory self-defence.[30] The chapter offers an insight into the tenets of the Bush Doctrine, discussing the Afghanistan invasion and then delving into the Iraqi invasion. In Chapter 5, the book will seek to set the parameters for state-sponsored terrorism through an evaluation of the tenets of state responsibility and the enshrined norms on the use of force contained in the UN Charter. Chapter 6 concludes with a general overview of the regime on the use of force past and focuses on the current climate. It notes generally that there is a need to rethink the existing rules on the use of force in an altered international security environment and importantly that viable solutions can be reached only by states maintaining the centrality of the UN even in the face of unconventional threats.

Notes

1　*General Treaty for the Renunciation of War*, signed at Paris, 27 August 1928, 94 L.N.T.S., 47; United States Statutes at Large Vol. 46, Part 2, 2343 (hereinafter *Kellogg-Briand Pact*).

2　Article I of the *Kellogg-Briand Pact*, ibid., provided:

> The High Contracting Parties solemnly declare in the names of their respective peoples that they condemn recourse to war for the solution of international controversies, and renounce it, as an instrument of national policy in their relations with one another.

3　Reprisal allows a state to commit an act that is otherwise illegal to counter the illegal act of another state. Retaliation is the infliction upon the delinquent state of the same injury that it has caused the victim. Retribution is a criminal law concept, implying vengeance, that is sometimes used loosely in the international law context as a synonym for retaliation.

4　See UN Charter, 59 Stat 1031, JS No 933, 3 Bevans 1153, done at San Francisco, 26 June 1945, arts. 39–51.

5　See James P. Rowles (1987), 'Military Responses to Terrorism: Substantive and Procedural Constraints in International Law', 81 *American Society of International Law Proceedings* 287, 310.

6　Mark Baker (1987), 'Terrorism and the Inherent Right of Self-Defence (A Call to Amend Article 51 of the United Nations Charter)', 10 *Houston Journal of International Law* 25.

7　Terrorism has existed for at least two millennia in one form or another and is likely to remain a fixture on political agendas, both domestic and international, for years to come. Originally terrorism had religious roots but reinvented itself in the 1800s, marking the rise of modern terrorism as nationalism, anarchism and other secular political movements emerged – terrorism was essentially antimonarchical, embraced by rebels and constitutionalists. During the 1920s and 1930s, terrorism became a tool of states, associated more with the repressive practices employed by totalitarian states than with the violence of non-state groups. After World War II, terrorism reverted to its previous revolutionary associations but still maintained an attraction for ideologically motivated groups. The late 1960s marked the resurgence of ideologically and/or religious driven international terrorism.

8   Bruce Hoffman, 'Terrorism', *Microsoft Encarta Online Encyclopedia* (2004), 14 March 2004 online at http://encarta.msn.com.

9   Jessica Stern (1999), *The Ultimate Terrorists*, Cambridge, Mass.: Harvard University Press, 4.

10   Between 1970 and 1995, on average each year brought 206 more incidents and 441 more fatalities. Stern, ibid., 6.

11   As Dr Bill Hoffman notes, 'Although commercial planes had often been hijacked before, this was the first clearly political hijacking.' Hoffman, 'Terrorism', ibid.

12   Many difficult issues surround the conflict, posing a number of complex issues including: Doesn't international law permit an insurgent force that is directed toward support of fundamental rights and rules? Aren't insurgents entitled to the right to use certain levels and types of force against a regime that represses their peremptory right to 'self-determination' and hence 'national liberation'? Isn't Israel bound necessarily to whatever its preservation and safety require? Hasn't a kind of holy war warrant been extended to the PLO where *jus ad bellum* judgments about the war of national liberation have swallowed up any concern for the war-conduct, *jus in bello* issues?

13   Shirlyce Manning (December 1995-January 1996), 'The United States' Response To International Air Safety', 61 *Journal of Air Law and Commerce* 505, 519.

14   Ronald Crelinsten and Alex P. Schmid (1992), eds, *Western Responses to Terrorism: A Twenty-Five Year Balance Sheet* 40.

15   See, e.g., Gregory Francis Intoccia (1987), 'American Bombing of Libya: An International Legal Analysis', 19 *Case Western Reserve Journal of International Law* 177; W. Michael Reisman (1999), 'International Legal Responses to Terrorism', 22 *Houston Journal of International Law* 3.

16   Wallace Warriner (1988), 'The Unilateral Use of Coercion under International Law: A Legal Analysis of the United States Raid on Libya on April 14, 1986', 37 *Naval Law Review* 49, 64.

17   See Commencement Address by President George Bush at the West Point Military Academy graduation, 1 June 2002, announcing an expansive new policy of pre-emptive military action. The speech can be accessed online at http://www.whitehouse.gov/news/releases/2002/06/20020601-3.html. (hereinafter West Point Commencement Speech); (last visited 1 May 2004).

18   Ibid.

19   Ibid.

20   Ibid.

21   George E. Bisharat (2003), 'Tyranny with Justice: Alternatives to War in the Confrontation with Iraq', 7 *Journal of Gender, Race and Justice* 1, 46. See also David Krieger and Devon Chafee (2003), 'Law Triumphs over Force: For the Moment', in Richard Falk and David Krieger, (eds.), *The Iraq Crisis and International Law*, Santa Barbara: Nuclear Age Peace Foundation, 7.

22   Bisharat, ibid., 46.

23   Philip Bobbitt (2002), *The Shield of Achilles: War, Peace and the Course of History*, New York: Knopf, 820–21.

24   Ibid. In a solemn observation, Patrick McLain notes that:

> The multilateral institutions of the nation-state should not, however, be discarded when the alternative offered by the United States is so standardless as to be tantamount to inviting the chaos of self-help.

Patrick McLain (2003), 'Settling the Score with Saddam: Resolution 1441 and Parallel Justifications for the Use of Force against Iraq', 13 *Duke Journal of Comparative and International Law* 233, 266.

25   Eyal Benvenisti, 'Iraq and the Bush Doctrine of Pre-emptive Self-Defence', Crimes of War Project, Expert Analysis, 1 June 2004 online at http://www.crimesofwar.org/expert/bush-benvenisti.html.

26   Ibid.

27   Thomas Franck, 'Iraq and the Bush Doctrine of Pre-emptive Self-Defence', Crimes of War Project, Expert Analysis, 1 June 2004 online at http://www.crimesofwar.org/expert/bush-franck.html.

28   Ibid.

29   Ibid.

30   President Bush noted that American security will require transforming the military to be ready to strike at a moment's notice in any dark corner of the world. He further added that 'All nations that decide for aggression and terror will pay a price.' West Point Commencement Speech.

Chapter 1

The Development of the Law Relating to the Use of Force in International Law

Introduction

The law of permissible uses of force in international law dates back to ancient Greek and Hindu law.[1] Following the Christianization of the Roman Empire, the use of force abroad was driven by the just war doctrine. Under this doctrine, force could be used as long as it complied with the divine will.[2] The foundation of this theory was that order was a deterrent to force, and force threatened order.[3] At the time, war was used to punish wrongs and restore the status quo. During this time, St. Augustine elaborated and gave authority to the concept of just war (*bellum justum*) and theorized that war for the purposes of aggression was unjust.[4] Natural law theory maintained that lawfulness of the use of force derived from the justness of its cause premised on the assumption that violations of natural law could be vindicated with force to the extent that justice permitted.[5]

The just war concept remained the dominant guide on lawful resort to war throughout the early centuries but developments in the 14th to 16th centuries rendered the already vague and easily manipulated concept almost meaningless in the face of the emergence of independent princes and national states.[6] As the state became supremely powerful in the Age of Absolutism, the demands of realpolitik, buttressed by legal positivist theories of state sovereignty, brushed aside natural law doctrines. The rise of state sovereignty and power made ideas of divine justice and its related set of criteria distinguishing lawful from unlawful war irrelevant. International practice of the 15th and 16th centuries exposed the unviability of this rule. It was impossible to determine in any particular case whose cause was just and whose not. As a result, the rule of just war which at the outset was understood as a legal restraint on war, was proving to be the opposite as international law increasingly became indifferent with regard to resort to war.

The just war theory lost its (virtual) war-preventing effects in the 17th century during the ferocious Thirty Years War (between Catholic and Protestant states) when it was dramatically recognized that recourse to war could be just for either side. In the midst of the war, a new standard on the use of force was articulated by Dutch lawyer Hugo Grotius, generally acclaimed as the Father of International Law[7] who redefined the just war theory as self-defence.[8] Under the new theory of self-defence, force was permissible to protect property and punish wrongs suffered by citizens.[9] In essence, Grotius refined the just war doctrine to exclude general evil contemplated by opposing states and required that some injury must have been suffered by the state that resorted to force. At the end of the war, the Peace Treaty of Westphalia was signed in 1648.[10] This treaty marked the rise of the modern nation-state and dispensed with the just war doctrine entirely,[11] replacing it with a universal concept of state sovereignty that eviscerated the source of just war actions.[12]

This chapter carries out a *tour de horizon* of the development of the various concepts relating to use of force in the era of the modern nation-state as well as the development of terrorism. Ironically, terrorism in modern times gained popularization through its use by the state as a tool of governance. However, it was to undergo several transformations in the course of the 19th and 20th centuries. The chapter covers the pre-collective security regime era as well as the collective security regimes constructed under the League of Nations and the United Nations which aimed to curb unbridled sovereign excesses very much evident during the many centuries when balance of power was the favoured stance. Through an introduction of the various forms of force, the chapter sets the stage for subsequent analysis and in particular the controversy over the UN Charter regime on the use of force and its relationship to customary international law. This remains a contested issue, considering that frequently states, especially in combating terrorism, have appealed to customary international law in the face of the restrictive UN Charter, which in any case does not mention nor address terrorism.

The Modern Nation-state and the Entrenchment of Force and Terrorism

The inauguration of the modern nation-state with the conclusion of the Peace Treaty of Westphalia[13] and the growing maturity of a state-centric international society, however, escalated the use of the institution of force, as the state-centric picture of the world was coloured by insecurity and fear of other states, necessitating individual states to look after their own security and possibly desire to dominate others by extending their hegemonic power. As modern international society developed, use of military force was seen as a normal feature of international relations and an important attribute of the state.

The institution of military force was gradually established as a central technique of influence in international relations through which states attempted to change their environment in accordance with determined aims and objectives or attempted to adapt to the environment. There was not a great deal of theorizing on the causes of war in general – as opposed to commentaries on particular wars – because most people thought that the causes of war, at least in the international system of the era, were obvious. 'States went to war for gain, or in self-defence because they were attacked by some other state acting for gain.'[14] Simply put, war was inherent in the nature of sovereignty – it was what states did, sometimes successfully, sometimes not.

Post-Westphalia international law, such as it was, imposed no effective restraints on nation-states and their leaders in starting and carrying out aggressive wars. 'Foreign policy was premised on a need to protect and advance something which was called "national interest" and, though clarity on this point has never been achieved, the tendency then and now was to define that notion primarily in terms of the state's power and well-being, and secondarily in terms of its citizenry's welfare.'[15] Thus national interests rather than 'moral abstractions' of principles and norms guided state action – a mode that favoured political expedience over appreciable gain in norms and principles.

> With imperialistic ambitions taking root, national interest came to encapsulate in part, extension of a state's territory and consolidation of hegemonic power. What varied was the degree of shrewdness in the calculation of self-interest by diplomats and politicians who dominated the discourse of international relations.[16]

By the 18th century, in Europe there had formed a system of self-conscious states ruled by statesmen who practised the diplomatic art of balancing power with power. War was still considered to be the sport of kings loosely hedged in by international law.[17] War was never absent in the international system as some nations sought to consolidate their hegemonies and others sought to reconfigure their governments. The advent of nationalism, and with it notions of statehood and citizenship based on the common identity of a people rather than the lineage of a royal family, was breeding serious antimonarchical sentiment and invigorating radical constitutionalists. In 1789, the French Revolution erupted, undergoing a number of phases from moderate to radical. The radical revolution with its reign of terror led to the popularization of the word 'terrorism' to describe a new system of government adopted during the French Revolution (1789–99). This marked the beginning of modern terrorism.

'The *regime de la terreur* (Reign of Terror) was intended to promote democracy and popular rule by ridding the revolution of its enemies and thereby purifying it.'[18] Unlike terrorism as it is commonly understood today, to mean a *revolutionary* or anti-government activity undertaken by non-state or subnational entities, the *regime de la terreur* was an instrument of governance wielded by the recently established French revolutionary *state*.[19] The revolutionary leader Maximilien Robespierre firmly believed that virtue was the mainspring of a popular government at peace, but that during the time of revolution it must be allied with terror in order for democracy to triumph. He famously proclaimed: 'Terror is nothing but justice, prompt, severe and inflexible; it is therefore an emanation of virtue.'[20] 'However, the oppression and violent excesses of the *terreur* transformed it into a feared instrument of the state. From that time on, *terrorism* has had a decidedly negative connotation.'[21] During this era, terrorism was internal and largely regarded as the sphere of the police and intelligence apparatus.

The ascendancy of Napoleon and his militaristic fixation in the aftermath of the French Revolution as the first modern military dictatorship with populistic trappings ensured that the focus in Europe remained on war and the balance of power system. By the 19th century, *raison d'etat* reigned supreme, as symbolized in the doctrines of Carl von Clausewitz.[22] In the absence of an international mechanism for enforcing international law, war was a means of self-help for giving effect to claims based on international law. Such was the legal and moral authority of this notion of war as an arm of the law that, in most cases in which war was resorted to in order to increase the power and possessions of a state at the expense of others, it was described by the states in question as undertaken for the defence of a legal right.[23]

Use of Military Force and the Modern Nation-state

The medieval theory of *bellum justum* had been developed by theologians and during its existence sat uneasily as a valid rule of public international law. During the early days of the modern nation-state, military force was in effect a sanction looked upon as a legal remedy of self-help.[24] This conception of war was intimately connected with the distinction which was established in the formative period of international law and which later become entirely extinct between just and unjust wars.[25] The birth of the modern international system was accompanied by the redefinition of the just war theory as self-defence by Dutch publicist Hugo Grotius. Accepted use of military force in the post-Westphalia world was premised on self-defence or reprisal.

Generally speaking, Professor Derek Bowett notes that self-defence and reprisals are forms of the same generic remedy, self-help.[26] However he points out the critical difference in function: the true function of self-help is to impose remedial or repressive measures in order to enforce legal rights rather than preserve or restore the status quo as is characteristic of self-defence.[27]

In a concise analysis of the basic tenets of these two forms of self-help, Michael F. Lohr notes the following three common preconditions:

> (1) The target state must be guilty of a prior international delinquency against the claimant state.
> (2) An attempt by the claimant state to obtain redress or protection by other means must be known to have been made, and failed, or to be inappropriate or impossible under the circumstances.
> (3) The claimant's use of force must be limited to the necessities of the case and proportionate to the wrong done by the target state.[28]

The difference between the two forms of self-help lies in their purpose. The use of force in self-defence is permissible for the purpose of protecting the security of the state and its essential rights, in particular the rights of territorial integrity and political independence, upon which that security depends. In contrast, reprisals are punitive in character; they seek to impose retribution for the harm done, or to compel a satisfactory settlement of a dispute created by the initial illegal act, or to compel the delinquent state to abide by the law in the future. But coming after the event, and when the harm has already been inflicted, reprisals cannot be characterized as a means of protection.

Self-defence

'Historically the law of self-defence was bound up with the amorphous right of self-preservation. The right of self-preservation was seen as preceding and underlying every other obligation. It was thought that all treaties were subordinated and subject to this basic and inherent right.'[29] It was implied and read into every treaty and contract, anything said to the contrary notwithstanding. This primary right could not be lost or bargained away; it was unalienable. In the 19th century, anticipatory self-defence was still very much a topical issue. In 1861, the English jurist Travers Twiss opined that that:

Of the primary or absolute rights of a nation the most essential, and as it were, the cardinal right, upon which all others hinge, is that of self-preservation. This right necessarily involves, as subordinate rights, all other rights which are essential as means to secure this principal end.[30]

With regard to the 'right of anticipating attack', the same author stated that:

When the safety of the state is at stake, the right of self-preservation may warrant a nation in extending the precautionary measures beyond the limits of its own dominions, and even in trespassing with that object on a neighbour's territory. As the right of self-preservation is prior and paramount to the right of dominion and property, in the case of individuals, so the right of self-preservation is prior and paramount to the right of territorial inviolability in the case of nations, and if ever these rights conflict, the former is entitled to prevail within the limits of the necessity of the case.[31]

Later in the 19th century, a leading international jurist Sir Robert Phillimore asserted that:

The right of self-preservation is the first law of nations, as it is of individuals. ... It may happen that the same right may warrant her in extending precautionary measures without these limits, and even in transgressing the borders of her neighbour's territory. For International Law considers the 'Right of Self-Preservation' as prior and paramount to that of Territorial Inviolability, and, where they conflict, justifies the maintenance of the former at the expense of the latter right.[32]

Essentially then, the right of self-preservation is called into being whenever the corporate existence of a state is menaced and corresponds to the individual right of self-defence. The danger may be internal, as in the case of insurrection or rebellion, or external, as in the case of invasion, either real or threatened. The general political and legal mindset in this period was that the right of self-preservation is the first law of nations, as it is of individuals. A society which is not in condition to repel aggression from without is wanting in its principal duty to its members of which it is composed, and to the chief end of its institution. All means which do not affect the independence of other nations are lawful to this end. No nation has a right to prescribe to another what these means shall be, or to require any account of her conduct in this respect.

As this author has noted elsewhere: 'The right of self-preservation had always been capacious enough to justify action beyond what was necessary for the maintenance of the integrity of territorial domain of a state.'[33] Commenting on the right of self-preservation and the occasional necessity to undertake anticipatory action in defence of the state and its interest, in 1880 William Edward Hall, in his masterpiece *A Treatise on International Law*, asserted that:

The right of self-preservation in some cases justifies commissions of acts of violence against a friendly or neutral state, when from its position and resources it is capable of being made use of to dangerous effects by an enemy, when there is a known intention on his part so to make use of it, and when, if he is not forestalled, it is almost certain that he will succeed, either through the helplessness of the country. or by means of intrigues with a party within it.[34]

Anticipatory Self-defence

In 1818, the US established the right to enter the territory of another state to prevent terror attacks, where the host is unable or unwilling to quell a continuing threat, when it sent troops into Spanish Florida. For years, southern plantation owners and white farmers had lost runaway slaves to the Florida swamps, with friendly Seminole and Creek Indians offering refuge to the slaves and leading raids against white settlers. The US government could do little about the problem because the swamps lay deep within Spanish Florida. Matters came to a head when the Seminole Indians in Spanish Florida demanded 'arms, ammunition and provisions or the possession of the garrison at Fort Marks'.[35]

President James Monroe directed General Andrew Jackson to proceed against the Seminoles, with the explanation that the Spanish were bound by treaty to keep their Indians at peace, but were incompetent to do so.[36] Jackson invaded Florida in 1818, burned Seminole villages, hanged tribal leaders, captured Pensacola and deposed the Spanish governor. He even executed two British citizens whom he accused of having incited the Seminoles to commit atrocities against American settlers.

The idea that if a state was unable or unwilling to effectively police its territory, then a victim state could reach across borders and do the necessary stopping was not an idle one. About two decades after President Monroe's directive, the US was again at the centre of military action premised on the same justifications that Monroe had advanced in ordering military action to curb the Seminole Indians. The incident involving British action on an American vessel during the unsuccessful rebellion of 1837 in Upper Canada against British rule, was to have a deep and lasting effect on the international regime on the use of force. During this Canadian insurrection the standard for justifiable anticipatory self-defence was more clearly established.[37] It is to this incident regarding *The Caroline* to which the chapter now turns.

The Caroline Incident   In 1837, anti-British sympathizers gathered near Buffalo, New York. A large number of Americans and Canadians were similarly encamped on the Canadian side of the border, with the apparent intention of aiding these rebels. The British, in anticipation of the action, carried out a pre-emptive strike to defuse the threat. *The Caroline*, an American vessel which the rebels used for supplies and communications, was boarded in an American port, at midnight, by an armed group, acting under orders of a British officer. The group set the vessel on fire and let it drift over Niagara Falls.

The US protested the incident, which claimed the lives of at least two US citizens. The British government replied that the threat posed by *The Caroline* was established, that the American laws were not being enforced along the border, and that the destruction was an act of necessary self-defence. In the controversy that followed, the US did not deny that circumstances were conceivable which would justify this action, and Great Britain admitted the necessity of showing circumstances of extreme urgency. The two countries differed only on the question of whether the facts brought the case within the exceptional principle. Charles Cheney Hyde summed up the incident by saying that 'the British force did that which the US itself would have done, had it possessed the means and disposition to perform its duty'.[38]

Where it is understood as 'anticipatory self-defence', the customary right to pre-empt has its modern origins in the *Caroline* incident which established that the serious threat of armed attack may justify militarily defensive action. In an exchange of diplomatic notes between the governments of the US and Great Britain, then US Secretary of State Daniel Webster outlined a framework for self-defence which did not require a prior attack. Military response to a threat was judged permissible so long as the danger posed was '*instant, overwhelming, leaving no choice of means and no moment of deliberation*'.[39]

> Until the Caroline case, self-defence was a political justification for what, from a legal perspective, were ordinary acts of war. The positivist international law of the 19th century rejected natural law distinctions between just and unjust wars. The Caroline case did nothing to prevent aggression, but it did draw a legal distinction between war and self-defence.[40]

As long as the act being defended against was not itself an act of war, peace would be maintained – a matter of considerable importance to relatively weak countries, as the US then was. The customary right of self-defence involved the assumption that the force used must be proportionate to the threat. The formula used by Webster in relation to the *Caroline* incident attracted writers by virtue of his insistence that self-defence must involve 'nothing unreasonable or excessive; since the act, justified by the necessity of self-defence, must be limited by that necessity, and kept clearly within it'.[41]

The Webster correspondence in reality merely stated a right of self-defence which had a more limited application than the vague right of self-preservation and the broad and political concept of self-defence found in 19th century thought and practice. Evidently the legal concept of self-defence comprehended proportionality as a special requirement in the law of nations, representing an attempt to create the necessary distinction between self-defence and self-help in reaction to an historical tendency to confuse them.

The *Caroline* criteria of necessity and proportionality became widely accepted as customary international law. However, the period between the *Caroline* incident and before the advent of the League of Nations remained of a diffuse character, reflecting the lack of the legal regulation of the use of force. A state, when exposed to a grave, imminent danger, was fully justified in committing any action liable to avert that danger, even if, under normal conditions, such action would constitute a wrong and a violation of international law. It can be concluded that customary law permitted anticipatory action in the face of imminent danger. The *Caroline* doctrine permitted preventive action in a context in which self-defence was equated with self-preservation.

There can be little doubt that the right of self-preservation and the doctrine of necessity comprehended anticipatory action. The particular fault of this seeming customary rule was that it provided no clear guidance as to the determination of cases in which anticipatory acts of force may be justified. Despite the Webster formula, the *Caroline case* was primarily verbal, lacking any well-established state practice to prop it up firmly. The *Caroline* doctrine was very much in tune with the general thinking of the 19th century as reflected in the works of leading jurists of the day, some of whose positions have been mentioned above. The acceptance of the notion of anticipatory self-defence carried over into the 20th century. In the opening years of the century, John Westlake, a leading international law scholar, reaffirmed the right of self-preservation and its collorary, the right to anticipatory self-defence.[42]

Reprisals/Retaliation

It is of significance to note that in the heydays of anticipatory self-defence, states also dealt with each other on the basis of reciprocity. There were no supranational institutions to make or enforce international law. States had the right to retaliate against states that failed to honour bilateral or multilateral arrangements through use of reprisals (retaliation by force) in ways that would otherwise have been considered illegal. 'In the absence of a supranational authority, this form of self-help was a way for states to get compensation for their losses, punish their offenders, and deter future violations.'[43]

'The concept of reprisal engendered considerable confusion. The term was often used imprecisely; actions could be labeled "reprisals" or "retaliation" when, in fact, the proper characterization should be self-defence, and vice versa.'[44] The historical development of peacetime reprisals and the customary international law governing the use of reprisals illustrate that such acts are more than simple retaliation. The principal objective of a reprisal is not to punish (although that may be an element) but rather to compel a change in state policy or obtain reparation for injury. Further, customary international law imposes strict limitations on when, and to what degree, force can be used.

Reprisal may be defined as an otherwise illegal act of self-help to coerce an action (for example, cessation of the offending action) or obtain redress (reparation) for a prior wrong under international law. Retaliation (retribution) differs from reprisal in that its sole purpose is to inflict punishment on the offender for a past wrong. Coercion is not its intent; and it seeks nothing beyond the satisfaction of imposing a measured response for some prior transgression.

The practice of states employing reprisals against opponents had its origin in the medieval practice of 'private reprisal'.

> When a subject of one feudal state considered him or her self wronged by a subject of another state, he or she was entitled to raise his or her grievance before his or her own sovereign. Upon a satisfactory showing that a wrong had been committed against him or her by the other party and that he or she had unsuccessfully sought redress in the territory of the wrongdoer, his or her own sovereign could issue a 'Letter of Marque and Reprisal'.[45]

Reprisal was soon to be transformed with the advent of the nation-state during the Middle Ages and the expansion of commercial contacts across national boundaries. Gradually private reprisals became a means of effecting foreign policy. States authorized citizens to carry out private acts of reprisal against citizens of other states to coerce these states into particular courses of action.

In the late Middle Ages, the development of the nation-state and the sophistication of international relations saw the official assumption of private reprisal by the state as a tool of foreign policy. The state would authorize its citizens to carry out private reprisals against a hostile nation for the sole purpose of coercing it into some desired course of action. In the 16th and 17th centuries this practice was so frequently employed that it resulted in a series of 'wars' of reprisal, in which seizures aimed at disruption of enemy trade, at provoking a foe to full-scale hostilities, or merely at filling the interval between war and peace. As might be expected, any pretext would be advanced to satisfy the previously stringent requirement of unredressed injury, as individual justice became subordinated to political interests.[46] With this development, the field of private reprisals proper became entangled with that of public reprisals. Private reprisals evolved into an arm of a state's foreign policy, becoming 'public reprisals'.

Like the resort to private reprisals in the early stages of its development, the recourse to public reprisals was at the outset not subject to any particular limitations. Usually, neither the size of the state's claim nor the severity of the reprisal, as a 'punishment of the offending state' inflicted 'to enforce a change in the opponent's policy', could be easily ascertained. Furthermore, neither the claimant nor the opponent were subject to any higher authority, as both were sovereign members of the decentralized international community. Hence, apart from the obvious limitation inherent in the seizure of vessels as the singular mode of force applied, no special characteristics gave rise to the idea of regulation and limitation of recourse to public reprisals.[47]

Gradually, the scope of public reprisals expanded as more and more specific actions were removed from the general concept of war and brought under the concept of reprisals. Nations quickly recognized the advantage of employing force short of war, and actions previously associated with waging war were gradually included within the term 'peacetime reprisals'. Military occupations and pacific blockades gained acceptance as forms of peacetime reprisal. Although violent reprisals were not abandoned,[48] coercive actions based on economic, diplomatic, financial or cultural pressure were more common. By the turn of the 19th century, peacetime reprisals had come to include a range of accepted measures including minor coercion, pacific blockade and temporary military occupation. As the concept of public reprisals extended in scope, norms limiting their legitimate use began to evolve. Major aspects of the limits to reprisals were to await the advent of the 20th century when the matter was subjected to the crucible of international law in the *Naulilaa Case*, perhaps the most frequently cited instance of armed reprisal.[49]

In October 1914, at a time when Portugal was still neutral during World War I, three German officials of the German colony of South-West Africa were killed by Portuguese soldiers at Naulilaa, a Portuguese station near the border between Portuguese Angola and the German colony. German authorities took the view that the Portuguese action constituted an international wrong. Accordingly, officials of the German colony, without much inquiry, initiated a series of assaults upon the Portuguese colony. These assaults, some six in number, inflicted severe property loss and personal injury on the Portuguese colony, eventually forcing the Portuguese to retreat within their own territory.

Fourteen years later, an arbitral panel viewed disfavourably the question of whether the German actions constituted a lawful reprisal on the grounds that: (1) no illegal action on Portugal's part had warranted recourse to reprisals; (2) such recourse ought to have been preceded by a request to remedy the alleged injury; and (3) the actions chosen were disproportionate to the alleged wrong.[50] Summing up the preconditions on the use of peacetime reprisals, the *Naulilaa Case*[51] established three criteria for lawful reprisals:

> (1) a prior violation of international law by the offending state;
> (2) a request for redress of the injury which has been refused or ignored by the offending state; and
> (3) an action which is proportionate to the original injury and which ceases once reparation has been obtained.[52]

The factors cited by the arbitrators in determining the validity of Germany's reprisal have come to be accepted as the customary international law governing resort to reprisal.[53]

The Inter-relation of Self-defence, Reprisal and Retaliation Reprisals are conceptually similar to self-defence in several ways. Both may be employed to meet a reasonably foreseeable threat. The action taken in each case must be both 'necessary' and 'proportional'. Both aim at preventing injury to the vital interests of the state. In addition reprisals may be considered both 'responsive' to a prior wrong and 'anticipatory' to a continuing course of wrongful conduct. But, unlike self-defence, reprisals have an additional requirement that action be taken to change the opponents' behaviour or obtain specific redress.

A second feature which distinguishes reprisals from acts of self-defence is the time in which the response is taken. Purely defensive actions will typically be closely related in time to the hostile act, whether threatened or in progress.[54] By contrast, reprisals are normally carried out after peaceful efforts are made to obtain redress or to prevent recurrences of the offending act. Consequently, a reprisal is typically undertaken after a longer period of time than the act of self-defence.

The true nature of reprisal and retaliation is a grey area judged from state practice. Absent a reasonable belief that the wrongful action is to continue, any response by the target state would amount to an act of retaliation (punitive only), rather than an act of reprisal whose purpose is to coerce the offending state to stop its hostile or illegal activity or to provide adequate reparation in compensation for the injury inflicted. The key difference is that reprisal allows a state to commit an act that is otherwise illegal to counter the illegal act of another state, while retaliation is the infliction upon the delinquent state of the same injury that it has caused the victim.

Retaliation is based on retribution – a criminal law concept, implying vengeance, that is frequently used loosely in the international law context as a synonym for retaliation. Customary law does not condone the use of force purely for purposes of retaliation or deterrence, but states have not been averse to playing fast-and-loose with the concept, weaving it in with self-defence. This means that often it is hard on paper to draw bright line distinctions, though in reality it might be otherwise.

Unsteady Steps Towards Limiting Use of Military Force

Though war was viewed in international law as a natural function of the state and a prerogative of its unrestricted sovereignty, the European settlement of 1814 and 1815 and the Final Act of the Congress of Vienna[55] re-established the notion of public order in Europe and the principle of Balance of Power. In the latter part of the 19th century, there appeared a view of war as a judicial procedure, a means of last resort after recourse to all available means of peaceful settlement had failed.[56]

The concert of Europe and the Congress system raised a strong presumption against unilateral changes in the status quo, with territorial changes through war depending upon collective recognition for their permanence and validity.[57] However, the essentially bilateral character of international rights and obligations meant states incurred little risk of collective sanction for launching an aggressive war.

The lack of collective sanctions and the intensified technical capacity of states to inflict widespread destruction against an enemy magnified the need for open avenues of peaceful dispute resolution, so that opportunities to avoid war at least could be available. Prior to the turn of the 19th century, war was a very formal business, with uniformed armies occupying clearly delineated territory, a code of conduct which was usually (although not always) observed, a formal declaration and a formal end – the peace treaty.[58] Under these circumstances, the need for outlawing war was not a priority on the agenda of statesmen and diplomats. However, as technological and strategic developments accelerated, the Clausewitzian notion of formal warfare dominated by set-piece battles was increasingly displaced as the 'nation-at-arms' concept matured, altering the face of war forever.[59]

The Hague Peace Conferences of 1899 and 1907 provided clear and definitive, albeit modest, effort on the part of states to establish regular means for the pacific settlement of disputes to allow parties to step back from the brink of war, as well as rules on the means and methods of warfare applicable if and when war broke out.[60] The Hague Conferences, and their movement towards pacific settlement of disputes, marked the beginning of the attempts to limit the right of states to use military force as an instrument of law and as a legally recognized means for changing legal rights.[61]

In Article I of Hague Convention III of 1907 Relating to the Opening of Hostilities, the contracting powers recognized that hostilities between them must not commence without a prior and unambiguous warning in the form of either a reasoned declaration of war or an ultimatum containing a conditional declaration of war.[62] Whereas Hague Convention III was, more than anything else, a formalization of the freedom to resort to war, Article I of Hague Convention II of 1907 Respecting the Limitation of the Employment of Force for the Recovery of Contract Debts (Drago-Porter Convention) contains a substantive, if modest, restriction upon that freedom.[63] The provision prohibits the recourse to armed force for the recovery of contractual debts. This prohibition, however, is subject to the debtor state's obligation not to reject or dodge an offer of arbitral settlement. Having accepted that offer, the state must not prevent the compromise from being concluded and is bound to comply with the subsequent award. The importance of this treaty lay in the fact that it sought to restrict the use of public reprisals which had rapidly escalated.[64]

Subsequent to the Hague Conventions, a similar modest restriction on the freedom to resort to war was introduced through the so-called Bryan Treaties,[65] concluded from 1913 onwards by the US with a number of other states. In 1916, nineteen such treaties existed.[66] The contracting parties undertook the obligation to submit all disputes to a conciliation commission and not to begin hostilities prior to the commission's report, which had to be delivered within one year. Prior to this, no prohibition on the use of force existed, so that states were free to resort to war. International law did not know of any rules about when it was permissible to wage war. If a state so decides, it had the prerogative of resorting to war at any time. Force was thus permitted in the relations between states without any conditions.

Technological advancements and the birth of the notion of total war, combined with a strong body of multilateral rules and norms governing war, marked the dawn of the 20th century – and the challenge of Clausewitzian conceptions of war. The landscape of war was set to undergo dramatic transformation. The combatant/non-combatant distinction was to be blurred and the immense bloodshed by new weapons and indiscriminate tactics of warfare was to inspire a need to discipline war excesses which were no longer confined to delineated battlefields. 'Previous conceptions of use of military force as a state prerogative and a legitimate and/or rational act of state as long as the war-making body had the authority to act were to be put in doubt with the common-sense view that war represented a breakdown, a malfunctioning, of the international system.'[67]

The 'Philosophy of Terror' and the Precipitation of World War I

Ironically it was in the shadow of the moves towards peaceful settlement of international disputes and the restriction of war that the metaphysics of modern terrorism developed. Terrorism gained wide popularity in the late 19th century when it was adopted by a group of Russian revolutionaries, Narodnaya Volya, or People's Will. The small group of Russian constitutionalists, founded in 1878 to challenge Tsarist rule, used the term to describe their violent struggle 'Terrorism then assumed the more familiar antigovernment associations it has today'.[68]

From this milieu a new era of terrorism emerged, in which the concept had gained many of the familiar revolutionary, anti-state connotations of today. Its chief progenitor was arguably the Italian republican extremist, Carlo Pisacane. Pisacane is credited with defining the theory of 'propaganda by deed' – an idea that has exerted a compelling influence on rebels and terrorists alike ever since.[69] 'The didactic purpose of violence,' Pisacane argued, 'could never be effectively replaced by pamphlets, wall posters or assemblies'.[70]

To Narodnaya Volya, the first organization to put into practice Pisacane's dictum, 'propaganda by deed' meant the selective targeting of specific individuals whom the group considered the embodiment of the autocratic, oppressive state. Hence their victims were deliberately chosen for their 'symbolic' value as the dynastic heads and subservient agents of a corrupt and tyrannical regime. The Narodnaya Volya's three years of terror culminated in the assassination of the reformist Tsar Alexander II on 1 March 1881. Importantly, the group also deeply influenced individual revolutionaries and subversive organizations elsewhere. To the nascent anarchist movement, the 'propaganda by deed' strategy championed by the Narodnaya Volya provided a model to be emulated.

'Within four months of the Tsar's murder, a group of radicals in London convened an "anarchist conference" which publicly applauded the assassination and extolled tyrannicide as a means to achieve revolutionary change.'[71] Anarchist organizations which proliferated in this era were responsible for a string of assassinations of heads of state and a number of particularly notorious bombings from about 1878 until the second decade of the 20th century.[72]

On the eve of World War I, with growing unrest and irredentist ferment welling up within the decaying Ottoman and Habsburg Empires, terrorism and its revolutionary connotations offered legitimacy to the actions of disaffected nationalists. It was against this background that the fuse that triggered World War I developed. A diverse group of Bosnian Serbs, disaffected with the Habsburg suzerainty, coalesced into the Mlada Bosna, or Young Bosnians. The militant student group had close ties to the intelligence service and military forces of Serbia, Austria's arch enemy in the Balkans. Like many contemporary state sponsors of terrorism, Serbia provided arms, training, intelligence, and other assistance to a variety of revolutionary movements in neighbouring nations. The obscure links between high government officials and their senior military commanders and ostensibly independent, nationalist terrorist movements provide a pertinent historical parallel to the contemporary phenomenon known as 'state-sponsored' terrorism.[73]

It was a member of Young Bosnia, Gavrilo Princip, a radical Bosnian Serb nationalist, who is widely credited with having set in motion the chain of events that led to World War I. On 28 June 1914, Princip, seeking to free his country from Austrian rule, assassinated Austrian archduke Franz Ferdinand, who was on an official visit to Sarajevo, Bosnia. This 'terrorist' incident lit the fuse that ignited World War I.[74]

The Era of the League of Nations

The senseless mayhem of World War I – the destruction of economic structures, dissipation of financial resources and undermining of political stability – wiped off the gloss from the traditional notion of war as a rational political act. The war was disastrous to both its initiators and the victims. Millions died pointlessly, regimes fell. The carnage forced modern industrial societies to question war as an instrument of national policy in the face of the obvious consequences of World War I in which the benefits of conquest (a major incentive in previous centuries) seemed trivial by comparison with the costs of war – large scale death and destruction, political instability and economic turmoil for all involved. It seemed obvious that war was no longer a profitable enterprise.

Resultant economic and political chaos, reinforced by increasing moral disquiet over the idea that states had a right to go to war or use force whenever they wanted to, provided the basis for focusing on the moral and legal responsibility for the outbreak of the war. The victory-at-whatever-cost mindset of the warring states was replaced by political-inspired calculus as to end objectives and 'rational' state egoism displaced virulent nationalism. The brutality of World War I had confirmed the fears of those who had campaigned for effective pacific resolution of disputes, and impelled the international community to create centralized international mechanisms to avoid such carnage in future. The development of pacific avenues for the resolution of disputes figured as a key element of the League of Nations, created after the end of the war.[75] It was a common belief that World War I was 'the war to end all wars', and that the League of Nations would usher a new world order that would prevent future wars and unjustified uses of force.[76]

The League of Nations represented an ambitious move to curb sovereign military excesses and guarantee world peace. It was during its chequered existence that two issues of significance that continue to plague the international community fell on the international agenda – terrorism and the limitation of the use of military force. With the formation of the League of Nations, the freedom of states to resort to military force became more and more restricted. The right of self-defence gained in significance, displacing the expansive right of self-preservation. The chapter turns to consider the major developments in the international regime on the use of force that occurred within the umbrella of the League of Nations as well as the attempted effort to address terrorism.

Restrictions on the Use of Military Force as a State Prerogative

It was during the era of the League of Nations adopted as part of the Peace Treaty of Versailles[77] that the concept of aggression (as an unlawful use of force)[78] appeared as the right of self-preservation fell into disrepute.[79] Under the League Covenant, the Council could issue recommendations to states in danger of going to war. If the Council failed to agree, however, the disputing parties were free to take whatever action they considered necessary for the maintenance of right and justice.

The legal developments of the period of the League had the result that, while the right of self-preservation no longer existed in its classical form, some of its content was preserved. This residual right was referred to as that of self-defence or legitimate defence. It was understood that this right of legitimate defence was subject to objective and legal determination and that it was confined to reaction to immediate danger to the physical integrity of the state itself. Attempts by governments to reserve the right of determining the existence of a necessity for self-defence including pre-emptive strikes did not meet with success. The acceptance of the existence of a right to self-defence, which was essentially a legally defined right, was, however, not accompanied by any precise definition of the content of the right.

The League Covenant was based on the ideal of terminating war by the obligation imposed on all members of the League to respect the sovereignty and territory of other members, and cooperation in guarding them against aggression whether from a peccant member of the League or from a non-member state. But this attempt still fell far short of establishing a general prohibition of war, even though Article 10 may, at first glance, suggest such an interpretation.[80] But if Article 10 is read together with Articles 12, 13 and 15, it becomes evident that the League Covenant, similar in this respect to the Bryan Treaties,[81] merely provided for a moratorium (or 'cooling-off period') for all cases of armed conflict. It was only in very special cases that it deprived League members of their freedom to go to war.

Recourse to war was definitely forbidden against a state complying with an award or a report that had been unanimously adopted by the Council (Articles 13(4) and 15(6)).[82] Since, in practice, most of the disputes submitted to the Council were not dealt with unanimously, this mechanism of the Covenant did not prove to be an effective prohibition of war. In addition major powers of the day did not give the League the support it needed. It has to be remembered that the US never belonged to the League, and that the Soviet Union, Germany, Japan and Italy – among the major world powers of the day – were members for only a short period of time. The end result was that the League lacked the capacity to enforce decisions with any hope that it would coordinate enforcement action by its members disappearing with a series of aggressive acts by major powers in the 1930s, which the League was incapable of addressing, paving the way for the outbreak of World War II.

Despite the League's many failures, one of its significant achievements was its robust efforts to restrict war that led to the adoption in 1928 of the International Treaty for the Renunciation of War as an Instrument of National Policy (the Kellogg-Briand-Pact).[83] The Pact capped the move towards the prohibition of war as an instrument of national policy and recognition of the right of self-defence as a legal right, thus tacitly excluding other previously accepted forms of self-help as avenues legitimating the use of military force.[84]

Although of outstanding importance, the Kellogg-Briand Pact had its shortcomings. The prohibition of war, for instance, failed to be linked to a system of sanctions. Its preamble simply declared that a state violating the Pact 'should be denied the benefits furnished by the Treaty'. An even more serious deficiency proved to be the fact that the prohibition, at least according to its wording, merely referred to war, and not to the use of force in general. In addition, the Pact, which was eventually ratified by 62 states, made an exception for self-defence, but failed to define it – with the result that the customary criteria set out in the *Caroline case* remained the only legal bases for the use of force in international affairs. Strong on principle but lacking an enforcement mechanism, the Pact was doomed to have little practical effect.[85]

Despite its shortcomings as a legal instrument, the Kellogg-Briand Pact signalled that the international community considered war and the use of military force in general to be an unacceptable means by which to further domestic priorities.[86] The Kellogg-Briand Pact was a decisive turning point in the development away from the freedom to wage war and towards a universal and general prohibition of war. The Pact was a watershed in history of legal regulation of the use of inter-state force. With the adoption of the Pact, international law progressed from *jus ad bellum* to *jus contra bellum*. It represented a symbolic step taken by the international community to prohibit the illegitimate use of military force in international relations and was accorded great importance by the Nuremberg and Tokyo Tribunals. It was within the dynamics of the post-World War II international military trials that the provisions of the Kellogg-Briand Pact were recognized as part of general customary international law.

Terrorism and the League of Nations

As noted earlier in the chapter, the birth of modern terrorism during the French Revolution represented practices of mass repression employed by the state, before metamorphosing into a revolutionary mechanism in the late 19th to early 20th century. By the 1930s, the meaning of modern terrorism had undergone a rebirth to re-emerge in its original form. It was now used less to refer to revolutionary movements and violence directed against governments and their leaders, and more to describe the practices of mass repression employed by totalitarian states and their dictatorial leaders against their own citizens.

Thus the term regained its former connotations of abuse of power by governments, and was applied specifically to the authoritarian regimes that had come to power in Fascist Italy, Nazi Germany and Stalinist Russia.[87] As Benito Mussolini, Italy's Fascist leader demurely noted in reaction to a claim of state-orchestrated terror campaigns: 'Terror? Never,' Mussolini insisted, dismissing such intimidation as 'simply ... social hygiene, taking those individuals out of circulation like a doctor would take out a bacillus'.[88]

Despite the rebirth of terror as an intrinsic component of Fascist and Nazi governance, it remained an integral operational component of many shadowy, radical organizations in various parts of Europe. In the face of lack of ample military power or political legitimacy, various radical nationalist organizations used terrorism as a major instrument in their overall strategy. It was through the actions of these groups that terrorism came to the League (and international) agenda amidst a background of the undermining of the collective security regime which the League had as the central pivot to curb aggression and other unwarranted uses of force.

On 9 October 1934, Mussolini, Italy's Fascist leader told cheering masses at the Piazza del Duomo in Milan, amidst a forest of green-white-red flags and Fascist standards, that the failure of Italy's wartime allies to concede to Italy her rightful place in the sun after World War I was a grave mistake. He promised that the time was near when Italy would obtain a treatment inspired by justice and adorn its rifles with the olive branch of peace. However he warned that should this not come about, Italy would adorn its rifles with the laurels of victory.[89] Importantly, the speech had an edge against Yugoslavia: 'We cannot maintain a passive attitude toward neighbouring countries. Our attitude is either friendly or hostile toward them.' On the same day that Mussolini made the speech, a double assassination was committed in Marseille: King Alexander I of Yugoslavia and Jean Louis Barthou, the Minister of Foreign Affairs of France, were killed by fanatic Croatian assassins[90] from the *Ustaši*, the terrorist and extreme nationalist Croatian Fascist organization.[91]

The organization was driven by a philosophy of racial and religious exclusiveness of the Croats. Smallish in numbers, and organized along military patterns, it fought against Yugoslav statehood by means of terror. In this and many other cases it enjoyed the support of Fascist Italy, which harboured their leadership while Hungary lent its territory to the *Ustaši* terrorist operations.[92] The organization was to gain added notoriety with the advent of World War II and intensify its activities after the change of the government in Belgrade and Italy's decision to join German aggression against Yugoslavia. Then they also obtained support of the Nazis,[93] and the advantage of direct access to military armaments, intelligence and training facilities. This state sponsorship which placed diplomatic, military and intelligence services at the organization's disposal, transformed it into a formidable organization. This clandestine arms provision and training, intelligence agents and cross-border sanctuary provide another pertinent historical parallel to the contemporary phenomenon of 'state-sponsored' terrorism.

The most important consequence of the double assassination was that terrorism crept onto the international agenda and induced the League of Nations in 1937 to adopt the first convention on terrorism.[94] Terrorism was defined as all 'criminal acts directed against a state and intended or calculated to create a state of terror in the minds of particular persons, or a group of persons or the general public'.[95] Importantly, certain customary norms of international law relating to the use of armed force, most notably the duty of states 'to prevent and suppress attempts to commit common crimes against life or property where such crimes are directed against other states',[96] contained in the Convention implicitly proscribed certain instances of terrorism. Twenty-four states became signatories to this convention, though it is telling that only one state, India, ratified it. Naturally in the volatile and charged nationalistic and militaristic atmosphere in Europe at the time, terrorism was not viewed as a separate generic issue that demanded attention in the same way that attempting to preserve the crumbling collective security regime and/or reinforce military alliances was. In any case Europe (and the world) was already heading down the slippery slope of excessive state hegemonic ambition that would lead to World War II in less than three years.

Force and the Regime of the UN Charter

The incompetence of the League of Nations in performing its functions and its practical termination was brought about by the series of aggressive acts carried out by the Axis powers during the 1930s and 1940s, which resulted in World War II and was later to move the Allied governments towards an effort to establish a new international organization in order to maintain world peace and security and to prevent aggression when World War II came to an end.

The problem of terrorism was not far from the conduct of World War II. The existence of numerous political groups (including sovereign states, guerrilla movements and transnational ethnic or cultural communities) that pursued their objectives through a mix of conventional political and diplomatic strategies, acts of war and selective terrorism was easily manifest. Similarly acts of terror violence by states played a major role in the German war effort against the Soviet Union and to a lesser role in the Anglo-American campaign against the Nazis. However, the landscape was different and these acts were viewed within the rubric of violations of the laws and customs of war rather than as a separate generic issue – this stance was to spill into the Cold War, with the focus being on groups whose exclusive or predominant political and military instrument is terrorism to the exclusion of state-orchestrated or state-supported terror violence. It is worth noting that the outbreak of World War II witnessed the surfacing claims and counterclaims by warring states based primarily on an exercise of self-defence and frequently an exercise of anticipatory self-defence as well as disguising of military actions through the procedural technicality of non-declaration of war.

In 1945, six years after the start of World War II, the Axis powers were on the verge of total defeat and one of the blackest pages in human history was about to close. By May 1945, Hitler's envisaged Thousand-Year Reich lay in ruins. By August, Japan was devastated, as the atomic bombs which the US dropped on Hiroshima and Nagasaki destroyed Japan's receding hope of carrying on its war of conquest.[97]

It was in the shadow of World War II that the victorious states negotiated both the establishment of the UN as well as the Nuremberg and Tokyo Tribunals. The final step in making the UN Charter was taken at Yalta, in 1945, by the 'Big Three' with victory in World War II in sight. All the Allied states, great and small, were invited to the United Nations Conference on International Organization, which met in San Francisco on 25 April 1945 to prepare the final instrument for the new international organization.[98] The 'Dumbarton Oaks Proposals' were taken as the basis for the discussions which were to lead to the UN Charter. The primary purpose of the new organization was 'to maintain international peace and security; and to that end to take effective collective measures for the prevention and removal of threats to the peace and the suppression of acts of aggression or other breaches of the peace'.[99]

Until the adoption of the UN Charter in 1945, there was no customary prohibition on the unilateral resort to force if circumstances warranted it, and for signatories to particular instruments, if certain preliminary procedures had been exhausted, states reserved the right to resort to force. The UN sought to impose limitations on the unilateral use of force in resolving international disputes, with the right of self-defence the only included exception to the prohibition of the use of force. Customary international law had previously accepted reprisal, retaliation and retribution as legitimate responses as well. Under the UN Charter, unilateral acts of force not characterized as self-defence, regardless of motive, were made illegal.[100]

The UN Charter introduced to international politics a radically new notion: a general prohibition of the unilateral resort to force by states.[101] The principle is encapsulated in its most authoritative form in Article 2(4) of the Charter. The UN Charter identified the structural defect of the international political system and created a network of institutions and procedures. Rather than standing by itself, Article 2(4) was part and parcel of a complex security system.

The UN Charter has as its primary goal the prevention of war – working with the political system to govern conflicts between states by outlawing a wide range of uses of force and defining permissible and lawful uses of force.[102] Surprisingly, in hindsight, the UN Charter does not expressly mention terrorism. The absence of an explicit recognition of terrorism in the UN Charter was later matched by the absence of a single definition of terrorism in either customary or conventional international law. As noted in the Introduction of the book:

> The UN Charter, while seeming to present a neat and tidy regime on the use of force, nonetheless reflects the drafters singular focus on creating a political system to govern conflicts between states. They did not contemplate the existence of international terrorists nor '... fully anticipate the existence, tenacity and technology of modern day terrorism'.

The UN Charter simply does not directly address the subtler modes in which terrorists began to operate in the post-World War II period.

It was, however, not long after the UN's formation, when the use of terrorism and the proliferation of terrorist organizations soon became a source of concern, as civil aviation and the safety of individuals became increasingly under threat from murder, kidnapping and hijacking. Early efforts to address terrorism, however, resulted in a definitional paralysis which subsequently throttled UN efforts to make any substantive progress on international cooperation against terrorism. This was as a result of another swing of the pendulum.

'Terrorism' was regaining its revolutionary connotations as the emergence of the Third World dominated UN and international discourse and the articulation of the right to self-determination. Terrorism was increasingly used and misused in reference to the violent revolts then being prosecuted by the various indigenous nationalist/anti-colonialist groups that emerged in Asia, Africa and the Middle East during the late 1940s and 1950s to oppose continued European rule.[103] Subsequently, many newly independent Third World countries and communist bloc states in particular adopted the 'politically correct' appellation of 'freedom fighters' as a result of the political legitimacy that the international community accorded to struggles for national liberation and self-determination.[104] Strong argument was made by the emerging Third World bloc that moves by the UN condemning 'terrorism' amounted to an endorsement of the power of the strong over the weak and of the established entity over its non-established challenger – in effect the UN would be acting as a defender of the status quo.

The UN Charter

Article 2 (4): The Proscription of Force   The UN Charter sought to address the shortcomings of the Kellogg-Briand Pact.[105] The prohibition of the use of force embodied in Article 2(4) of the UN Charter not only proscribes war, but any use or threat of force in general. Apart from the now obsolete clauses concerning the former enemy states, the UN Charter contains only two exceptions to the prohibition of force, namely Security Council enforcement actions pursuant to Chapter VII, and the right to individual and collective self-defence laid down in Article 51.

Article 2, paragraph 3 of the Charter provides that: 'All members shall settle their international disputes by peaceful means in such a manner that international peace and security and justice are not endangered.'[106] Paragraph 4 then elaborates on the need for peaceful resolution of disputes: 'All members shall refrain in their international relations from the threat or use of force against the *territorial integrity* or *political independence* of any state, or in any other manner inconsistent with the purposes of the UN.'[107]

The terms 'territorial integrity' and 'political independence' are not intended to restrict the scope of the prohibition of the use of force. Rather, the two given modes of the use of force cover any possible kind of trans-frontier use of armed force. Thus an incursion into the territory of another state constitutes an infringement of Article 2(4), even if it is not intended to deprive that state of part of its territory and if the invading troops are meant to withdraw immediately after completing a temporary and limited operation. In other words, 'integrity' has to be read as 'inviolability' proscribing any kind of forcible trespassing. Therefore most forms of the exercise of armed force already fall under the first two forms of the prohibition of force. Gaps that may possibly be left are filled by the remaining form which outlaws the threat or use of force 'in any other manner inconsistent with the Purposes of the UN'.

The pivot on which present day *jus ad bellum* hinges is Article 2(4) of the charter which articulates the principle of the prohibition of force in international relations. Article 2(4) avoids the term 'war'. The use of force in international relations proscribed in the article includes war and transcends war to cover forcible measures short of war. Today Article 2(4) constitutes the basis of any discussion of the problem of the use of force. Its predominant significance has been emphasized by authors who label it 'the corner stone of peace in the Charter'[108] and 'the heart of the UN Charter's basic rule of contemporary public international law'.[109]

Undoubtedly, the wording of Article 2(4) constitutes a considerable improvement when compared with Article I of the Kellogg-Briand Pact.[110] The use of force in general is prohibited, rather than only war. Furthermore, the prohibition is not confined to the actual use of force, but extends to the mere threat of force. Finally, the prohibition is, at least in theory, safeguarded by a system of collective sanctions against any offender (Articles 39–51).

The principle of prohibition of the threat or the use of force, well enshrined in Article 2(4) of the UN Charter, has been further elaborated by several consensual law-making decisions of the UN General Assembly including, in particular, the 1970 Declaration on the Principles of International Law Concerning Friendly Relations[111] and the 1974 Declaration on the Definition of Aggression.[112] The 1970 Declaration on Friendly Relations, besides restating Article 2(4) of the UN Charter, emphasizes that such threat or use of force 'shall never be employed as a means of settling international issues'.[113] It characterizes a war of aggression as a 'crime against peace, for which there is responsibility under international law'.[114] V.S. Mani notes:

> Indeed, this responsibility is both delictual and criminal – the criminal responsibility befalls not only the state perpetrating the aggression but also the high functionaries of the state including those of the armed forces at whose instance the aggression was mounted. The Friendly Relations Declaration also postulates the principle of the inviolability of boundaries and other 'international lines of demarcation'.[115]

Mani goes on to note that:

> The Friendly Relations Declaration further reminds every state of its duty 'to refrain from organizing or encouraging the organization of irregular forces or armed bands, including mercenaries, for incursion into the territory of another state'. This postulate is also reiterated as part of the principle of non-intervention in the same declaration.[116]

Despite reaffirmations of the prohibition of force in a number of international instruments, the scope and content of the prohibition of the use of force in contemporary international law cannot be determined by an interpretation of Article 2(4) alone. Rather, the provision must be read in its context with Articles 39, 51 and

53. Here the problem arises that those articles contain a number of terms which, though related to one another, differ considerably in their meaning. Thus notions such as 'use or threat of force', 'threat to the peace', 'breach of the peace', 'act of aggression', 'armed attack' and 'aggressive policy' are used, but do not receive any further explanation in the Charter. Neither legal writings nor state practices have so far clarified these terms beyond doubt. Nor have attempts within the framework of the UN yet led to a satisfactory interpretation.

The Concept of Armed Attack   Paragraph 7 of the Preamble to the Charter states as one of the goals of the UN 'that armed force shall not be used, save in the common interest'. Article 44 supports the view that the Charter uses the term 'force' where it clearly means 'armed force'. The prevailing view is further corroborated by a teleological interpretation of Article 2 (4): were this provision to extend to other forms of force, states would be left with no means of exerting pressure on other states that violate international law. The *travaux preparatoires* of the UN Charter illustrate the fact that only military force is the concern of the prohibition of the use of force.[117]

This conclusion is confirmed by the Friendly Relations Declaration, adopted by the UN General Assembly on 24 October 1970, which contains an interpretation of the fundamental Charter Principles.[118] When interpreting the principle that states shall refrain in their international relations from the threat or use of force, the Declaration deals solely with military force. Apart from that, the Declaration stipulates as a further principle the obligation not to intervene in matters within the domestic jurisdiction of another state. It is in this context that the Declaration reads: 'No state may use or encourage the use of economic, political or any other type of measures to coerce another state.'[119] By doing so, the Declaration underlines the fact that the scope of Article 2(4) is restricted to armed force. Economic and other types of coercion are not covered by Article 2(4) but by the general principle of non-intervention.

The terms 'aggression' and 'armed attack' are central to the UN Charter regime on the use of force. Only an unambiguous definition would ward off arbitrary interpretations. However, despite the bias of the interpretation of the terms towards military force, the terms still lack clear-cut universally accepted definitions; thus the problem persists. The UN has been striving since 1950, first in the ILC, then in four subsequent special committees of the General Assembly, for a definition of these terms.[120] With the adoption of the 1974 resolution on aggression, this undertaking, for the time being, came to an end. However, to begin with, the 'Definition of Aggression' constitutes a mere recommendation and not binding law, since it is a resolution of the General Assembly. Secondly it determines the notion of 'act of aggression' embodied in Article 39 of the Charter, rather than that of an 'armed attack' as used in Article 51.[121] Lastly, the *travaux preparatoires* of the Definition illustrate that a definition of armed attack was not intended.[122]

The Use or Threat of Force   The prohibition of the use or threat of force forms yet another significant plank in remedying the shortcomings in the Kellogg-Briand Pact which does not expressly prohibit threats. With regard to threat of force, this generally consists of an express or implied promise by a government of a resort to force conditional on non-acceptance of certain demands of that government. If the promise of resort to force occurs in conditions in which no justification for the use of force exists, the threat itself is illegal.

Threats vary according to their nature and magnitude. The types of weapons likely to be used in an attack is an aspect of the nature of a threat, as well as the methods of delivery. At the inception of the UN, it would appear that the focus was almost exclusively on conventional weapons, in view of the fact that only the major powers had the capability to develop WMDs. But several decades later, this technology would soon be in the hands of any state that was determined enough. As will be seen later in the book, new problems were created. The question became whether suspected or actual development of chemical and biological weapons would automatically attract the military wrath of countries able and capable of launching military campaigns in view of the devastating capability of these weapons. In the post-Cold War era, another question was tied in – did a history of supporting terrorists and the potential supply of WMDs to terrorists by rogue states justify pre-emptive threats and pre-emptive use of force. These issues will be addressed in Chapters 4 and 5.

Article 51: The State's Right to Respond in Self-defence

Having proscribed forcible self-help, the UN Charter nevertheless permits those state actions that are reasonably necessary in its own self-defence when faced with an 'armed attack'.[123] This defensive right exists until the Security Council mobilizes to halt the attack.[124] The term 'armed attack' (French: '*agression armee*') represents the key notion of the concept of self-defence pursuant to Article 51. In the final analysis, its interpretation determines how far unilateral force is still admissible.

In the *Nicaragua Case*, the International Court of Justice held that: 'an armed attack must be understood as including not merely action by regular armed forces across an international border, but also the sending by or on behalf of a state of armed bands, groups, irregulars or mercenaries, which carry out acts of armed force of such gravity as to amount to "(inter alia) an actual armed attack conducted by regular forces or its substantial involvement therein"'.[125] The Court thus gave its judicial imprimatur to Article 3(g) of the Declaration on the Definition of Aggression. In effect, in customary international law, the prohibition of armed attacks may apply to the sending by a state of armed bands to the territory of another state, if such an operation, because of its scale and effects, would have been classified as an armed attack rather than a mere frontier incident had it been carried out by regular armed forces.

Based on a literal reading of the UN Charter, the meaning of armed attack is taken and presumed to be ordinarily self-evident. It clearly does not mean an incident created by irresponsible groups or individuals, but rather an attack by one state upon another. Purely internal disorders, revolution or attacks by non-statal entities fall outside the definition. However, if a revolution or an attack by a non-statal entity were aided and abetted by an outside power, such assistance might possibly be considered an armed attack. Since the phrase 'armed attack' strongly suggests a military offensive, it is very doubtful if it applies to the case of aid to revolutionary and other groups and forms of trespass which do not involve offensive operations by the forces of a state. Sporadic operations by armed bands would also seem to fall outside the concept of 'armed attack'. It is conceivable that a coordinated and general campaign by powerful bands of irregulars, with obvious or easily proven complicity of the government of a state from which they operate, would constitute an 'armed attack', more especially if the object were the forcible settlement of a dispute or the acquisition of territory.

As straightforward as Article 51 appears, its application has sparked considerable debate in much the same way as the concepts of 'armed attack' and 'use or threat of force' – the question of interpretation. Article 51 provides: 'Nothing in the present Charter shall impair the inherent right of individual or collective self-defence ...'[126] The key battleground in interpreting this provision is the word 'inherent'.

While the Charter does not indicate what rights are 'inherent', the inclusion of this term was considered significant by the drafters of the Charter. The initial draft of Article 51 made no mention of this 'inherent right', but it was changed to make the definition of self-defence acknowledge that right.[127] Two schools of thought have developed with regard to the scope of Article 51 – those who take the literal, or restrictive, approach and those who take the expansive view that Article 51 is considerably broader than its terms. Depending on which position one takes, self-defence may be viewed either as solely predicated as a responsive act to a current attack or as a broader notion encompassing anticipatory acts to an imminent threat of attack.

The Restrictionist Approach   The restrictionists adhere to the argument that 'inherent right' does not modify self-defence in any meaningful way, requiring some incursion beyond national borders before the right is activated.[128] In any case they point out that a critical question is left open that paves the way for abuse if the right is accepted: How far in advance of such an attack may a state employ such an active, or anticipatory, defence? The restrictionist approach cites the absolute prohibition of resort to forcible self-help as set out in Article 2(4) subject only to the limited exception contained in Article 51. This exception permits recourse to self-defence only when faced with actual 'armed attack'. The argument is that the article does not contemplate anticipatory or pre-emptive actions by a state so threatened. Rather, it requires a state to refrain from responding with like force unless actively involved in repelling an armed attack.[129]

If the correctness of the view that Article 51 of the UN Charter is the authoritative definition of the right of self-defence and is not qualified or supplemented by the customary law since it subsumes the same is accepted, then states are bound by the black-letter law of the Charter and have less extensive grounds to support armed force undertaken other than within the framework of the UN Charter.[130] The phrasing of Article 51 was almost certainly not regarded as a novel development of the law by the delegations at San Francisco, and generally speaking by 1945 self-defence was understood to be justified only in case of an attack by the forces of a state. And quite apart from this consideration, the Charter may be regarded as objective or general international law.[131]

The Counter-Restrictionist Approach   The counter-restrictionist approach adopts an expansionist view. Proponents interpret this to mean that the Charter recognizes and includes those rights of self-defence that existed under customary international law prior to the drafting of the UN Charter.[132] The counter-restrictionists argue that 'inherent right' is used to preserve the meaning of 'self-defence' as it existed prior to the founding of the United Nations: customary international law as it existed in 1945.[133] They round up with the assertion that self-defence actions may be taken both in anticipation of a given threat and in immediate response to actions directed at the vital interests of the target state.[134]

The argument is premised on the fact that under customary international law, the right of self-defence was judged by the standard first set out in the 1837 case of *The Caroline*[135] which established the right of a state to take necessary and proportional actions in anticipation of a hostile threat. Proponents in recent years have cited the impracticability of applying a literal interpretation of Article 51 in an age of advanced weapons and delivery systems and heightened terrorist activity throughout the world. Adherents argue the absurdity of requiring a state to refrain from taking action on its own behalf when an opposing state is preparing to launch an attack.[136] Given the devastating potential of modern weapons and the swiftness of their delivery to intended targets, denying a state the right to act in advance of a pending attack effectively denies any defence at all. The same rationale applies to states threatened with impending terrorist attacks on their citizenry or property.

Professor Michael Byers explains that customary law traditionally recognized a limited right of pre-emptive self-defence according to the '*Caroline* criteria' – 'a necessity of self-defence, instant, overwhelming, leaving no choice of means and no moment for deliberation' and the action taken must not be 'unreasonable or excessive'.[137] Professor Martti Koskenniemi notes that the right of self-defence articulated in the UN Charter 'should be read rationally against the useful purpose the rule is intended to serve'.[138] Koskenniemi argues that the purpose of Article 51 was 'to protect the sovereignty and independence of the state',[139] and therefore that a state that feels its sovereignty and independence to be threatened by the actions of another country might be entitled to use force against that country, even if the country's hostile actions had not yet risen to the level of an actual armed attack.

Anticipatory Self-defence

The two antagonistic arguments relating to the status of self-defence under international law remain very much alive upon a review of state practice. As early as 1956, Israel sought to justify its military action across the UN armistice line against the *fedayeen* on the basis of anticipatory self-defence. Both the UN and the wider international community rejected this argument. The anticipatory self-defence argument met with a somewhat better reception in 1967 when the Israelis attacked Egypt and Syria in anticipation of an all-out attack by the Arab states on Israel.

'Israel justified the strikes that initiated the 1967 Six-Day War on the basis that Egypt's blocking of the Straits of Tiran was a prior act of aggression.'[140] The United Nations seemed moved by these appeals. As Professor Louis Rène Beres notes: '... both the Security Council and the General Assembly refused to condemn Israel for its 1967 pre-emptive attacks against certain Arab states, thereby signifying implicit approval by the UN of Israel's lawful resort to anticipatory self-defence.'[141] But the permissive international reaction was an exception since most states refrained from claiming pre-emptive self-defence – a claim standing on very slippery legal ground in favour of self-defence 'proper'.

International opinion on the impermissibility of anticipatory self-defence was never clearer than when Israel attacked an Iraqi nuclear reactor at Osirak in 1981, leaving it in a pile of ruins. Against a backdrop of Iraqi efforts to develop nuclear weaponry, Israel, fearing that it might eventually be targeted, covertly sent fighter jets to Iraq. They sneaked into Iraq undetected and reduced the Osirak nuclear reactor to rubble in a few seconds of precision bombing. The world was outraged and rose up in one voice to condemn the act, despite Israel's vehement argument that the attack was justified based on the right of anticipatory self-defence.[142] The international community's reaction is eloquently captured by Jonathan Steele thus:

> The world was outraged by Israel's raid on June 7 1981. 'Armed attack in such circumstances cannot be justified. It represents a grave breach of international law,' Margaret Thatcher thundered. Jeane Kirkpatrick, the US ambassador to the UN and as stern a lecturer as Britain's then prime minister, described it as 'shocking' and compared it to the Soviet invasion of Afghanistan. American newspapers were as fulsome. 'Israel's sneak attack ... was an act of inexcusable and shortsighted aggression,' said the New York Times. The Los Angeles Times called it 'state-sponsored terrorism'. The greatest anger erupted at the UN. Israel claimed Saddam Hussein was trying to develop nuclear weapons and it was acting in self-defence, which is legal under Article 51 of the UN Charter. Other countries did not agree. They saw no evidence that Iraq's nuclear energy programme, then in its infancy and certified by the International Atomic Energy Agency as peaceful, could be described as military, aggressive or directed against a particular country. In any case, pre-emptive action by one country against another country which offers no imminent threat is illegal.[143]

The Security Council condemned Israel's 1981 bombing of the Osirak reactor, which Israel justified as an anticipatory response to Iraqi threats to develop nuclear weapons to be used against it.[144] The Security Council unanimously passed Resolution 487 damning the Israeli action as illegal – strong condemnation indeed, especially given that the US (a key stumbling block to any Council efforts to censure Israel) was party to it.[145] Moreover, the US, under the authority of the Arms Control Act of 1968, suspended arms shipments to Israel on the grounds that those arms were to be used for defensive purposes only.[146] Invoking the standards of customary international law in general, and the *Caroline* factors in particular, the opposition to the bombing as self-defence was based on the fact that the Iraqi threats, as well as their construction of the reactor, did not amount to an 'armed attack' on Israel. It is notable that in this as well as later Security Council condemnations of Israeli action, the premeditation evident in the execution of the military operation was considered an argument against accepting the offered justification of self-defence.[147]

Politicians, policymakers and the world at large were unanimous in sensing that Israel's pre-emptive strike was taking the world down a slippery slope. If pre-emption was accepted as legal, the fragile structure of international peace would be undermined. Any state could attack any other under the pretext that it detected a threat, however distant. Notwithstanding the apparent crystal clear position taken by the Security Council and the international community, the argument both by states and scholars regarding the principle that states enjoy the 'inherent' right to

defend themselves from armed attacks is far from settled. This matter will be
addressed in further detail in Chapters 3, 4 and 5 within the context of various
defining events.

The UN Charter and Other Forms of Forcible Self-help

Major Phillip A. Seymour notes that:

> Prior to the *Naulilaa* decision in 1928, international law imposed few constraints, if any,
> on state reprisals. Though the League of Nations had been unsuccessful in fashioning
> restraints, it did signal a shift in state philosophy in fostering a growing awareness that a
> central corporate authority may provide an effective means of resolving disputes between
> states, thus reducing the need to seek recourse through violent methods. This belief
> persisted through World War II and found expression in the UN Charter. While the League
> of Nations had addressed its proscriptions in terms of wartime practices, the UN Charter
> instead proscribed the 'threat or use of force' by member states, a prohibition which
> applied in peacetime. In doing so, it sought to extinguish a state's right, except in very
> limited circumstances, to use forcible self-help.[148]

The text of the UN Charter represents a conventional rejection of the just war
theories of retribution buttressed by Article 2(3) of the Charter which requires states
to settle disputes peacefully. The Charter neither acknowledges nor even mentions
reprisals. Many commentators believe retaliation and reprisals to be illegal under the
UN Charter, citing the language of Articles 2 and 51.[149] Taken together, Articles 2 and
51 comprise a minimum order in the sense that they protect only the primary interest
in freedom from aggression and the right of self-defence as a sanction.[150] This view
is set forth by Professor Ian Brownlie: 'The provisions of the Charter relating to the
peaceful settlement of disputes and no resort to the use of force are universally
regarded as prohibiting reprisals which involve the use of force.'[151] These authorities
conclude that the UN Charter prohibits all forms of forcible self-help other than the
exercise of self-defence within the meaning of Article 51. An assertion that, in the
post-UN Charter era, reprisals are illegal under international law because they are
punitive, rather than legitimate, actions of self-defence seems well supported.

It would be difficult to conform acts of reprisal with the overriding dictate in the
Charter that all disputes must be settled by peaceful means. Indeed, the use of
reprisals represents a regression to the discredited just war theory. The purpose of
international bodies such as the League of Nations and the UN was to limit the use
of force in international matters and to provide a forum for the resolution of conflict
in international matters so as to prevent the need for war. To permit reprisals would
thwart the very goal to which states have committed themselves through
membership of the UN.[152]

The Declaration on Friendly Relations   More support for the assertion that
reprisals and other forms of forcible self-help are illegal comes from the Declaration
on Principles of International Law concerning Friendly Relations and Co-operation
among States in accordance with the Charter of the United Nations.[153] This
Declaration, which among other things provides a quasi-interpretation of the UN
Charter, seems to suggest that members of the UN, including the US, have legally

renounced the use of peacetime reprisals/retaliations. The first principle provides that '[s]tates shall refrain in their international relations from the threat or use of force against the territorial integrity or political independence of any state, or in any other manner inconsistent with the purposes of the United Nations'.[154] 'One of the duties imposed under this principle is to refrain from acts of reprisal involving the use of force. On its face, this would seem to flatly reject the use of reprisals under all circumstances.'[155]

It should be remembered, however, that the duty to refrain from acts of reprisal must be construed in the context of the rest of the language of the Declaration. The Declaration constantly speaks of the duties of states toward one another. A terrorist organization operating within the territorial boundaries of a sympathetic state cannot fairly be included within the definition of a 'state' for purposes of this Declaration. Although the Declaration imposes a duty to refrain from acts of reprisal/retaliation, it also imposes a duty 'to refrain from organizing, instigating, assisting or participating in acts of civil strife or terrorist acts in another state or acquiescing in organized activities within its territory directed towards the commission of such acts'.[156] The duty with respect to reprisal does not exist in a vacuum. If another state, despite warnings, repeatedly breaches the duty to refrain from involvement in state-sponsored terrorism, absent other effective prescribed alternatives, does that mean that the targeted state no longer owes a duty to refrain from the use of peacetime reprisal? This will be yet another issue subjected to detailed discussion in subsequent chapters of the book.

Security Council Practice   It is of great significance that the UN Security Council has condemned reprisals/retaliation as 'incompatible with the purpose and principles of the United Nations'.[157] The Council's rationale has been that reprisals are illegal because member states foreswore the use of force in resolving international disputes and because reprisal does not fall within the Council's understanding of 'self-defence'.

The Security Council expressed its view of the status of reprisals in 1964 when it censured Great Britain for carrying out a reprisal against the Yemeni town of Harib in retaliation for alleged Yemeni support of the anti-colonial struggle in Aden. By a vote of 9-0, with two abstentions, the Security Council determined that it '[c]ondemns reprisals as incompatible with the purposes and principles of the United Nations'.[158] The Council's rationale was that the members of the UN contracted not to use force to achieve solutions to international controversies.[159]

The history of Security Council action from the UN's inception to the 1980s supports the view that, until that point, the restrictionist view rejecting the legitimacy of any reprisal, retaliation or anticipatory self-defence dominated international law in practice. As such, the Council and many legal authorities seem to have adopted the 'restrictive' interpretation of the Charter discussed earlier. It should be noted, however, that both the General Assembly and the Security Council appear to have subsequently adopted a policy inconsistent with their spoken opposition to reprisals, as not all acts of reprisal result in Security Council condemnation.[160]

The Council has generally not condemned acts of reprisal which it considered 'reasonable', while voting to condemn actions considered excessive or disproportionate. In so doing, the Council has appeared to indicate its tolerance of proportionate acts of reprisal. The status of reprisals may therefore be viewed as illegal *de jure* but accepted *de facto*, provided they meet the requirement of proportionality. Thus it would appear that there is a contrary view that the Charter does not prohibit forcible self-help, i.e. reprisals, entirely. As Michael F. Lohr observes:

> An argument can be made that resorts to reprisals are both legal and desirable under the Charter. First, Security Council practice implies the recognition of the legitimacy of some type of reasonable reprisal. There is however an inconsistency between the Security Council's alleged principle of the illegality of all armed reprisals and the Council's practice in not condemning a particular reprisal because it appeared reasonable. A practice of condemning only unreasonable or disproportionate reprisals is, in effect, an affirmation of the right of states to resort to reasonable reprisals.[161]

As a consequence of the Council's selective condemnation, the troubling question of whether any other forcible form of self-help outside of self-defence is permitted under the Charter thus persists.[162] Reprisals are not an isolated notion; they are but one aspect of the broader subject matter constituting both peacetime and belligerent reprisals.[163] The case of self-defence is in general clear-cut since international law recognizes the right of a state to resort to force when responding to the threat or use of force. The case for a legitimate exercise of self-defence can most clearly be justified in law in response to an armed attack. It is the use of reprisals that is most problematic considering it is fluid and on uncertain legal ground in the face of inconsistent state pronouncements and practice in relation to it.

Conclusion

It was the failure of the League to enforce the constraints on the waging of warfare that paved the way for sovereign excesses leading to the outbreak of World War II. Amidst the backdrop of the Nuremberg and Tokyo trials, in 1945, a new world order was seemingly inaugurated by the coming into force of the UN Charter. The Charter sought to craft and guarantee a new system of international peace and security. The end of the war saw the birth of the UN and another effort to put in place an international security regime to guarantee peace. With the adoption of the UN Charter, the course of events and legal developments subsequent to World War II reinforced the importance of the right of self-defence.

With the lessons of the League's failure in mind, the drafters sought to foreclose unilateral use of military force by entrusting the Security Council with a monopoly on determination of instances where this was permissible and authority to act (through force or other sanction). Knowing that the Council could never respond promptly to every act of aggression, they also included an exception for self-defence. But in addition to the two restrictions of necessity and proportionality recognized under customary law in relation to self-defence, three new restrictions were introduced: a state could act in self-defence only if subject to an 'armed attack'; acts of self-defence had to be reported immediately to the Council and the right to respond ended as soon as the Council took action.

This was a constitutional moment in international affairs: an anarchic world of self-help and temporary alliances was being transformed into a nascent system of governance. The linkage of self-defence with a 'right of self-protection' was no longer admissible, hence the UN Charter's basic thrust in establishing the illegality of self-help and reiterating the obligation to settle disputes peacefully, a position reflected in the League of Nation's Covenant but forcefully re-articulated in the UN Charter. Considering that Articles 2(4) and 51 of the UN Charter seek to protect the primary interest in freedom from aggression and the right of self-defence as a sanction, after World War II, armed reprisals and other forms of retaliatory military action were officially banned.

> The Charter granted the Security Council a quasi-monopoly on force, limited only by the right of states to act in self-defence in response to 'an armed attack.' In the event of a provocation short of an armed attack, states are expected to trust the Security Council to respond properly – with economic sanctions or force or whatever other measure it deems appropriate.[164]

Though the UN Charter recognizes that force may be necessary to restore order and that states are entitled to defend themselves against aggression, this right is stated to be 'inherent' and customary international law is the yardstick upon which the degree and manner of self-help should be measured. It is the interpretation of this particular word that has created a legal quagmire. In the face of the UN Security Council's inability to control the spread of international terrorism, debate as to the status of previously accepted military responses under customary international law remains strong.

The US position (shared by several other states) has always been that actions protective of national interests and citizens, rather than being illegal punitive acts, are a means of offering hope of securing a lasting, peaceful resolution of international conflict by guaranteeing that entities and states that injure another state's interests will not be allowed to do so with impunity.[165] Layered on this issue is the fact that the prohibition of the use of force in contemporary international law is burdened with seemingly uncertain wording of the relevant provisions of the UN Charter and an unclear relation to one another. These ambiguities leave room for individual states to interpret the Charter provisions in accordance with their particular political interests. This has had the counter-productive effect of states seeking to stretch the concept of self-defence beyond its clear and defined parameters in order to serve as a legal basis for actions which can be described more accurately, and more honestly, as reprisal or retaliation.

On another front, the relation between Charter law and customary international law continues to present a headache after the eloquent pronunciation of the International Court of Justice in the *Nicaragua Case* that the customary international law was not subsumed by Charter law.[166] Logically, there are two possibilities – the liberty of state to use military force has survived intact in customary international law (as have related concepts such as reprisals) or in view of the centrality of the UN Charter as a quasi-constitution of a radically recrafted international system, it changed the contours of customary international law and thus this exists subject to the changes.

Overall inconsistent international community reaction to uses of force to counter terrorism and unclear legal justifications for military action by victim states has contributed in undermining any clearly accepted or permitted use of military force as a counter measure. Subsequent chapters will carry out a detailed analysis and critique of use of military force to counter terrorism, juxtaposing the nature of force against the international legal framework with particular reference to the UN Charter.

Notes

1   See Sebastian Junger (1999), 'The Forensics of War', *Vanity Fair*, October, 144.

2   See Malcolm N. Shaw (4th ed., 1997), *International Law*, Cambridge: Cambridge University Press, 777–78.

3   Ibid., 778.

4   Ian Brownlie (1963), *International Law and the Use of Force by States*, Oxford: Clarendon Press, 5-6; Shaw, ibid., 778; Leah Campbell, (2000) 'Defending against Terrorism: A Legal Analysis of the Decision to Strike Sudan and Afghanistan', 74 *Tulane Law Review* 1067, 1075–1076.

5   See F. Vitoria (1557), *De Indis et De Jure Belli Relectiones*, the work of the very celebrated Spanish theologian in *Classics of International Law* (1917, Vol. 7), Washington DC: The Carnegie Institution of Washington; B. Ayala, *De Jure et Officiis et Discipline Miltari Libri Tres* (1582) in *Classics of International Law* (1912, Vol. 2), Washington DC: Carnegie Institution of Washington. See further P. Haggen-Macher (1983), *Grotius et al Doctrine de la Guerre Juste*, Paris: Presses Universitaires de France; J. B. Scott (1934), *The Spanish Conception of International Law and of Sanctions*, Washington DC: Carnegie Endowment for International Peace,; J. B. Scott (1928), *The Spanish Origin of International Law*, Oxford: Clarendon Press; Hugo Grotius, *De Jure Belli ac Pacis* ((1625), Bk. 11, Ch. 11 in *Classics of International Law* (1913–25, Vol. 3), Washington DC: Carnegie Institution of Washington.

6   With the emergence of independent princes and national states, scholars argued that a prince recognizing no *de facto* superior had the right to declare war. In essence, to be just a war was now not only confined to the vague motive of a just cause but also extended to a war waged by one who had the power to declare it. See Brownlie, 7–13.

7   There were many publicists before Grotius who wrote on special parts of the international Law. Consequent to the centrality of war in international relations, these early authoritative treatises on international law focused on the laws of war and peace in a bid to regulate war and outlaw the international anarchy that was inherent in the sovereign right of war. These publicists are referred to by Oppenheim as 'Forerunners of Grotius'. Although Grotius owes much to Gentilis, he is nevertheless the greater of the two and bears by right the title of Father of International Law. Lassa Oppeinheim (1st ed., 1905), *International Law: A Treatise (Peace)* Vol. I, London: Longmans & Green, 171.

8   See Hugo Grotius (1646), *De Jure Belli ac Pacis Libri Tres*, Bk. I, Ch. I, § II, Reprinted in (J. B. Scott ed. and Francis W. Kelsey trans., 1925), *The Classics of International Law* Vol. 2, Washington DC: Carnegie Institution of Washington, 172.

9   Ibid.

10   The treaty of Westphalia concluded the Thirty Years War and marked the first attempt by nation-states in Europe to establish a collective agreement as to use of force. See, e.g., Antonio Cassese (1986), *International Law in a Divided World*, Oxford: Clarendon Press; New York: Oxford University Press, 34–35.

11   Leah Campbell (2000), 'Defending Against Terrorism: A Legal Analysis of the Decision To Strike Sudan And Afghanistan', 74 *Tulane Law Review* 1067, 1076.

12   Coming at the end of the period of violent religious wars in Europe, the treaty sought to establish a balance of power among states that was to last until 1914.

13   See Adam Watson (1992), *The Evolution of International Society: A Comparative Historical Analysis*, London: Routledge, which is one of the best guides to the origins of the Westphalia system.

14   Chris Brown (2001), *Understanding International Relations*, New York: Palgrave, 9.

15   Jackson Maogoto (2004), *War Crimes and Realpolitik: International Justice from World War I into the 21st Century*, Boulder: Lynne Rienner Publishers, 3.

16   Ibid., 3.

17   The wars of the 18th century included the Great Northern War, the War of the Austrian Succession (1740–1748), and the Seven Years War (1757–1763). The Great Northern War at the beginning of the century is waged by Peter the Great of Russia against Sweden and saw the establishment of Russia as a Great Power in Europe.

18   Bruce Hoffman, 'Terrorism', Microsoft Encarta Online Encyclopedia (2004), 14 March 2004 online at http://encarta.msn.com.

19   It was designed to consolidate the new government's power by intimidating counter-revolutionaries, subversives and all other dissidents whom the new regime regarded as 'enemies of the people'.

20   Quoted in Bruce Hoffman (1998), *Inside Terrorism*, New York: Columbia University Press, 16.

21   Bruce Hoffman, 'Terrorism'.

22   The Prussian General von Clausewitz (1780–1831) wrote *Vom Kriege* (*On War*) between 1816 and 1830, advocating 'absolute war'. To von Clausewitz, war was a natural expression of the competition between states and its value lay in sorting out the weak from the strong. C. von Clausewitz (1976), *On War* (1832) (M. Howard and P. Paret eds. and trans.), Princeton, NJ: Princeton University Press.

23   See e.g. Herscht Lauterpacht (1966), *The Function of Law in the International Community*, Hamden: Archon Books, 364–365.

24   Herscht Lauterpacht (ed.) (1952), *Oppeinheim's International Law: Disputes, War and Neutrality*, London: Longmans, Vol. II, 202.

25   Ibid., 217–222.

26   Derek Bowett (1972), 'Reprisals Involving Recourse to Armed Force', 66 *American Journal of International Law* 1, 3.

27   Ibid.

28   Michael F. Lohr (1985), 'Legal Analysis of US Military Responses to State-Sponsored International Terrorism', 34 *Naval Law Review* 1, 13.

29   Jackson Maogoto (2004), 'New Frontiers, Old Problems: The War on Terror and the Notion of Anticipating the Enemy', 51 *Netherlands International Law Review* 1, 16.

30   Travers Twiss (1861), *The Law of Nations Considered as Independent Political Communities. On the Right and Duties of Nations in Time of Peace*, Oxford: The University Press, 144, Section 99.

31   Ibid., Section 102, page 149.

32   Robert Phillimore (1879–89), *Commentaries Upon International Law*, London: Butterworths, Ch. 10 (CCXI).

33   Maogoto, 'New Frontiers, Old Problems', 17.

34   William Edward Hall (1880), *A Treatise on International Law*, Oxford: Clarendon Press, 273.

35   J. Moore (1906), *A Digest of International Law as Embodied in Diplomatic Discussions, Treaties and other International Agreements, International Awards, the*

Decisions of Municipal Courts, and the Writings of Jurists, Washington DC: Government Printing Office, Vol. 2, 404.

36   Ibid.

37   Ibid., 409–14. The *Caroline* incident, often called the *Caroline* 'case', was not resolved through the judicial process but rather through diplomatic correspondence (hereinafter *Caroline* incident).

38   C. Hyde (2nd ed., 1945), *International Law: Chiefly as Interpreted and Applied by The United States*, Boston: Little, Brown, Vol. 1, 240.

39   Ibid., at 221 (internal quotations omitted) (quoting Myres S. McDougal and Florentino P. Feliciano [1961], *Law and Minimum World Public Order: The Legal Regulation of International Coercion*, New Haven: Yale University Press, 217).

40   Michael Byers (2002), 'Jumping the Gun', 24 *London Review of Books*, (25 January), 14.

41   C. Hyde (2nd ed., 1945), *International Law: Chiefly as Interpreted and Applied by the United States*, Boston: Little, Brown, Vol. 1, 221, quoting Myres S. Mcdougal and Florentino P. Feliciano (1961), *Law and Minimum World Public Order: The Legal Regulation of International Coercion*, New Haven: Yale University Press, 217.

42   He noted that:

> A State may defend itself, by preventive means if in its conscientious judgment necessary, against attack by another State, threat of attack, or preparations or other conduct from which an intention to attack may reasonably be apprehended.

John Westlake (1904–07), *International Law*, Cambridge: The University Press, i. 299.

43   Stephanie Giry (February 2003), 'New World, Old Law: Would a Unilateral Strike against Iraq Ever have been Legal', *Legal Affairs* 21.

44   Philip A. Seymour (1990), 'The Legitimacy of Peacetime Reprisal as a Tool against State-Sponsored Terrorism', 39 *Naval Law Review* 221, 225.

45   Ibid.

46   E. Colbert (1948), *Retaliation in International Law*, New York: King's Crown Press, 47.

47   F. Kalshoven (1971), *Belligerent Reprisals*, Leyden: Sijthoff, 4.

48   A. Hindmarsh (1933), *Force in Peace: Force Short of War In International Relations*, Cambridge, Mass.: Harvard University Press, 75. An extreme example of a violent peacetime reprisal occurred in 1853 when a US naval vessel bombarded and nearly destroyed Greytown, Nicaragua in response to wrongs committed upon the persons and property of Americans in that town.

49   *Naulilaa Case (Portugal v Germany)* R. Int'l Arb. Awards (1928)Vol. 2, 1011.

50   Ibid., 1026.

51   Ibid.,1011.

52   Ibid.

53   H. Waldock (1952), 'The Regulation of the Use of Force by Individual States in International Law', 2 *Recueil Des Cours* 451.

54   J. Stone (1958), *Aggression and World Order; A Critique of United Nations Theories of Aggression*, Berkeley, University of California Press, 245.

55   C. K. Webster (2nd ed, 1934), *The Congress of Vienna, 1814–1815*, London: H.M. Stationery Office; H. Nicolson (1961), *The Congress of Vienna: A Study in Allied Unity; 1812–1822*, London: Constable.

56   Ian Brownlie (1963), *International Law and the Use of Force by States*, Oxford: Clarendon Press, 21.

57   Ibid., 19–20.

58   Brown, *Understanding International Relations*.

59   Maogoto, *War Crimes and Realpolitik*, 24–5.

60   See the Hague Conventions of 1899 and 1907 on the Pacific Settlement of Disputes. The texts are reproduced in J. B. Scott (ed.) (1908), *Texts of the Peace Conferences at The Hague, 1899 and 1907*. For reports on the proceedings, see J. B. Scott, (ed.) (1917), *The Reports to The Hague Conferences of 1899 and 1907*, Oxford: Clarendon Press.

61   Herscht Lauterpacht (ed.) (1952), *Oppenheim's International Law: Disputes, War and Neutrality*, London: Longmans, Vol. II, 179.

62   Treaties and Other International Agreements of the United States of America 1776–1949, Vol. 1 Multilateral 1776–1917, Department of State Publication 8407, Washington DC: Government Printing Office, 1968. Convention reprinted in D. Schindler and J. Toman (1988), *The Laws of Armed Conflicts*, Dordrecht: Nijhoff Publishers, 57–59.

63   36 Stat. 2241; Treaty Series 537. Treaties and Other International Agreements of the United States of America 1776–1949, Vol. 1 Multilateral 1776–1917, Department of State Publication 8407, Washington DC: Government Printing Office, 1968.

64   History contains many examples of state-ordered peacetime reprisals. For example, between 1813 and 1899 US military or naval landing forces were employed abroad on at least forty-six occasions. Whether the measures used were taken to prevent impending injury or to secure reparation for wrongs already committed, they were defended as a necessary ultimate means of enforcing international obligations. The severity of this ranged from basic maritime blockades to extensive destruction. Hindmarsh, 75.

65   'Treaties for the Advancement of Peace', in (1939) 33 *American Journal of International Law* 861(supplement).

66   Ibid.

67   Maogoto, *War Crimes and Realpolitik*.

68   Hoffman, *Inside Terrorism*, 18.

69   'The propaganda of the idea is a chimera,' Pisacane wrote. 'Ideas result from deeds, not the latter from the former, and the people will not be free when they are educated, but educated when they are free.' Violence, he argued, was necessary not only to draw attention to, or generate publicity for, a cause, but to inform, educate and ultimately rally the masses behind the revolution. Quoted in Hoffman, *Inside Terrorism*, 17.

70   This doctrine that was to shape terror was also shared by German radical Karl Heinzen (1809-1880). To Heinzen's way of thinking, the revolutions of 1848 had failed because the revolutionaries had been insufficiently ruthless. And like Johann Most, another German radical, Heinzen hoped that technology, and specifically new explosives like dynamite, would compensate for what was lacking in the willpower of the laggardly masses. (Most was the inventor of the letter bomb and other terrorist refinements, and extolled 'propaganda by deed' in his newspaper, *Freiheit*.)

71   Hoffman, *Inside Terrorism*, 70. In hopes of encouraging and coordinating worldwide anarchist activities, the conferees decided to establish an 'Anarchist International' (or 'Black International').

72   For example, the Russian group, the Social Revolutionary Party, conducted a campaign of bombing and assassination from 1902 until 1911.

73   The active and often clandestine support, encouragement and assistance provided by a foreign government to a terrorist group.

74   See John F. Murphy (1980), 'Terrorism: Documents of International and Local Control', 74 *American Journal of International Law* 711, 713 (Book Review) (noting that 'the origin of the First World War can be traced to an act of transnational assassination arising out of revolutionary terrorism').

75   The *Covenant of the League of Nations* was incorporated in the *Treaty of Peace Between the Allied and Associated Powers and Germany, Peace Treaty of Versailles*, concluded at Versailles, 28 June 1919, 2 Bevans 43.

76   Maogoto, *War Crimes and Realpolitik*, 57.
77   *Treaty of Peace between the Allied and Associated Powers and Germany (Peace Treaty of Versailles)* concluded at Versailles, 28 June 1919.
78   Brownlie, 351–352.
79   Aggression was synonymous with an armed attack, the unlawful use of force, which justified action in self-defence. The assertion that the right of self-defence justified preventive action in the face of potential threats to the interests of states was seen as a relic of the vague and obsolete right of self-preservation or the doctrine of self-help which the war had helped credit.
80   The *Covenant of the League of Nations* was incorporated in the *Treaty of Peace Between the Allied and Associated Powers and Germany, Peace Treaty of Versailles*, concluded at Versailles, 28 June 1919, 2 Bevans 43 (hereinafter *League Covenant*).
81   'Treaties for the Advancement of Peace', in (1939) 33 *American Journal of International Law* 861 (supplement).
82   *League Covenant.*
83   *General Treaty for the Renunciation of War* (hereinafter *Kellogg-Briand Pact*), signed at Paris, 27 August 1928, 94 L.N.T.S. 57, 46 Stat 2343, T.S. No 796; United States Statutes at Large Vol. 46, Part 2, 2343. Signed initially on 27 August 1928 by the representatives of 15 states, entered into force 24 July 1929. By the time it entered into force, the *Kellogg-Briand Pact* had been signed and ratified/acceded to by a total of 59 states, including all the states (major and minor) that were subsequently to comprise the Axis Powers, almost all the states comprising the international community at that time. A list of the signatory countries as at 24 July 1929 is set out in Ferencz, note 20, pp.190–192.
84   *Kellogg-Briand Pact*, ibid., states:

> [P]ersuaded that the time has come when a frank renunciation of war as an instrument of national policy should be made to the end that the peaceful and friendly relations now existing between their peoples may be perpetuated;
> Convinced that all changes in their relations with one another should be sought only by pacific means and be the result of a peaceful and orderly process, and that any signatory Power which shall hereafter seek to promote its national interests by resort to war should be denied the benefits furnished by this Treaty...
> Have decided to conclude a Treaty;
> Article I: The High Contracting Parties solemnly declare in the names of their respective peoples that they condemn recourse to war for the solution of international controversies, and renounce it as an instrument of national policy in their relations with one another.
> Article II: The High Contracting Parties agree that the settlement or solution of all disputes or conflicts of whatever nature or of whatever origin they may be, which may arise among them, shall never be sought except by pacific means.

85   The pact never made a meaningful contribution to international order, although it was invoked in 1929 with some success, when China and the USSR reached a tense moment over possession of the Chinese Eastern RR in Manchuria. Ultimately, however, the pact proved to be meaningless, especially with the practice of waging undeclared wars in the 1930s (e.g. the Japanese invasion of Manchuria in 1931, the Italian invasion of Ethiopia in 1935, and the German occupation of Austria in 1938). See generally R. H. Ferrell (1952, reprint 1968), *Peace in Their Time*, New York: W.W. Norton.
86   The Pact, though, had a number of weaknesses:

1. Issue of self-defence was not recognized or addressed.
2. No limits were agreed upon as to legality of war as instrument of international policy.

3. Prohibitions of war did not embrace the whole of international community.

4. Forcible measures short of war were eliminated from consideration.

5. Reinvention of war in Article 1 circumscribed to relations between contracting parties *inter se.*

87   The most sinister dimension of this form of 'terror' was that it became an intrinsic component of Fascist and Nazi governance, creating a system of government-sanctioned fear and coercion. The 'Great Terror' that Stalin was shortly to unleash in Russia both resembled and differed from that of the Nazis.

88   Information online at http://www.hungary.com/corvinus/lib/eckh/eckh01.htm (visited 14 June 2004).

89   Information online at http://www.hungary.com/corvinus/lib/eckh/eckh01.htm (visited 14 June 2004).

90   'These were the first shots of the Second World War,' writes Anthony Eden. Sir Anthony Eden (1962), *Facing the Dictators; The Memoirs of Anthony Eden, Earl of Avon*, Boston: Houghton Mifflin, 119.

91   This party originated from the extremist Croatian Law Party founded by Ante Starčević – also the founder of the idea of a 'Greater Croatia', which claimed a racial and religious exclusiveness of the Croats, and advocated their right to territorial expansion.

92   John F. Montgomery (1947), *Hungary, the Unwilling Satellite*, New York: Devin-Adair Co.

93   The crimes *Ustaši* later committed during World War II in their own country gained them infamy in the whole civilized world – online at http://www.hungary.com/corvinus/lib/eckh/eckh01.htm (visited 14 June 2004).

94   League of Nations, *Convention for the Prevention and Punishment of Terrorism*, OJ 19 (1938) 23; League of Nations Doc. C.546 (I). M.383 (I) 1937V (1938), which contains an annex calling for the establishment of an international criminal court.

95   *Convention for the Prevention and Punishment of Terrorism*, 16 November 1937, art. I(2), 19 League of Nations OJ 23 (1938).

96   Lassa Oppenheim (9th ed, 1996), *International Law* (Robert Jennings and Arthur Watts, eds.) Vol. 1, 400.

97   World War II was the most cruel and devastating conflict in history. In terms of lives lost, geographical extent, and cities reduced to ashes, the struggle defies rational comprehension. Over 27 million combatants were killed, 17 million wounded and nearly 20 million captured or missing. Civilian populations were more affected by this war than any other in the past. Maogoto, *War Crimes and Realpolitik*, 83.

98   Leland M. Goodrich and Anne P. Simons et al (1969), *Charter of the United Nations*, New York: Columbia University Press, 4-8.

99   See 'Proposals of the Delegation of the Republic of Bolivia for the Organization of a System of Peace and Security', Doc 2, G/14, May 5, 1945 para 7, reproduced in Benjamin Ferencz (1975), *Defining International Aggression, The Search For World Peace: A Documentary History And Analysis*, Dobbs Ferry, NY: Oceana Publications, Vol. I, 313.

100   See *UN Charter*, 59 Stat 1031, JS No 933, 3 Bevans 1153, done at San Francisco, 26 June 1945, arts. 39–51.

101   Various legal instruments have reinforced the prohibition of the use of force since the adoption of the *UN Charter*, 59 Stat 1031, JS No 933, 3 Bevans 1153, done at San Francisco, 26 June 1945. These include:

1. Art 5 of the *Pact of the Arab League* and reaffirmed by the *Inter-American Treaty of Reciprocal Assistance*, signed in Rio de Janeiro on 2 September 1947.

2. *Charter of the Organization of American States* of 1948 (Bogota Charter), art 5 condemns aggression, art 15 no intervention, art 18 no use of force except in self defence.

3. The five principles of peaceful co-existence (known as Panch Shila). First formulated in the agreement of 29 April 1954 between India and the PRC.

4. The final communiqué of the Afro-Asian conference at Bandung of 24 April 1955 gave approval to ten principles as the basis for promotion of world peace and cooperation.

102   See James P. Rowles (1987), 'The Legal and Moral Adequacy of Military Responses to Terrorism: Substantive and Procedural Constraints in International Law', *American Society of International Law, Proceedings of the 81st Annual Meeting* 307, 310.

103   Many countries from Asia to Africa and the Middle East owe their independence at least in part to nationalist political movements that employed terrorism against colonial powers.

104   The argument was that anyone or any movement that fought against 'colonial' oppression and/or Western domination should not be described as 'terrorists', but were properly deemed to be 'freedom fighters'. This position was perhaps most famously explained by the Palestine Liberation Organization (PLO) chairman Yasser Arafat, when he addressed the United Nations General Assembly in November 1974. 'The difference between the revolutionary and the terrorist,' Arafat stated, 'lies in the reason for which each fights. For whoever stands by a just cause and fights for the freedom and liberation of his land from the invaders, the settlers and the colonialists, cannot possibly be called terrorist ...'

105   *Kellogg-Briand Pact.*

106   See United Nations (1968), *Yearbook of the United Nations*, Vol. XXII, app II.

107   *UN Charter*, art 2(4) (emphasis mine).

108   Douglas Eisner (1993), 'Humanitarian Intervention in the Post-Cold War Era', 11 *Boston University International Law Journal* 195; Bartram Brown (2000), 'Humanitarian Intervention at a Crossroads', 41*William and Mary Law Review* 1683.

109   Brown, ibid.; Oscar Schachter (1984), 'The Right of States to Use Armed Force', 82 *Michigan Law Review* 1620.

110   Article I of the *Kellogg-Briand Pact*, op.cit., provides:

The High Contracting Parties solemnly declare in the names of their respective peoples that they condemn recourse to war for the solution of international controversies, and renounce it, as an instrument of national policy in their relations with one another.

111   G.A.Res. 2625, 25 U.N. GAOR Supp. (No. 28), U.N. Doc. A/8028 (1970).

112   G.A. Res 3314 (XXIX), U.N. GAOR, 29th Sess, Supp No 31, pp.142–43, U.N. Doc A/9631 (1974). This Resolution has been severely criticized by a number of scholars for leaving too many loopholes. See e.g. Allegra Carpenter (1995), 'The International Criminal Court and the Crime of Aggression' 64(2) *Nordic Journal of International Law-Acta Scandinavica Juris Gentium* 223, 242.

113   G.A.Res. 2625, 25 U.N. GAOR Supp. (No. 28), U.N. Doc. A/8028 (1970).

114   G.A.Res. 2625, 25 U.N. GAOR Supp. (No. 28), U.N. Doc. A/8028 (1970).

115   V.S. Mani (1999), 'Kargil – International Law – II', Embassy of India (Washington DC), available at http://www.indianembassy.org/new/NewDelhiPressFile/ Kargil_June_1999/2kargil_International_Law.htm.

116   Ibid.

117   For instance at the San Francisco Conference, a proposal by Brazil of 6 May 1945, to extend the prohibition of force to economic coercion, was explicitly rejected.

118   *Declaration Concerning Friendly Relations.*

119   Ibid.

120   For a concise survey of efforts to define aggression encompassing both the League and

Charter eras, see Jackson Maogoto (2002), 'Aggression: Supreme International Offence Still in Search of Definition', 6 *Southern Cross University Law Review* 278.

121 This follows from paragraphs 2 and 4 of the Preamble, as well as from Article 6, pursuant to which the Definition does not contain any regulation of the right of self-defence in response to an armed attack.

122 In the special committee that worked out the definition, the US, supported by other Western state along with the Soviet Union, expressed strongly opposed tendencies to define 'armed attack'.

123 See Brownlie, 432–433. Professor Ian Brownlie has categorized several art. 51 exceptions to the restrictions on the use of force. They are as follows:

1. acts of self-defence;
2. acts of collective self-defence;
3. actions authorized by a competent national organ (e.g. the United Nations Security Council);
4. where treaties confer rights to intervene by an ad hoc invitation, or where consent is given by the territorial sovereign;
5. actions to terminate trespass;
6. necessity arising from natural catastrophe; and
7. measures to protect the lives or property of a state's nationals in a foreign territory.

124 See *UN Charter*, art. 42 (which provides that the Security Council 'may take such action by air, sea or land forces as may be necessary to maintain or restore international peace and security') and art. 43 (which provides that the member states will make forces and facilities available to the Security Council to facilitate the restoration of international peace and security).

125 I.C.J. Reports 1986, note 10 at 103.

126 *UN Charter*, art. 51.

127 Ruth B. Russell (1958), *A History of the UN Charter; The Role of the United States, 1940–1945*, Washington DC: Brookings Institution, 698–699.

128 See Sean M. Condron (1999), 'Justification for Unilateral Action in Response to the Iraqi Threat: A Critical Analysis of Operation Desert Fox', 161 *Military Law Review* 115, 115, 151–155, nn. 215; see, also, Yoram Dinstein (2nd ed, 1994), *War, Aggression, and Self-Defence*, 202 (drawing the distinction between imminence and immediacy).

129 Stone, 94–95.

130 Brownlie, 279.

131 Firstly, it has received the adherence of every recognized independent state with the states expressly accepting the principles and obligations of the Charter. Secondly, the provisions of the Charter have had strong influence on state practice since 1945 and the terms of Article 51, or very similar terms, have appeared in several important multilateral treaties and draft instruments. Thus art. 3 of the *Inter-American Treaty of Reciprocal Assistance* of 1947 provided for individual or collective self-defence in case of an 'armed attack'. (43 *American Journal International Law* (1949), Supplement 53.) Arts. 18 and 25 of the Bogota Charter of 1948 are primarily concerned with reaction to the use of force but the latter article refers ambiguously to 'an act of aggression that is not an armed attack' and is concerned only with the application of 'measures and procedures', whilst the former merely refers to 'the case of self-defence in accordance with existing treaties or fulfilment thereof'. (46 *American Journal International Law* (1952), Suppl, 43.) The Draft Declaration on Rights and Duties of States adopted by the International Law Commission in 1949 provided in art 12 that 'every State has the right of individual or collective self-defence against armed attack'. The Report of the Commission states that the language is based upon that employed in art. 51 of the UN

Charter. Though discussions of the article by the Commission indicated differences of opinion as to the legality of preventive action prior to an actual attack, all members regarded the right of self-defence as exercisable through the medium of armed force only in the case of the threat of armed attack or actual attack, i.e. as a reaction to the use of force.

132 Blum (1986), 'The Legality of State Response to Acts of Terrorism', in Binyamin Netanyahu, (ed.) *Terrorism: How the West Can Win,* New York: Farrar, Straus, Giroux, 137.

133 See Condron, 160. This position is similar to the position advocated in Part V, but with a distinction akin to the distinction between original intent originalism and original meaning originalism in constitutional law.

134 Stone, 245.

135 Moore, 409–14.

136 See generally Mark Baker (1987), 'Terrorism and the Inherent Right of Self-Defense (A Call to Amend Article 51 of the United Nations Charter)', 10 *Houston Journal of International Law* 25.

137 Michael Byers, 'Iraq and the "Bush Doctrine" of Pre-emptive Self-defence', 10 December 2003, online at http://www.crimesofwar.org/expert/bush-byers.html.

138 Martti Koskenniemi, 'Iraq and the "Bush Doctrine" of Pre-emptive Self-defence', 10 December 2003, online at http://www.crimesofwar.org/expert/bush-koskenniemi.html.

139 Ibid.

140 Michael Byers (2002), 'Terrorism, the use of Force and International Law after 11 September', 51 *International Comparative Law Quarterly* 401, 410, 410.

141 Louis René Beres (1999), 'Implications of a Palestinian State for Israeli Security and Nuclear War: A Jurisprudential Assessment', 17 *Dickinson Journal of International Law* 229, 283.

142 The United Nations Security Council condemned the Israeli attack on the Iraqi nuclear reactor in a unanimous resolution adopted 19 June 1981. For an excellent discussion of the history of United Nations' responses to various Israeli anti-terrorist campaigns, see William V. O'Brien, 'Reprisals, Deterrence and Self-Defence in Counter-terror Operations', (1990) 30 *Virginia Journal of International Law* 421, 462–63.

143 Steele, Jonathan, 'The Bush Doctrine Makes Nonsense of the UN Charter', *The Guardian* (London), Comment, 7 June 2002, available at http://www.guardian.co.uk/bush/story/0,7369,728870,00.html (visited 1 August 2004).

144 36 U.N. SCOR (2288th mtg) U.N. Doc S/PV.2288 (1981) 57; S.C. Res 487, 36 U.N. SCOR, Res and Decs at 10, U.N. Doc. S/INF/37 (1981) (The US voted for the Resolution).

145 See U.N. SCOR Resolution 487, 1981 *United Nations Yearbook* 282, UN Sales No E.84.I.1.

146 *Arms Control and Disarmament Act* of 1968, 22 USC, ss 2751–2794 (1982).

147 U.N. SCOR Resolution 487.

148 Philip A. Seymour (1990), 'The Legitimacy of Peacetime Reprisal as a Tool against State-Sponsored Terrorism', 39 *Naval Law Review* 221, 227.

149 Guy B. Roberts (1987), 'Self-Help in Combating State-Sponsored Terrorism: Self-Defence and Peacetime Reprisals', 19 *Case Western Reserve Journal of International Law* 243, 282.

150 McDougal and Feliciano, *Law and Minimum World Public Order,* 121-24; W. T. Mallison Jr and S. V. Mallison (1973), 'The Concept of Public Purpose Terror in International Law: Doctrines and Sanctions to Reduce the Destruction of Human and Material Values', 18 *Howard Law Journal* 412, 419.

151 Brownlie, 281.

152   See Roberts, 286. In the case of Israel, however, the US has sometimes insisted, before condemning a reprisal by Israel, that the terrorist act that prompted the reprisal also be condemned. See O'Brien, supra note 139 at 433.
153   *Declaration on Principles of International Law Concerning Friendly Relations and Co-operation among States in accordance with the Charter of the United Nations*, G.A. Res 2625, 25 U.N. GAOR Supp. (No 28), U.N. Doc A/8028 (1970); *United Nations Yearbook* (1970).
154   Ibid.
155   Philip A. Seymour (1990), 'The Legitimacy of Peacetime Reprisal as a Tool against State-Sponsored Terrorism', 39 *Naval Law Review* 221.
156   Ibid.
157   Brownlie, 281.
158   Richard Falk (1969), 'The Beirut Raid and the International Law of Retaliation', 63 *American Journal of International Law* 415, 429 and n. 37.
159   McDougal and Feliciano (1958), 'Legal Regulation of the Right to International Coercion', 68 *Yale Law Journal* 1063, 1063–64.
160   See Barry Levenfield (1982), 'Israel's Counter Fedayeen Tactics in Lebanon: Self-Defence and Reprisal Under Modern International Law', 21 *Columbia Journal of Transnational Law* 7, 35.
161   Michael Lohr (1985), 'Legal Analysis of US Military Responses to State-Sponsored International Terrorism', 34 *Naval Law Review* 1, 32–33.
162   See *UN Charter*, art. 51,
163   'The simple idea of retaliation is as old as the customs underlying the *lex talionis*.' E. Colbert (1948), *Retaliation in International Law*, 10 n.1.
164   Stephanie Giry (February 2003), 'New World, Old Law: Would a Unilateral Strike against Iraq Ever have Been Legal', *Legal Affairs* 21.
165   See Arthur Rovine (1974), 'Contemporary Practice of the United States Relating to International Law', 68 *American Journal of International Law* 720, 736 (statement of Acting Secretary of State Rusk).
166   In the *Nicaragua Case*, when the ICJ stated clearly that the adjudication did not rest on law of the Charter, the court perhaps created more problems than it solved as it re-ignited debate on the accepted options on the use of force, especially in a period when the US and Israel were increasingly turning to military force to combat terrorism as its reach and lethality increased.

Chapter 2

Countering Terrorism:
An Evaluation of the Law Enforcement
and Conflict Management Approaches

Introduction

Despite wide universal acceptance of terrorism as an international crime, confusion over a precise definition of terrorism and its corollary state-sponsored terrorism has hampered any effective development in the discourse regarding acceptable and permitted countermeasures. General agreement by states at a philosophical level on what constitutes terrorism masks serious disagreements in practice. Not surprising since factors contributing to the utility of terrorism are many. In its simplest terms, terrorism as a weapon has proven to be cheap and to have a synergistic effect in its impact. Like other forms of low-intensity warfare, terrorism is ambiguous. The fact that it throws its victims off balance and that they must grope for an appropriate means of response, or a determination if any response is appropriate, only increases its effectiveness.

'In its modern manifestations, terror is the totalitarian form of war and politics. It shatters the war convention and the political code. It breaks across moral limits beyond which no further limitation seems possible.'[1] Whether civilian or non-civilian, there is no immunity from terrorism. Terrorists kill anyone. In essence, the terrorist respects no law – not criminal law, moral law, the law of peace or the law of war. In short, they do not play by any rules.[2] It seems that terrorists should either be thought of as acting within the scope of the criminal law, in which case they might be accused of violating criminal law, or they should be thought of as acting within the scope of 'war and peace', in which case they might be accused of violating either the law of war or the law of peace.[3] However, they do not seem to fall clearly in either scenario; thus despite being law violators, they have situated themselves in an impossible place, located somewhere outside of the law.[4]

States have historically initiated a legal response as their first reaction to international terrorist activities. From the legal perspective, managing the terrorist threat requires identification of the threat and a selection from within the range of counter terrorism measures usually within the framework of international conventions that generally provide for prosecution through the *aut dedere, aut judicare* – extradite or prosecute – mechanism and state responsibility concept. These legal mechanisms are primary examples of legal responses used by states against international terrorists.[5]

Legal means to combat terrorism often prove to be insufficient mechanisms for deterring future terrorist attacks.[6] As a consequence, states have sought to wean themselves from a sole reliance on this paradigm. Though states have worked in earnest to develop new strategies within the rubric of domestic and international law to deal with terrorism, one important option that does not fall within the range of generally accepted legitimate options is the use of military force. Use of military force as a countermeasure against terrorism is generally held to be inconsistent with the UN Charter regime on the use of force and poses a great dilemma.

This chapter commences with a general introduction of the two dominant counter-terrorism management paradigms. It then grapples with the difficult issue of the definition of terrorism and state-sponsored terrorism. It notes the difficulties that have prevented a universal definition or consensus as well as the consequences – the UN's seeming awkward and ambivalent treatment of the issue. It notes that some of the UN's constituent parts (governments and international civil servants) and influential elements in the UN firmament (would-be governments, non-governmental organizations, and individuals) have viewed terrorism variously as a social, political or religious phenomenon.[7]

The chapter then evaluates counter-terrorism measures from both a domestic and international perspective and the attendant strictures and implications. In particular the chapter carries out its analysis in the context of the law enforcement and conflict management paradigms. The law enforcement paradigm applies the law (whether domestic or international) within the context of domestic penal process, while the conflict management paradigm seeks to make use of force – whether lethal or non-lethal and thus engages the international regime on the use of force and state responsibility, and frequently (in the case of non-lethal military force) co-opts the domestic penal process. Review of these counter-terrorism measures will illuminate the issues as well as set the stage for subsequent chapters which will focus on one particular facet – the contentious conflict management paradigm.

Counter-terrorism Management Paradigms

The Law Enforcement Paradigm

Until recently, the law enforcement approach predominated counter-terrorism responses.[8] This approach considers terrorist events as purely criminal acts to be addressed by the domestic criminal justice system and its components. This entails domestic criminal law which is clearly within the authority of individual nations, and grants no status – other than that of common criminal and common crime – to either those who commit terrorist acts or to the acts themselves. The crimes charged – murder, kidnapping, hijacking and arson – reflect domestic criminal law with little or no reference to the terrorist motives of the defendants or the international character of their organizations.

> Equally important, a law enforcement response to terrorist acts ensures due process. When the evidence is insufficient, allegations are dropped or fail in court, resulting in a dismissal of the charges or findings of not guilty. The use of military force, on the other hand,

provides no due process to those killed or injured, and creates a greater risk of harm to innocents caught up in the battle. The law enforcement approach is a more precise instrument and one much more capable of meting out individualized justice.[9]

Despite the clear-cut positives that the domestic legal enforcement framework offers, it has proved to be inadequate. The possibility of dismissed charges or acquitted defendants is all too real and frequent. The absence of an effective international police agency and the reality that police capability of many states is either both corrupt and ineffective or the state willingly harbours terrorists renders this approach good in theory and hopeless in practice. Besides the fact that extradition regimes are far from satisfactory, there is no effective international tribunal to deal with terrorist acts.

The Conflict Management Paradigm

Despite numerous anti-terrorism conventions, extradition agreements, and other forms of jurisdictional cooperation, rising impunity for terrorists and terrorist entities led states (notably Israel and the US) in the mid-1980s to suggest that terrorist acts might be approached from a conflict management (and thus use of force) perspective, rather than exclusively from a law enforcement viewpoint.[10] In support, Neil C. Livingstone argues that legal means do not conform to the new nature of the international terrorism threat, and the legal strategy does not deter international terrorists from acting.[11]

In the face of the apparent inability of the Security Council to control the spread of international terrorism during the Cold War era, several states (particularly the US and Israel) sought to circumvent the provisions of the UN Charter or to stretch them, arguing that they would legitimately use military force to counter terrorism. Several states argue that in the face of the seriousness of contemporary potentially devastating terrorist threats, there seems an urgent need to take action before a terrorist attack occurs rather than respond to an attack through the legal process paradigm.[12] 'It has been argued that international law actually plays into the hand of terrorists. They protect themselves by exploiting various lacunae in the law and use these to their advantage. Further, it is argued that if it is desired to wage war against terrorism, then terrorists must be seen, not as criminals, but as persons jeopardizing national security.'[13]

The lack of a clear-cut definition for international terrorism means that domestic agencies best suited to implement an anti-terrorist strategy cannot be ascertained and even if they can, it leads to a leaky patchwork that entails the courts and the intelligence services. Often the kind of evidence tendered cannot stand in a court of law or cannot be divulged without compromising a state's intelligence gathering. As a consequence, the belief is that only the use of armed force will result in the degree of decisive action that will minimize the likelihood that offenders will go unpunished. The law of armed conflict deals with terrorist acts in a manner similar to the domestic law of various nations – as criminal acts. It recognizes terrorists as engaging unlawfully in combatant activity, characterizes them as unlawful combatants, and denies them legitimacy 'by identifying them as perpetrators of acts contrary to the fundamental international humanitarian law that serves as a basis of the law of armed conflict'.[14] However, it differs significantly by sanctioning military strikes, thus engaging the law of armed conflict and negating due process and its safeguards.

The perceived threat that transnational terrorism poses to states impacts the laws and policies used to thwart it.[15] Terrorists now use more sophisticated and devastating weapons,[16] seeking targets that inflict the greatest damage on human life and property.[17] 'Terrorists now look to multi-millionaires and entire nations for financial support.'[18] With large 'war chests' terrorists have steadily developed their capabilities with a lethal combination of professionalism and advanced weaponry – weapons that are increasingly technically advanced and more difficult to detect. 'The advanced weapons available to terrorists pose an alarming national security threat, providing terrorists with the ability to destabilize entire regions ... and to inflict massive harm against [] citizens and property.'[19]

The challenge to states and the international community is compounded when states (actively or passively) support terrorism, thus enhancing the capabilities of terrorist organizations, as well as their ability to avoid both domestic and international enforcement regimes paving the way for impunity. This has contributed to the ascendance of the view that terrorists, though criminals, are persons jeopardizing national security and thus necessitating the use of military force. This view has become especially dominant in the post-September 11 international climate with the US branding the bid to combat terrorism as a 'War on Terror' and noting that it will be a long and difficult struggle and a very different kind of war. This is in the face of the reality that the enemy is not comprised of soldiers of a state, the enemy 'soldiers' wear no uniforms and have no fixed bases. They pursue uncertain goals but with a very certain weapon – terror.[20]

Terrorism and the UN: An Ambivalent Relationship

The UN came into being at a time when the seeds for the dissolution of imperial and colonial possessions had been sown. As mentioned in Chapter 1, in the early years of the UN, there were numerous national liberation struggles. Many acts of 'terror-violence'[21] occurred in the context of armed conflicts, specifically in the context of de-colonization and wars of national liberation.[22] At first, these acts were labelled 'terrorism' by colonial powers as they sought to cling to their colonial possessions through military violence. Soon the language changed as self-determination became increasingly recognized at the international level as a group right. In any case acceptance of the right to self-determination crowded out the methods of terror frequently employed by both parties. As Professor M. C. Bassiouni astutely observes:

> The reason may well be that unlawful terror-inspiring methods used by national liberation fighters were the most effective means available to them to combat the more powerful colonial powers. Furthermore, because of the inherent political nature of these conflicts, the use of terror-violence became hopelessly mired in politics. Thus, the legitimacy of the cause seeped into the illegitimacy of the means employed. In short, it was a reversion to the Machiavellian concept that the 'end justifies the means.'[23]

Though most armed struggles for national liberation ended in the 1970s, new ones emerged, which concerned the rights of self-determination by ethnic groups seeking secession from the states in which they lived.[24] Regrettably, the world community remained unable to find ways to peacefully resolve these conflicts, which gave rise to massive victimization.[25] New and emerging states were mired in civil strife and internecine power struggles in which 'terror' was a tool. In addition, ideological and geopolitical differences between states was fueling the proliferation of ideologically motivated non-statal entities, frequently with uncertain agendas but always certain about their methods – terror.

Ideological and political quagmires laid down fertile ground for a dichotomy of terrorism to come into being. In the 1960s and 1970s, focus on terrorism mainly targeted ideologically motivated individuals and small groups. The international community increasingly targeted manifestations of individual and small group acts of 'terror-violence', sidestepping the politically volatile issue of state/insurgent sponsored and orchestrated 'terror-violence'.[26] Attacks by individuals and small groups soon came to comprise the category of 'terrorists'.[27] These attracted international attention and gained prominence in the 1960s with the hijacking of several commercial airliners and again in 1972 at the Munich Olympic Games with the kidnapping and assassination of nine Israeli athletes by Black September terrorists.[28]

The trend towards ever more convoluted semantic obfuscations to side-step terrorism's pejorative overtones was most clearly demonstrated in the exchanges between Western and non-Western member states of the United Nations following the 1972 Munich Olympics massacre. The then UN Secretary-General, Kurt Waldheim, raised the issue at the General Assembly noting that the UN should not remain a 'mute spectator' to the acts of terrorist violence then occurring throughout the world but should take practical steps that might prevent further bloodshed.

While a majority of the UN member states supported the Secretary-General, a disputatious minority, mainly the ascendant Third World bloc, derailed the discussion, arguing that 'people who struggle to liberate themselves from foreign oppression and exploitation have the right to use all methods at their disposal, including force'. As a consequence individual and small group acts of terror increasingly gained attention while terror orchestrated by states or insurgents slipped out of the international legal agenda into the interstices of politico-diplomatic chicanery. Not surprising. It was the height of the Cold War and the two superpowers, engaged in wars of proxy, were busy supporting or laying fertile ground for 'terror-violence', albeit under the guise of supporting national liberation movements and furthering the right of self-determination.

In order to mobilize consensus, the international community adopted a piecemeal approach to combating terrorism, choosing to target very specific acts of terrorism, occurring in specific situations, circumstances or places and generally providing for extradition and prosecution regimes. With a large segment of international society vulnerable to random and unexpected terrorist threats, in the wake of repeated attacks on international civil aviation,[29] the international community reacted with a series of international conventions adopted between 1969 and 1988.[30] A rash of assassinations and kidnappings of diplomats from the 1960s to the 1990s brought about the adoption of several multilateral conventions.[31] Similarly a rapid increase in the kidnappings of civilian hostages for ransom brought about the adoption of a specialised UN Convention in 1979.[32]

Against this background, UN efforts began to tentatively address state-sponsored terrorism. In 1971, the UN General Assembly passed the United Nations Declaration on Principles of International Law Concerning Friendly Relations and Co-operation among States in accordance with the Charter of the United Nations. The Declaration affirmed the duty of all states 'to refrain from organizing, instigating, assisting or participating in ... terrorist acts in another State'.[33] By the 1980s, with international terrorism coming of age and proliferating, the General Assembly took the big step of passing a resolution condemning terrorism, entitled, in part, Measures to Prevent International Terrorism.[34] It 'unequivocally condemned, as criminal, all acts, methods and practices of terrorism wherever and by whoever committed ...'[35]

However, these resolutions and declarations, while important, have one key plank missing – an accepted definition of terrorism and/or terrorist acts. Thus they provide scant insight into the essential characteristics of terrorist violence. These declarations are similar to existing multilateral anti-terrorist conventions in that they reflect a pragmatic, *ad hoc* approach that criminalizes specific practices without reference to the underlying political objectives of the offenders. However, a seemingly insurmountable obstacle to such cooperation and response has been the lack of international consensus as to an acceptable definition of terrorism, mainly due to the 'politically charged nature of terrorist activity', and the related question of whether definitions of terrorism can or should encompass national liberation movements.[36] In this charged climate, the nations of the Third World and the then communist Eastern European bloc nations rejected attempts to condemn or criminalize all political violence irrespective of the political context of the act or the political motivation of the actor. One commentator noted:

> [W]hile terrorism may be perceived in the West ... as a humanitarian problem, this is not the way it is perceived by most of the rest of the world. Most countries regard international terrorism as basically a political manifestation of the struggles against regimes such as South Africa, Rhodesia, and Israel...[37]

Many, if not a majority, of Third World and communist nations achieved independence from colonial domination through wars of national liberation or from established regimes by violent revolutionary struggle. As a consequence many of these nations argued (and occasionally still do) that otherwise impermissible violence may be legitimate in the context of revolutionary or anti-colonial struggle. The representative of Mauritania captured this mindset during a debate in the UN General Assembly in 1979 when he stated:

> ['terrorism' should not] be held to apply to persons denied the most elementary human rights, dignity, freedom, and independence ... and whose countries objected to foreign occupation ... such peoples should not be blamed for committing desperate acts which in themselves were reprehensible; rather the real culprits were those responsible for causing such desperation.[38]

Similarly, the 1979 UN Ad Hoc Committee on Terrorism Report[39] underscored ideological or geopolitical divisions which centred around the efforts of Third World nations to distinguish national liberation movements from acts of international terrorism.[40] The Committee recommended instead that the UN try to eliminate the causes of terrorism, including colonialism, racism and situations involving alien occupation; the United States rejected this position.[41] In the absence of a blanket condemnation of all forms of political private actors committed to remedying perceived injustice through violence predictably reject the 'criminal terrorist' label that states attach to their conduct, and appeal to higher moral concepts for justification.

Anatomy of Terrorism

Defining Terrorism

As noted in Chapter 1, the term 'terrorism' is of French origin and was first coined in connection with the Jacobin 'Reign of Terror',[42] a period of the bloody French Revolution in which the French State asserted its authority by knitting a fabric of fear over the populace through the summary executions of thousands. However, it was not until 1934, following the assassination of French statesman Jean Louis Barthou and King Alexander of Yugoslavia, that terrorism entered the international agenda.[43] This event induced the League of Nations to draft the first ever penal instrument making terrorism an international offence – the Convention for the Prevention and Punishment of Terrorism (CPPT).[44] The CPPT defined terrorism in a broad way, as 'criminal acts directed against a state and intended or calculated to create a state of terror in the minds of particular persons, or a group of persons or the general public'.[45] The CPPT never entered into force. Nevertheless, certain customary norms of international law relating to the use of armed force, most notably the duty of states 'to prevent and suppress attempts to commit common crimes against life or property where such crimes are directed against other states',[46] implicitly proscribed certain instances of terrorism.

During the early years of the UN the distinction between terrorists and revolutionaries was the subject of much disagreement.[47] The volatile Cold War era loomed large over any effort to establish a firm international definition of terrorism as it relates to states that sponsor or support terrorists. The UN was presented with its greatest opportunity to bring terrorism within the ambit of the UN Charter through the key 1974 UN General Assembly Resolution defining 'aggression', Resolution 3314.[48] Sidestepping the volatile issue, the UN elected to ignore using the word 'terrorism', choosing instead to classify the activities of states who send, organize or support 'armed bands, groups, irregulars, or mercenaries, which carry out acts of armed force against another State'[49] as engaging in unlawful aggression in direct violation of the UN Charter. During the 1970s and 1980s, the attempts of the UN to define the term failed, mainly due to differences of opinion between various members about the use of violence in the context of conflicts over national liberation and self-determination. In spite of its failure to define terrorism, in 1985 the UN General Assembly adopted Resolution 40/61,

[u]nequivocally condemn[ing], as criminal, all acts, methods and practices of terrorism wherever and by whomever committed ... call[ing] upon all States to *fulfil their obligations under international law* to refrain from organizing, instigating, assisting or participating in terrorist acts in other States, or acquiescing in activities within their territory directed towards the commission of such acts.[50]

Similar language can be found in a number of subsequent General Assembly and Security Council resolutions over the last thirty years, many of which state that terrorism is contrary to the purposes and the principles of the UN and represents a 'threat to international peace and security'.[51] Various definitions of terrorism refer to unlawful force as opposed to lawful force. However, the problem arises on the fundamental aspect of the definitions – the distinction between unlawful and lawful force.

In choosing to avoid defining terrorism conclusively, the UN has either used it in a more general sense or selected specific acts as constituting terrorist activity.[52] Consequently, the international community has taken a piecemeal approach and addressed the problem of international terrorism by identifying particular criminal acts inherently terrorist in nature to be prevented and punished by domestic law. The result has been the adoption of numerous global treaties, regional conventions, and bilateral agreements, which are relevant to the suppression of international terrorism, and corresponding domestic laws that implement those arrangements.[53]

To date, efforts by the UN to draft a single broad definition of terrorism acceptable to all states, such as that found in the CPPT have failed.[54] Conventional international law on terrorism is presently limited to a relatively small number of widely accepted conventions that proscribe particular types of terrorism, which likely reflect customary norms of international law.[55] The most common types of terrorism covered by these conventions include crimes against the safety of civil aviation and maritime navigation, the taking of hostages, the use of nuclear and chemical weapons, and crimes against internationally protected persons.[56] Some basic features that might contribute to an acceptable and working definition can be gleaned from the following definitions which encapsulate various aspects of terrorism:

- The unlawful use or threatened use of force or violence by a revolutionary organization against individuals or property with the intention of coercing or intimidating governments or societies, often for political or ideological purposes.[57]
- The unlawful use of force or violence against persons or property to intimidate or coerce a government, the civilian population, or any segment thereof, in furtherance of political or social objectives.[58]
- Premeditated, politically motivated violence perpetrated against non-combatant targets by subnational groups or clandestine agents.[59]
- Violent criminal conduct apparently intended: (a) to intimidate or coerce a civilian population; (b) to influence the conduct of a government by intimidation or coercion; or (c) to affect the conduct of a government by assassination or kidnapping.[60]

The synthesis of these elements is broadly consistent with most definitions in academic literature, which generally require two elements: actual or threatened violence against civilians or persons not actively taking part in hostilities and the implicit or explicit purpose of the act being to intimidate or compel a population, government or organization into some course of action.[61] This broad definition is supported by a proposed convention drafted by the International Law Association, which defines an international terrorist offence as:

> *any serious act of violence or threat* thereof by an individual whether acting alone or in association with other persons, organizations, places, transportation or communications systems or against members of the general public *for the purpose of intimidating* such persons, *causing injury to or the death* of such persons, disrupting the activities of such international organizations, of causing loss, detriment or damage to such places or property, or of interfering with such transportation and communications systems in order to undermine friendly relations among States or among the nationals of different States or *to extort concessions from States.*[62]

As Professor Jeffrey Addicott notes:

> Despite the lack of a fixed universal agreement defining terrorism, the essential goal of terrorism is readily identifiable. As the root word implies, the goal of terrorism is to instil fear in a given civilian population by means of violence. In the oft-repeated Chinese proverb, the objective of the terrorist is to kill one and frighten 10,000. While specific acts of terrorism may appear to be mindless and irrational, terrorism is the antithesis of confused behaviour. Terrorism is a goal – directed, calculated, and premeditated use of force.[63]

Defining State-sponsored Terrorism

Historically, rules on the lawful use of force developed within a framework of state-to-state relationships. This poses a problem when this framework is applied to terrorist acts. James Terry states that: 'Terrorism's uniqueness lies in its use of armed force against targets that would be exceptional or aberrational in regular warfare, with results that have little relationship to traditional military necessity.'[64] He notes that involvement in terrorist activity by states may result from both practical and ideological influences. For example, where traditional forms of warfare are considered overtly costly or would result in uncertain outcomes, terrorism may be regarded as an appropriate substitute. This may result in state provision of a range of support mechanisms to militia, paramilitary groups or other non-statal entities adopting violence (more often than not in the form of terror) as a vehicle to achieve their aspirations, whether they be revolutionary, political or ideological in character. The support ranges from propaganda, financial aid and training to intelligence, weapons and even direct involvement.[65]

However, just like terrorism, the notion of state-sponsored terrorism lacks a universal definition. Furthermore, the confusion over a precise definition of state-sponsored terrorism is in large part reflective of the basic disagreement over the elements of terrorism itself. There are, however, certain basic elements of state-sponsored terrorism: a politically subversive violent act or threat thereof; a state sponsor; an intended political outcome; and a target, whether civilian, military or material, whose death, injury or destruction can be expected to influence to some degree the desired political outcome.[66]

State sponsorship of terrorism involves both acts of commission and omission.[67] This can range from a state directly supporting the terrorist attacks, to less direct state involvement such as providing training, financing, or support one way or another. This may include a toleration of particular terrorist groups which base their activities in a state's territory.[68] From as far back as 1977, commentators suggested that the attempt 'to hold states responsible in damages for the acts of terrorists when such acts can be attributed to them represents a strategic use of traditional international law norms which may produce short-run benefits and ... contribute to long-run interests of the world community'.[69]

This position has been actively pursued by the International Law Commission (ILC)[70] in its quest to codify customary international law relating to state responsibility in its Draft Articles on Responsibility of States for Internationally Wrongful Acts.[71] Articles 8 and 11 codify the relevant rules pertaining to state responsibility for terrorist acts committed by private persons. Article 8 is the classic formulation of the *de facto* agency principle. It reads: 'The conduct of a person or group of persons shall be considered an act of a State under international law if the person or group of persons is in fact acting on the instructions of, or under the direction or control of, that State in carrying out the conduct.'[72]

Historically, the ILC has firmly insisted that in order to meet this test, it must be proved in each and every case that the person or persons 'had really been charged by the State organs to carry out that specific act'.[73] In contrast, Article 11 does not require proof of a state's prior knowledge, instruction or control of a terrorist act in order to attribute a private person's conduct to the state. Under this rule, conduct ordinarily not attributable to a state under antecedent articles shall nevertheless be attributed to a state if they acknowledge such conduct as their own.[74] Elaborating on this rule, Scott Malzahn notes that it:

> differs from the classic formulation of the de facto agency principle in that the private person is not acting on behalf of the state at the time of the act's commission, rather state responsibility is based on the state identifying the conduct and either expressly or impliedly making the conduct its own at some later date.[75]

The Law Enforcement Paradigm: Terrorism as a Crime

In response to the massacre of Israeli athletes at the 1972 Munich Olympics, the UN called for legal suppression by its members of violent acts of terrorists through the ratification of the Convention for the Prevention and Punishment of Certain Acts of International Terrorism.[76] However, many nations, primarily Western states, voted against this resolution due to its bias toward, and legitimizing of, violent national liberation movements.[77] They took issue with the fact that the Arab and Soviet blocs, along with other allies, were attempting to shield radical movements, with which they sympathized and supported, from being classified as terrorist – thereby protecting them from international condemnation and punishment.[78]

Classifying international terrorism as a crime creates a dilemma because '[a] criminal act of terrorism to some will embody a legitimate act of self-determination to others'.[79] At times states have not strictly applied the definition of international terrorism to foreign acts, recognizing some terrorist acts as legitimate claims of groups seeking self-determination. This method of defining terrorism is based on a political standard that leaves policymakers the discretion to decide which violent acts are acceptable and allows for the subjective definition of some terrorist groups as revolutionaries.[80]

> For many decades the world has been trying to develop laws to prevent and punish terrorist acts. The original problem was to devise a single definition that would appeal to all nations. Obviously this remains unlikely, if not impossible. The next obstacle was to make new laws respecting both the old and new forms of terrorist attacks.[81]

Contemporary multilateral anti-terrorism conventions began to enter the world scene in 1963. In 1970, the UN passed the United Nations General Assembly's Declaration on Principles of International Law Concerning Friendly Relations and Co-operation among States in Accordance with the Charter of the United Nations.[82] This resolution held that: '[E]very state has the duty to refrain from organizing, instigating, assisting, or participating in acts of civil strife or terrorist acts in another State or acquiescing in organized activities within its territory directed toward the commission of such acts when the acts . . . involve a threat or use of force.'[83] 'The problem remained, however, as to what each state considered a "terrorist" act. This failure essentially took the bite out of this, and many other, conventions.'[84]

The 1970s and 1980s were decades rife with politically motivated violence such as hijacking and hostage taking; the international community sought to regulate the political violence through multilateral conventions: the Convention on Offences and Certain Other Acts Committed on Board Aircraft (Tokyo Convention),[85] the Convention for the Suppression of Unlawful Seizure of Aircraft (Hague Convention),[86] the Convention for the Suppression of Unlawful Acts Against the Safety of Civil Aviation (Montreal Convention),[87] the Convention on the Prevention and Punishment of Crimes Against Internationally Protected Persons (Protection of Diplomats Convention),[88] and the Convention Against the Taking of Hostages (Hostage Taking Convention).[89] Under these conventions air hijacking, attacks on diplomatic personnel, and hostage taking became international crimes. Although only the Hostage Taking Convention specifically refers to terrorism,[90] all five multilateral conventions attempt to regulate acts of violence which are popularly perceived as terrorism.[91]

The efforts at the international level to criminalize terrorism were also reflected in regional initiatives. An important effort was undertaken in 1971 by the Organization of American States' Convention to Prevent and Punish the Acts of Terrorism Taking the Forms of Crimes Against Persons and Related Extortion That Are of International Significance. This Convention tried to remove political ideologies from the definition of terrorism by reclassifying the offences as 'common crimes of international significance'. The Convention developed a class of crimes known as 'common crimes of international significance' which encompass: kidnapping, murder, or other assaults against the life or personal integrity of, or extortion related to such crimes against, 'those persons to whom the state has the duty to give special protection according to international law'.[92] If the state refuses to extradite the offender, the Convention requires that the state prosecute domestically 'as if the act had been committed in its territory'.[93]

The Extradite or Prosecute Mechanism

The overarching enforcement mechanism of each of these conventions is the requirement that states either extradite or prosecute the offenders. This pervasive 'extradite or prosecute' scheme indicates that the purpose of the multilateral anti-terrorist conventions is to punish and deter private actors rather than agents of states. This mechanism requires states to investigate and prosecute serious offences. If a custodial state declines to extradite an alleged offender, it is required to submit the case to its competent authorities for the purpose of prosecution.

The international treaties prohibiting various acts of terrorism specify the obligation of states to extradite or prosecute perpetrators of acts defined as crimes under international law. The purpose of the principle *aut dedere, aut judicare* – extradite or prosecute – is to ensure that those who commit crimes under international law are not granted safe haven anywhere in the world. These treaties show a tendency in international law to require states to investigate and prosecute serious offences.

In 1985, the Seventh United Nations Congress on the Prevention of Crime and the Treatment of Offenders adopted a resolution on Criminal Acts of a Terrorist Character.[94] The resolution provided an umbrella of illegitimate international violence, which categorized such criminal acts as aircraft hijacking and sabotage, attacks on internationally protected persons and hostage taking.[95] This resolution was later incorporated into the General Assembly Resolution 40/61 of December 1985, which 'unequivocally condemned, as criminal, all acts, methods and practices of terrorism whenever and by whomever committed'.[96]

> After decades of terrorist violence that resulted in thousands of deaths and injuries, affecting territories of nations across the globe and international and sovereign airspace, the UN took a long overdue step in the fight against terrorism. Groups that once hid behind the shield of legitimacy while attacking innocents in restaurants, train stations, shopping plazas, ships and airplanes, lost their pretext. The acts which fell previously through the cracks of the multiple definitions were not to be specified, but labeled criminal as a whole.[97]

During the debate, fifty-seven countries participated by speaking out on the subject of terrorism prevention.[98] Israel said, 'no cause could justify acts of terrorism or serve as a pretext for states to escape obligations under international law'. International terrorism was aimed at destroying the rule of law.[99] Belgium, on behalf of the European Community, Spain and Portugal stated, 'the prevention and punishment of criminal acts should be ensured, and the taking of hostages and other crimes must no longer be treated as "acts whose political character protected their perpetrators from extradition or prosecution".'[100] Sweden, on behalf of the Nordic countries, said, 'the legitimacy of a cause such as the struggle for self-determination and independence, did not in itself legitimize the use of certain forms of violence, especially violence against innocent persons. There must be no safe haven for terrorists'.[101]

The resolution also asked 'all states to take appropriate measures at the national level with a view to the speedy and final elimination of the problem, such as the harmonization of domestic legislation with existing international obligations, and the prevention of the preparation and organization in their respective territories of acts directed against other states'.[102] States were also encouraged to 'refrain from organizing, instigating, assisting or participating in terrorist acts in other states, or acquiescing in activities within their territory directed towards the commission of such acts'.[103] They were further urged to cooperate by exchanging relevant information in combating terrorism.[104] The world had officially accepted terrorism, not as an expression of political ideologies, but as a crime.

Bases of Extra-territorial Criminal Jurisdiction

Considering that terrorism acts frequently affect more than one state, the traditional nationality and territorial link that facilitates the operation of domestic criminal jurisdiction is supplemented by three additional bases that seek to grant states extra-territorial jurisdiction in recognition of the limitations of the two classic jurisdiction bases. The three international law principles that support the legal theory of extra-territorial jurisdiction are: the protective principle, the passive personality principle and the universality principle.[105] The chapter now turns to consider these bases in the context of terrorism.

The Protective Principle   The protective principle provides jurisdiction on the basis of a perceived threat to national security, integrity, or sovereignty[106] by an extra-territorial offence.[107] The protective principle permits a state to punish a limited class of crimes (excluding such offences as violating laws against political expression) committed outside its territory by persons who are not its nationals: offences directed against the security of the state or other offences threatening the integrity of governmental functions that are generally recognized as crimes by developed legal systems.[108] The focus of the protective principle is the nature of the interest that may be injured, rather than the place of the harm or conduct.[109] Therefore, the conduct need only be a potential threat to the asserting state's interests or citizens.[110]

This jurisdictional concept has been used as the basis of many counter-terrorism laws. Thus, for example, the legislative history of the *Omnibus Diplomatic Security Act*[111] enacted by the US Congress reveals that the drafters borrowed from some of the language in the protective principle. Congress realized that one-half of the terrorist incidents in the previous seventeen years were aimed at US interests and citizens.

> Congress stated that governmental functions were threatened, including: the protection of its citizens, the ability to maintain foreign policy, interstate and foreign commerce, and business travel and tourism. This is an expansive reading of the principle which enables the US and other nations to assert jurisdiction over essentially all attacks against its citizens and interests even though there is no effect occurring within the territory of the forum state.[112]

States too have included terrorist-based offences in their penal laws. For instance, under the *Israeli Penal Law (Offenses Committed Abroad)*, 'the Courts in Israel are competent to try under Israeli law a person who has committed abroad an act which would be an offense if it had been committed in Israel and which harmed or was intended to harm the State of Israel, its security, property or economy or its transport or communications links with other countries'.[113] This law embraces the protective principle of jurisdiction and is in part the result of terrorist orchestrated activities.

The Passive Personality Principle   The passive personality principle allows the extension of jurisdiction over offenders who victimize citizens of the particular nation seeking jurisdiction.[114] The passive personality principle permits a state to apply its laws to an act committed outside its territory by a person who is not its citizen, when the victim of the act was its national.[115] 'This principle has been increasingly accepted worldwide as it is applied to terrorist and other organized attacks on a state's nationals by reason of their nationality, or to assassination of a state's diplomatic representative or other officials.'[116]

One of the first cases utilizing the passive personality principle against a terrorist was *United States v. Benitez*.[117] In that case, the court held that the passive personality principle could be used to establish jurisdiction in a case against a terrorist, not a US citizen, who had robbed, assaulted and conspired to murder US Drug Enforcement Agency (DEA) agents in Columbia.[118] In *US v Yunis*, District Judge Barrington Parker commented on the international law duty of states to prosecute or to extradite persons accused of terrorist offences, in this case hijacking. Under the US *Hostage Taking Act*,[119] since two of the passengers on a Royal Jordanian Airlines hijacked by Yunis were US citizens, the US was able to assert jurisdiction as 'the offender or the person seized or detained (was) a national of the US'.[120]

The Universality Principle   The most broadly worded principle is the universality principle. The universality principle is premised on the finding that acts of terrorism are crimes against humanity, thus allowing a state to prosecute an offender on behalf of the world.[121] This principle permits a state to define and prescribe punishment for certain offences recognized by the community of nations as of universal concern, such as piracy or hijackings, where there is no connection between the territory and the offence or of nationality with the persons involved.[122] 'Like the pirate of yore, the terrorist is imagined to be the enemy of all (civilized) mankind and therefore subject to capture by any state and subject to every state's jurisdiction.'[123]

Therefore, the location of the terrorist act is irrelevant as are the nationalities of both the offender and offended. The crimes encompassed by this principle are considered so brutal that any state within the community of nations may prosecute the accused.[124] The history of crimes, the treaties and conventions to combat terrorism, and domestic laws of all nations, 'when considered as a whole, make it clear that terrorism – including hostage taking or kidnapping or wanton acts of violence against innocent civilians – is really a composite term including all of the separately universally condemned offenses, and thus triggers the universality theory of jurisdiction'.[125]

Whether or not the universality principle applies to 'treaty crimes', which predominantly includes terrorist-related offences, remains a subject of great debate and not infrequently controversy.[126] The general tenor of domestic jurisprudence acknowledges that terrorism is an activity that attracts international condemnation. Nonetheless the highly political nature of acts of terrorism often permit them to be viewed as either a legitimate means of political protest or a criminal offence.[127] Thus, domestic jurisprudence generally shies away from recognizing universal jurisdiction as establishing the basis for prosecuting overseas terrorist crimes.

The Use of Non-lethal Military Force: Apprehension of Terrorists in International Space

Even though most states have voluntarily undertaken to prosecute or to extradite persons for the most common terrorist crimes, such as air piracy and sabotage, '[w]hen States violate these obligations, and especially when they are implicated in the conduct of the terrorists involved, other States are seriously affected'.[128] This in turn means that states are left in some cases with no option for ending the threat from such terrorists short of violating in some manner the territorial integrity of the state that has violated its own international responsibilities. This has been particularly the attitude taken by Israel and the US, who suffer and continue to suffer from repeated terrorist activity both within and without their territory.

A state which directs agents or allied entities to attack diplomats abroad or to take hostages within its own borders obviously will not order the extradition or prosecution of these perpetrators.[129] Often, the sad reality is that some nations of the world refuse to condemn terrorism and/or condone it. Thus '... the impact of political considerations in the extradition process, and the various degrees of assistance and support some nations provide to terrorist groups, make it virtually impossible to gain custody of terrorists using traditional methods'.[130] As a result, barring extraordinary intervention, perpetrators can escape criminal sanctions for the conduct outlined in the anti-terrorist conventions. Nations, victimized by terrorists, are sometimes left with no choice but to assert themselves forcefully to apprehend terrorists and bring them to trial.

In view of the reality that some states deliberately harbour terrorists or choose to circumvent their obligations under international conventions, this has led to James Bond-style operations designed to secure perpetrators or masterminds of terrorist activities through a highly controversial form of action that violates territorial sovereignty, commonly called 'abduction'. An abduction is the forcible, unconsented removal of a person by agents of one state from the territory of another state. Professor M. Cherif Bassiouni's assertion that international abductions violate international law by disrupting world order and infringing upon sovereignty and territorial integrity of other states is illustrative of customary international law.[131] Yet this is customary law, which is subject to change and modification by continued practice within the international community.[132] In fact, some countries [notably Israel and the US] have changed their posture with respect to this approach, and abductions have become recognized – though not accepted – under international law.[133]

Under international law, once a government has notice that its territory is being used for the preparation of hostile acts in or against another state, it must take effective steps to prevent those acts in order to satisfy its duty under international law[134] or risk frustrated states resorting to the extraordinary measure of abduction. The political and legal reality, however, is that abductions are controversial, politically risky, and dangerous to the individuals assigned the task. The forcible removal of a person, especially one being protected by a state hostile to the state conducting the abduction, will be treated as criminal conduct, amounting at the least to a kidnapping. In the course of such an operation, individuals may be killed, leading to charges of murder. Where the state from which the person is taken is not hostile but refuses to extradite the person seized for reasons of policy, an abduction is likely to cause a severe strain on relations. Almost invariably, the state responsible for an abduction has apologized for the violation of the other state's sovereignty, and often the individual seized is returned to the state from which he/she was taken.[135]

The Conflict Management Paradigm: Terrorists as Warriors

A basic rule of customary international law, which was adopted in Article 33 of the UN Charter, states that in the settlement of any dispute that may threaten world peace and security, an attempt must first be made to resolve the dispute by peaceful means. Though in conflicts between states it is necessary to exhaust all possible 'tools of peace',[136] negotiations between a terrorist organization and a state cannot be conducted for a number of reasons, the primary one being that the very existence of such negotiations recognizes the legitimacy of the organization and the legitimacy of its activities – a result that the state shuns.[137] Additionally, negotiations with the state may be rendered impractical due to:

> The inability to influence terrorist groups by traditional diplomatic and economic means, their decentralized and transnational character, their lack of accountability to constituencies to which governments are traditionally accountable, their clandestine nature, and their eagerness to acquire and willingness to use weapons of mass destruction, ...[138]

Even more problematic is the fact that some states 'instead of enforcing their domestic law against or extraditing terrorists, protect, train, support, or utilize terrorist groups to advance policies they favor. Some states ... are simply unable to exercise authority over terrorists, even if they were inclined to do so'.[139] Some states have argued that they have a prerogative to utilize force to defend themselves against threats resulting from breaches of international responsibility. As then US Secretary of State George P. Shultz predicted in 1984: 'We can expect more terrorism directed at our strategic interests around the world in the years ahead. To combat it, we must be willing to use military force.'[140]

Some argue that the notion that self defence relates only to a use of force that materially threatens a state's 'territorial integrity or political independence', as proscribed in Article 2(4), ignores the Charter's preservation of the 'inherent' scope of that right. Nations such as Israel and the US have 'traditionally defended their military personnel, citizens, commerce, and property from attacks even when no threat existed to their territory or independence'.[141] This stance is premised on the long-standing consideration that the military facilities, vessels and embassies of a nation are its property, and for some purposes its territory.[142]

Attacks on a nation's citizens cannot routinely be treated as attacks on the nation itself; but where a citizen is attacked because he/she is a citizen of a particular state, in order to punish his/her state of nationality or to coerce his/her state into accepting a political position, it would appear that the attack is one in which the victim state has a sufficient interest to justify extending its protection through necessary and proportionate actions. No nation should be limited to using force to protect its citizens, from attacks based on their citizenship only to situations in which the attacks occur within its territorial boundaries.

Terrorists: Combatants or Non-Combatants

For many decades, Israel has regarded terrorist acts – real or perceived – as acts of war. In the 1980s, the US followed suit, increasingly perceiving transnational terrorism as acts of war.[143] Like an enemy in a war, terrorists aim to kill and attack strategic governmental and non-governmental targets.[144] Although terrorism does not exactly comport with the definition of war,[145] scholars classify it as irregular or low-intensity warfare that involves armed attacks against both government and non-government personnel for political purposes.[146] Thus, approaching terrorism as a war[147] may be a more appropriate tack because the military is better equipped for low-intensity warfare and is not limited by restrictions placed on law enforcement.[148]

Because an act that one state considers terrorism, another may consider as a valid exercise of resistance, it is difficult to prepare effective legal principles to deter terrorism.[149] Demonstrating the problem is the much used but still practical cliché that 'one man's terrorist is another man's freedom fighter'.[150] In an attempt to put this cliché to rest, one author has suggested that the difference between terrorists and freedom fighters is that terrorists kill innocent civilians, while freedom fighters save lives and fight at the risk of their own lives 'until liberty wins the day'.[151] This, though a logical observation, is not overly consonant to reality. The main difficulty lies in the fact that each time an incident occurs, the international community cannot consistently interpret whether the act was a terrorist attack or a legitimate act of a freedom fighter.[152]

The Terrorist in Action: Hero or Villain? In December 1973, the UN General Assembly passed Resolution 3103 which granted legitimacy to conflicts involving the struggle of people against colonial and racist regimes by labeling them as 'armed conflicts'.[153] One year later, the UN adopted a Definition of Aggression, which justified terrorist activities when terrorism is waged on behalf of self-determination movements or directed against colonial and racist regimes.[154] These initiatives granted a limited amount of legitimacy to groups who are responsible for acts that have been labeled 'terrorism'. Many groups have tried to fall into the UN definitions by claiming that their actions are legal expressions of their rights.

> Due to this uncertainty, many groups are waging destruction upon sovereign nations and claiming, and thereby receiving impunity, that they are engaged in a legitimate and legal

war and that they are only fighting for their freedom. The variety of classifications used, resolutions adopted, and laws enacted only increase the difficulty in differentiating between a terrorist act and a legal and legitimate act of a freedom fighter.[155]

The interface of the law, politics and morality creates difficult problems. From a political and moral point of view: should consideration be given to the motives of the terrorist organization? From a legal perspective: if the objectives the terrorist organization wishes to achieve may be regarded as justified, does this justification become relevant to the nature of the prohibited act? These two broad queries are not posed to beg the question but rather to highlight that even the UN itself and by extension the international community, has been unable to apply seemingly clear-cut legal standards to the issue for obvious reasons – frequently terrorist acts are tightly bound up with moral and legal considerations making bright line, logical legal assessments and conclusions hazy.

Slippery Ground: The Terrorist in the Law of Armed Conflict Framework   Terrorism is generally directed at persons who are not combatants and who are completely innocent.[156] Frequently though, terrorist activities also target military personnel or government officials largely owing to the 'symbolic' value of these individuals who represent important pillars of the state – security and governance. The conundrum is that terrorism is generally conducted by persons who do not fall within the category of combatants, but they are also not in the nature of non-combatants or protected persons.[157]

The definition of the term 'civilians' or 'civilian population' appears in Article 50 of Additional Protocol I of the Geneva Convention of 1977:

> 1. A civilian is any person who does not belong to one of the categories of persons referred to in Article 4 (A) (1), (2), (3) and (6) of the Third Convention and in Article 43 of this Protocol. In case of doubt whether a person is a civilian, that person shall be considered to be a civilian.
> …
> 3. The presence within the civilian population of individuals who do not come within the definition of civilians does not deprive the population of its civilian character.[158]

In an analysis of the implications of the provisions of the aforementioned article, Professor Emmanuel Gross observes:

> Prima facie, as this Article is formulated in the negative, one may think that if certain persons do not fall within the category of combatants, they must be civilians. However, in my opinion, it would not be right to interpret the Article in this way as the drafters of the Convention did not intend to grant terrorists the status of civilians. In addition, the defenses granted to civilians are broader than the defenses granted to combatants.[159]

To be a civilian who does not belong to the armed forces and who is not a combatant is one thing. To be a civilian who fights against those whom he/she regards as his/her enemy is something else completely. International law distinguishes between those who participate in the armed conflict and those who do not[160] as do the various Geneva Conventions.[161] Generally, soldiers fall within the former definition, as indeed do members of other armed militias.[162] These

Conventions afford defences to combatants who have been captured by the enemy during the course of the fighting.[163] Those captured fighters are deemed to be prisoners of war.[164] However, the various Geneva Conventions do not refer to the legal status of civilians who do not fall within the scope of the term 'combatant', yet take an active part in the fighting. 'This phenomenon is completely disregarded by the various Geneva Conventions.'[165]

Notwithstanding that the notion of classifying 'freedom fighters' as combatants for all purposes was not adopted or accepted by the Geneva Conventions in 1949, when the latter were formulated, recognition of the need for such a development grew. Accordingly, in 1977, this issue was added to Additional Protocol I to the original Geneva Conventions.[166] Additional Protocol I amended the Geneva Conventions 'to embrace a new type of combatant, one who had not been recognized as a combatant within the classic structure of European wars, and grant him the rights of a prisoner of war, on the condition that he conducted himself in accordance with the rules applicable to combatants under international law'.[167]

The amended Geneva Conventions now provided prisoner of war protection for fighters who did not fall within the classic structure of conventional wars – the guerilla fighter. Even with regard to these other groups, it is contemplated that the fighters are 'rebel groups' or 'non-state actors' such as organized armed militia or paramilitary groups with an element of organization and command structure approximate to or inherent in armed forces, especially of a political or revolutionary colour. Importantly, they should conduct themselves in accordance with the rules of combat in international law in order to benefit from the various protections.[168]

It is evident from the final draft of the Protocol that the

> protection of the interests of the civilian population was preferred over full protection of freedom fighters. The requirements that those freedom fighters refrain from intermingling with the civilian population, that they wear uniforms or other recognizable means of identification, and that they carry their weapons openly, were specifically intended to ensure that other parties to the conflict would know against whom they were fighting. These requirements were meant to ensure that civilians who were not combatants would not be endangered.[169]

On the basis that Additional Protocol I expanded the definition of combatants to include freedom fighters as bearers of rights under the Convention many countries (including Israel, the US and the United Kingdom) have all refused to sign Additional Protocol I. The argument is, *inter alia*, that the Article would enable terrorist organizations to be recognized as combatants, and thereby allow them to be granted the rights of prisoners of war. In their view it was not desirable to grant terrorists rights such as the right not to be tried for their actions.[170] Professor Frits Kalshoven, in a panel dealing with the question 'Should the Law of War Apply to Terrorists?',[171] asserted that terrorist organizations and terrorists are not entitled to the status of combatants:

> In these circumstances, a simple statement that the law of armed conflict is applicable to terrorists seems of little practical utility. Who would be bound by such an instrument, and to what effect? Would, for instance, the authorities acquire any additional legal powers that

they do not already possess under their constitutional provisions? Would they become bound to respect any special rights of terrorists not ensuing from existing human rights instruments? Again, are we to assume that terrorists must respect the law of armed conflict – with its express prohibition on acts of terror?[172]

Terrorists are not entitled to the broad protection given to civilians under international law, and at the same time are not combatants. The difficult question then becomes what are the legal and justifiable means of fighting the menace of terrorism.

Two questions arise: is it proper to regard terrorists as combatants, and thereby grant the terrorists the protection due to combatants, *a fortiori*; and is it improper to regard terrorists as civilians who are not combatants, and grant them even more extensive rights?[173]

Argument has been made that attacking terrorists using military force is not an issue in which the law needs to or can intervene. In other words, it is said that the issue is not justiciable, at least from an institutional point of view.[174] This position was supported by an Israeli court in *Motti Ashkenazi v Minister of Defense*[175] The bold statement by the Court in the case, however, seems at odds with the dictates of international law. Any use of military force by a state generally engages the law of armed conflict. This in turn means that the operational policies of a state ought to be constrained by international law and judged by the standards established by the law of armed conflict. There is no doubt that decisions of whether or not to undertake military action are executive decisions which domestic courts may not be in a position to adjudicate; however these decisions ought to accord with international law rather than a sweeping invocation of 'national security' as though this trumps laid down international standards. Thus the question of the status of the terrorist still persists once military force is deployed, since it activates the application of the law of armed conflict.

Limited Lethal Military Force: Assassinations or 'Surgical Strikes'

In countering terrorism, intelligence agencies have increasingly devoted significant resources to following individual terrorists – the leaders and operational masterminds. They do so through following a 'footprint' – this may include the transmission of a mobile telephone or the tracing of an e-mail. Once their whereabouts are established, they are targeted with precision missiles whether they are in moving vehicles or buildings. In the last few years, Israel has managed to eliminate many Palestinian leaders through limited missile strikes targeting moving vehicles, houses or even rooms in houses. They see this as having several advantages: pulverizing tactical and organizational capability, pre-empting attacks, meting out justice to operational commanders and limiting collateral damage that inevitably results from large-scale military incursions.

The meaning of the term 'assassination' in historical context, and in the light of its usage in the laws of war, is, simply, any unlawful killing of particular individuals for political purposes. This rule seems consistent with the views of early writers of international law. Enemy combatants who fall into the hands of a state, for example, may not be summarily executed, however heinous their personal misdeeds.[176] Hague Convention IV of 1907, which is part of customary international law, prohibits the killing of individuals belonging to the other side, through the use of treacherous or deceitful means, during the course of the war:[177]

In addition to the prohibitions provided by special Conventions, it is especially forbidden –

(i) To employ poison or poisoned weapons;
(ii) To kill or wound treacherously individuals belonging to the hostile nation or army;
...
(vii) To destroy or seize the enemy's property, unless such destruction or seizure be imperatively demanded by the necessities of war;
(viii) To declare abolished, suspended, or inadmissible in a court of law the rights and actions of the nationals of the hostile party.[178]

This prohibition has been reaffirmed in Article 37 of Additional Protocol I to the Geneva Conventions of 1949.[179] The matter, however, is not as black and white as the law might seem to suggest. What about situations where a state attempts to resolve the problem by peaceful means? Apparently then, the lack of cooperation or the inability of a concerned entity to prevent terrorist operations would prompt the victim state to defend itself. But then what would be the parameters or the nature of the defence? Do suicide bombers (in training or enroute to an operation), for example, present an immediate threat triggering the *Caroline* formula?

The use of force in a foreign territory to defend against terrorists will sometimes take the form of an attack aimed at one or more individuals. The standard by which the propriety of such attacks should be judged is the same applied to more general attacks. Attacks aimed at specific individuals potentially involve claims of 'assassination', which is prohibited under international law. When such attacks are lawful under international law, and therefore are not an 'assassination', they are often less damaging to innocent persons than bombings and other less discriminate actions. Prohibiting 'assassination', however, is legally, militarily and morally sound. Assassination is in essence intentional and unlawful killing – murder – for political purposes.[180]

Evidently from a tactical point of view, a limitation on assassination undoubtedly disadvantages states in a contest with states or groups that routinely resort to murder, even of citizens having nothing to do with their political objectives. The life and death question is – can there be a proper use of assassination? The controversy associated with such debates – and the natural desire of officials to avoid controversial issues – leads them (and the agencies they represent) to shy away from such actions. However, Israel has consistently viewed the use of so called 'surgical strikes' targeting terrorist leaders (real or perceived) and masterminds as a necessary instrument in its national security planning process and operations.

It is accepted that in domestic cases of terrorism, the state is entitled to use force against terrorists operating within its own territory. However, even this entitlement is subject to constraints. If no imminent danger is anticipated, it is forbidden to use force against the terrorists. A terrorist may not be killed for his/her past actions, thereby preventing him/her from realizing his/her right to a fair trial.[181]

In other words, force may not be used against a terrorist as a punitive act, but only as a pre-emptive act. Similarly, the state is subject to a number of human rights that are provided in customary international law.[182] Whether or not the assassination of terrorists or perceived terrorists is justified presents not just a legal dilemma but a moral one. Professor Emmanuel Gross argues that:

> If the killing of terrorists will prevent the death, or serious injury, of many innocent people, then, at least according to the principle of moral utilitarianism, it would seem possible to kill them. The justification of any action as proper, according to this approach, is determined by whether the action will lead to the best possible result among all the possible outcomes in that situation. In other words, one must aspire to the maximum general good in each and every situation. If the good result ensuing from the performance of the act outweighs the bad ensuing from it, then it must be performed, irrespective of whether the act entails killing, torture, or the like.[183]

Large-scale Military Force: Terrorism as an Act of War

The UN Charter has as its primary goal the prevention of war – working with the political system to govern conflicts between states by outlawing a wide range of uses of force and defining permissible and lawful uses of force.[184] The UN Charter contains only two exceptions to the prohibition of force, namely Security Council enforcement actions pursuant to Chapter VII, and the right to individual and collective self-defence laid down in Article 51. Considering that the UN Charter does not expressly mention terrorism, the prohibition of the use of force embodied in Article 2(4) of the UN Charter sits uneasily with the particular realities of the nature of use of force by terrorists, since the drafters of the Charter had a singular focus in regulating state-to-state use of force. However, this has not prevented some grounds to be articulated within the Charter regime (sometimes firm, sometimes infirm) in relation to using military force as a counter-terrorism measure.

State Responsibility   In general, large-scale military force is almost inevitably tied to state responsibility as various incidents have demonstrated, whether it be the bombing of Tunis by Israel in 1985[185] or more recently the post-September 11 military campaigns against Afghanistan and Iraq.[186] In certain circles, there is a feeling that the rules relating to state responsibility and self-defence are sufficiently robust and flexible to permit a broad range of counter-terrorism measures. Though transnational terrorists now occur in the form of stateless entities that possess most of the attributes of a state – wealth, willing forces, training, organization, and potential access to weapons of mass destruction nonetheless they sit uneasily within the state-centric international regime on the use of military force. In practice, the reach and lethality of these entities does depend on some form or other of state support and this linkage provides a plank that triggers the operation of the international regime on the use of force, as was evident in the decision to bomb Libya in the mid 1980s or more recently the military campaign against Afghanistan.

Under customary international law, a state is normally responsible for those illegalities which it has originated. A state bears responsibility for acts injurious to another state committed by private individuals when the illegal deeds proceed from the command, authorization, or culpable negligence of the government. It is beyond dispute that states are directly responsible under international law to control terrorists operating within their borders, as is the fact that states have a responsibility to refrain from actively supporting terrorist organizations. As early as 1970, the UN General Assembly, in Resolution 2625,[187] made it clear that a state's mere acquiescence in terrorist activity emanating from its soil is a violation of the state's international obligations.

The violation of international norms by a state provides grounds for the wronged state to use force lawfully in order to right the wrong or to prevent future wrongs. Though states are generally not permitted to use force under international law against other states that harm them wrongfully,[188] the covert or overt support of terrorists by a state may engage state responsibility and thus trigger the application of military force as a countermeasure. In order to justify military force against terrorists in another country and thus by extension on the state sponsor, the actions of the terrorists under a teleological reading of the UN Charter would ordinarily have to rise to the level of an armed attack. Acts not rising to this level do not justify a forcible response under international law, because the military action would violate, without legal justification, the territorial integrity of the state in which the terrorists are located. Because an attack against the terrorists violates the territorial integrity of the host state, the 'armed attack' of the terrorists must be attributable to that state. Only then can force be used against the terrorists in that state or against the forces of that state itself. However, this position should be taken with a word of caution:

> Placing responsibility for acts of terrorism is more than merely a problem of proof. Controversy and uncertainty exist as to the extent to which States that protect or support terrorist groups can legally be held responsible for the acts of such groups. Furthermore, terrorist groups commonly seek to avoid responsibility for the acts of their members.[189]

The active support by a state of a terrorist entity, such as was evident in the relationship between the Taliban government and Al-Qaeda, offers a textbook example of state-sponsored terrorism. In reality, such scenarios are extremely rare, with most contemporary state-sponsored terrorism taking the form of provision of covert support and the terrorist actions manifesting themselves in sporadic attacks against a nation's interests or citizens against a wider background of a sustained terror campaign. This has led some scholars to argue that injuring civilians in a foreign country may amount to an attack, as required by Article 51 of the UN Charter, i.e. an attack in response to which one may engage in self-defence.[190] This is based on the equation of an armed attack on nationals abroad with that on the state itself, since it is the population that makes up a state. Forcible protection of a state's national interests, though often a justification in military responses to terrorism, nonetheless is a controversial issue as it seeks to assimilate the interests/citizens to the territorial domain of a state and thus trigger the self-defence argument in circumstances which run counter to the traditional grounds of invoking this right.

Anticipatory Self-defence/Pre-emptive Strike Another ground on which use of military force is pegged is the issue of defusing potential attacks through pre-emptive military action targeting terrorist training camps and infrastructure. The right of anticipatory self-defence had been invoked by a number of states, sometimes accepted, but more often than not rejected. The primary stumbling block to anticipatory self-defence is that terrorist attacks – even on a global scale – do not rise to the level of sustained combat. Indeed, the very effectiveness of such attacks depends on a state not knowing when – or how – such attacks will next occur. This in turn presents the international regime on the use of force with a major headache since the nature of the terrorist threat makes 'anticipating the enemy' a sound tactical move based on both logical and practical premises.

Argument (supported by some international scholars) points to the fact that when a terrorist attack is about to be launched, the state under attack may take action, including the use of force, against those responsible, in order to prevent the anticipated future harm. Argument is further made that in the light of the fact that the world and military capabilities have changed in recent years, Article 51 of the UN Charter should be interpreted in a broader manner and in the light of its contents and purpose, so as also to enable self-defence in the face of future terrorist attacks or repeated terrorist attacks. In essence, terrorism is deemed to be indirect acts of aggression by the state which hosts the terrorists, and as the language of Article 51 does not require that the armed attack be direct, indirect activities of this type may also be deemed to be an armed attack.[191]

To the extent that the lethality of a terrorist act can be equated to an indirect or direct act of aggression, it may be approximated to a threat to national security, triggering the engagement by the victim state of military force. The terrorist threat to national security may be a legitimate consideration in the decision whether the state under attack may and even should defend itself. Indeed, the manner in which Article 51 is drafted does not provide a particularly suitable basis for a response against a terror attack launched from a foreign state. But in certain cases, this right to act in self-defence will arise in any event.

The use of anticipatory defence to defuse potential terrorist attacks against a nation's interests and/or citizens finds even stronger support in the real potential danger posed by terrorist groups that may acquire and be in possession of weapons of mass destruction. Some scholars believe that a right of truly anticipatory self-defence has emerged outside of Article 51 in light of the availability of WMDs.[192] Professor Thomas Franck accounts for the emergence of a viable doctrine of anticipatory self-defence through 'the transformation of weaponry to instruments of overwhelming and instant destruction. These [weapons] [bring] into question the conditionality of Article 51, which limits states' exercise of the right of self-defense to the aftermath of an armed attack. Inevitably, first-strike capabilities begat a doctrine of "anticipatory self-defense".'[193] This issue will be covered in greater depth in subsequent chapters.

This section of the chapter has deliberately traversed in general detail the issues that are at the centre of the discourse of terrorism as an act of war triggering the use of lethal military force. The various issues raised in this section of the chapter will be fleshed out in greater detail and subjected to rigorous analysis in subsequent chapters. Overall though, it is of note from the above sketch that, over the last two decades, the capabilities of terrorists and other state and non-state entities that support terrorists have prompted a gradual move towards looking at terrorist acts as acts of war in addition to the classical view of crime. This glacial move was, however, hastened with the events of September 11 (discussed at length in Chapters 4 and 5) marking a crossing of the rubicon. Engaging the military against global terrorists as a means of availing greater intelligence-gathering capability and, importantly, decisive action now occupies an important part in the legal and political discourse in both domestic and international arenas.

Conclusion

The law plays an important role in marking the limits and conditions on measures used to protect national security against terrorism. Though states may propose counter-terrorism measures, they must consider both their operational practicality and legality. The rules of international law must and do evolve to meet new and changing circumstances. But this evolution is circumscribed by necessity and accomplished only by the explicit and implicit agreement of the world community.

Having evaluated the various counter-terrorism measures, the book now embarks on a comprehensive discussion and analysis of the conflict management approach. It is the cold-blooded and indiscriminate nature of acts of terrorism that generated a general desire by nations to act swiftly and decisively, frequently at the expense of due process and justice. Absent alternatives, a state seems to be justified to act swiftly and forcefully with enough facts to justify its actions in order to minimize terrorist action. However, the reality is that the regime on the use of force exists and was designed to guard against just this sort of action. The real and terrible threat of terrorism has led states down paths that were initially best left unexplored and shaken important aspects of the international regime on the use of force in various ways.

Notes

1   Emmanuel Gross (2001), 'Thwarting Terrorist Acts By Attacking The Perpetrators or Their Commanders as an Act of Self-Defense: Human Rights Versus The State's Duty To Protect Its Citizens', 15 *Temple International and Comparative Law Journal* 195, 233.

2   Ileana M. Porras (1994), 'On Terrorism: Reflections on Violence and the Outlaw', 12 *Utah Law Review* 119, 139.

3   Ibid.

4   Ibid., 142.

5   See, e.g., *Omnibus Security and Antiterrorism Act* of 1986, Pub. L. No. 99–399, 100 Stat. 855 (providing a basis for the United States to prosecute terrorists for acts committed against Americans overseas); see also Ethan A. Nadelmann (1990), 'The Role of the United States in the International Enforcement of Criminal Law', 31 *Harvard International Law Journal* 37, 64–71 (noting the United States' efforts to renegotiate extradition treaties in order to prosecute international terrorists).

6   Tyler Raimo (1999), 'Winning at the Expense of Law: The Ramifications of Expanding Counter-Terrorism Law Enforcement Jurisdiction Overseas', 14 *American University International Law Review* 1473, 1478.

7   For UN perspectives on terrorism in the mid-1980s, see Abraham D. Sofaer (1986), 'Terrorism and the Law', 64 *Foreign Affairs* 901, 903–06.

8   M. Cherif Bassiouni (2002), 'Legal Control of International Terrorism: A Policy-Oriented Assessment', 43 *Harvard International Law Journal* 83, 88-96.

9   Greg Travalio and John Altenburg (2003), 'Terrorism, State Responsibility, and the Use of Military Force', 4 *Chicago Journal of International Law* 97, 99.

10 Ibid.

11 See 'Proactive Responses to Terrorism: Reprisals, Preemption, and Retribution', in Charles W. Kegley, Jr. (ed.) (1990) *International Terrorism*, New York, NY: St. Martin's, 240 (commenting on the different interpretations of international terrorism).

12 See 143 Cong. Rec. H651–03 (daily ed. 26 February 1997) (describing law enforcement proactive measures as 'prevention, immediate incident response, and post-incident response').

13 Gross, 'Thwarting Terrorist Acts', 202; see also Abraham D. Sofaer (1989), 'The Sixth Annual Waldemar A. Solf Lecture in International Law: Terrorism, the Law, and the National Defense', 126 *Military Law Review* 89, 89–90.

14 Richard J. Erickson (1989), *Legitimate Use of Military Force Against State-Sponsored International Terrorism*, Maxwell Air Force Base, Ala.: Air University Press, 63.

15 See Agencies' Efforts to Fight Terrorism: Hearings before the Subcommittee on National Security, International Affairs and Criminal Justice of the House Committee Government Reform and Oversight, 105th Cong. (1998), available in LEXIS online, Cong. Rec. [hereinafter Agencies' Efforts To Fight Terrorism] (statement of Richard Davis, Director of National Security Analysis, National Security and International Affairs Division) (asserting that since the 1970s, the United States' policy toward terrorism abroad has evolved concurrently with the perception and nature of the terrorist threat).

16 See Counter-terrorism Policy Hearings Before Senate Judiciary Committee, 105th Cong. 123 (1998) [hereinafter Counter-terrorism Policy Hearings] (announcing that the trend of international terrorism is to inflict the maximum amount of destruction to property and human life and create a sense of terror to gain media recognition).

17 See Tim Weiner (1998), 'Man With Mission Takes On the U.S. at Far-Flung Sights', *New York Times*, (21 August), A1 (noting that Osama bin Laden, president of 'Terrorist University', provides major assistance to terrorist organizations and Islamic groups from his $250 million fortune).

18 Raimo, 1479.

19 Ibid., 1480.

20 See, e.g., Robert D. McFadden (2001), 'A Nation Challenged: In Profile; Bin Laden's Journey From Rich, Pious Boy to the Mask of Evil', *New York Times*, (30 September), B1.

21 M. Cherif Bassiouni (2000), 'Assessing "Terrorism" Into The New Millennium', 12 *DePaul Business Law Journal* 1.

22 Richard R. Baxter (1975), 'The Geneva Conventions and Wars of National Liberation', in M. Cherif Bassiouni (ed.), *International Terrorism and Political Crimes*, Springfield, Ill.: Thomas, 120; Jiri Toman, 'Terrorism and the Regulation of Armed Conflicts', in *International Terrorism and Political Crimes*; 'Deception and Deterrence in "Wars of National Liberation": State-Sponsored Terrorism and other forms of Secret Warfare', in *International Terrorism and Political Crimes*; Donald M. Snow (2nd ed., 1997), *Distant Thunder: Patterns of Conflict in the Developing World*, Armonk, NY: M.E. Sharpe.

23 Bassiouni, 'Assessing "Terrorism"', 3.

24 See Hurst Hannum (1996), *Autonomy, Sovereignty, and Self-determination: The Accommodation of Conflicting Rights*, Philadelphia, PA : University of Pennsylvania Press.

25   One such case is the conflict in the Former Yugoslavia. See Letter Dated 24 May 1994 from the Secretary-General to the President of the Security Council, U.N. SCOR, 49th Sess, U.N. Doc S/1994/674 (1994); see also Final Report of the Commission of Experts Established Pursuant to Security Council Resolution 780 (1992), U.N. online at gopher:// gopher.igc.apc.org:7030/11/annexes.

26   M. Cherif Bassiouni, 'A Policy-Oriented Inquiry into the Different Forms and Manifestations of International Terrorism', in M. Cherif Bassiouni (ed.) (1988), *Legal Responses to International Terrorism: US Procedural Aspects XV*, Dordrecht; Boston: Norwell, MA: M. Nijhoff; W. T. Mallison Jr and S. V. Mallison (1973), 'The Concept of Public Purpose Terror in International Law: Doctrines and Sanctions to Reduce the Destruction of Human and Material Values', 18 *Howard Law Journal* 412. However, the recently adopted *United Nations International Convention for the Suppression of the Financing of Terrorism* holds State Parties accountable for engaging in the financing of terrorist acts. Such accountability evidences an international movement towards recognizing State actors as subject to international crimes of terror-violence. *International Convention for the Suppression of the Financing of Terrorism*, G.A. Res 109, U.N. GAOR 6th Comm, 54 Sess, 76th mtg, Agenda Item 160, U.N. Doc A/54/109 (1999).

27   Though there are no reliable statistics, a number of official and non-official publications provide estimates. The most reliable source is the US Department of State's annual report assessing international terrorism. For the latest of these reports, see Office of Counter terrorism, Department of State (2001), *Patterns of Global Terrorism 2000*, Washington DC: Government Printing Office, (Appendix C). Available online at http://www.state.gov/s/ct/rls/pgtrpt/2001/, 21 September 2004.

28   Cindy C. Combs (2nd ed. 2000), 'Terrorism', in Charlyce Jones Owen et al. (eds), *Terrorism in the Twenty-First Century*, Upper Saddle River, NJ: Prentice Hall, 168.

29   See, e.g., Alona Evans (1969), 'Aircraft Hijacking: Its Cause and Cure', 63 *American Journal of International Law* 695.

30   *Convention on Offences and Certain Other Acts Committed On Board Aircraft* (Tokyo Convention), opened for signature 14 September 1963, 704 U.N.T.S. 219; *Convention for the Suppression of Unlawful Seizure of Aircraft* (Hague Convention), opened for signature 16 December 1970, 860 U.N.T.S. 105; *Convention for the Suppression of Unlawful Acts Against the Safety of Civil Aviation* (Montreal Convention), opened for signature, 23 September 1971, 974 U.N.T.S. 177; *Protocol for the Suppression of Unlawful Acts of Violence at Airports Serving Civil Aviation*, ICAO Doc. 9518; reprinted in 27 ILM 627.

31   *Convention on the Prevention and Punishment of Crimes Against Internationally Protected Persons, Including Diplomatic Agents*, opened for signature 14 December 1973, 1035 U.N.T.S. 167; *Convention on the Safety of United Nations and Associated Personnel*, G.A. Res 59, U.N. GAOR, 49th Sess, U.N. Doc A/49/59 (1994). See also, *Convention to Prevent and Punish Acts of Terrorism Taking the Form of Crimes Against Persons and Related Extortion that are of International Significance*, OAS Doc A/6/Doc 88 rev 1, corr1 (2 February 1971) reprinted in 10 I.L.M. 255.

32   *International Convention Against the Taking of Hostages*, U.N. G.A. Res. 34/154 (XXXIV), U.N. GAOR, 34 Sess, Supp No 46 at 245, U.N. Doc A/34/146 (1979) reprinted in 18 ILM 1456.

33   1979 *Declaration on Principles of International Law Concerning Friendly Relations and Cooperation among States*, G.A. Res 2625, U.N. GAOR, 25th Sess, Supp No 28, U.N. Doc A/8028 (1970) 123.

34   *Measures to Prevent International Terrorism*, G.A. Res 61, U.N. GAOR, 40th Sess, Supp No 53, at 301, U.N. Doc A/40/53 (1986).

35   Ibid., 302.

36   Lyal S. Sunga (1997), *The Emerging System of International Criminal Law: Developments in Codification and Implementation*, The Hague; Boston: Kluwer Law International, 192–93, 201; see also Louis Rene Beres (1995), 'The Meaning of Terrorism: Jurisprudential and Definitional Clarifications', 28 *Vanderbilt Journal of Transnational Law* 239, 248; Michael Reisman (1999), 'International Legal Responses to Terrorism', 22 *Houston Journal of International Law* 3, 9–13.

37   Ernest H. Evans, 'American Policy Response to International Terrorism: Problems of Deterrence', in Marius H. Livingston (ed.) (1978) *International Terrorism in the Contemporary World*, 376, 381–82.

38   U.N. GAOR, General Comm, 27th Sess, 19th mtg, U.N. Doc A/C.6/SR/1362 (1979) 24. For a more recent reflection on the UN understanding of terrorism, consider a comment in February 2001 by a Malaysian representative to the ad hoc committee of the General Assembly created to draft a comprehensive convention on terrorism. Speaking on behalf of the Organization of the Islamic Conference, the representative said that a definition of terrorism was desirable so that terrorism could be 'differentiated from the legitimate struggles of people under foreign occupation for national liberation, as recognised by the relevant resolutions and declarations of the United Nations'. Committee on Terrorism Takes Up Draft Comprehensive Anti-Terrorism Convention, Press Release, Ad Hoc Committee on Assembly Resolution 51/210, 5th Sess 19th mtg, U.N. Doc L/2971 (2001).

39   U.N. GAOR, 34th Sess, Supp No 37, U.N. Doc A/34/37 (1979).

40   Ibid., 32.

41   Ibid.

42   See John Murphy (1989), 'Defining International Terrorism: A Way Out of the Quagmire', 19 *Israel Yearbook on Human Rights* 13, 14.

43   Joel Cavicchia (1992), 'The Prospects for an International Criminal Court in the 1990s', *Dickinson Journal of International Law* 223, 225.

44   *Convention for the Prevention and Punishment of Terrorism* (1938) 19 *League of Nations Official Journal* 23 (*CPPT*).

45   Ibid., 23.

46   Lassa Oppenheim (9th ed., 1996), *International Law* (Robert Jennings and Arthur Watts, eds), London: Longmans, Vol, 1, 400.

47   For example, when Nelson Mandela first visited the US, he was on the State Department's list of international terrorists. Mandela is now a Nobel Peace Prize Laureate and pre-eminent international statesman. In the Middle East, another 'international terrorist', Yasser Arafat, won the Nobel Peace Prize, but questions remain as to whether he is an architect of peace or a purveyor of terrorism. As recently as February 2001, Mr Hasmy, a Malaysian representative to the Ad Hoc Committee of the General Assembly created to draft a comprehensive convention on terrorism, spoke on behalf of the Organisation of the Islamic Conference and commented that a definition of terrorism was desirable so that terrorism could be 'differentiated from the legitimate struggles of peoples under colonial or alien domination and foreign occupation for self-determination and national liberation, as recognised by the relevant resolutions of the United Nations': *Measures to Eliminate International Terrorism,* U.N. GAOR, 56th sess, 14th plen mtg, 11, U.N. Doc A/56/PV.14 (2001).

48   *Definition of Aggression*, G.A. Res 3314, U.N. GAOR, 29th Sess, 2319th plen mtg, Annex, Supp No 31, 142, U.N. Doc A/Res/3314 (1974).

49   Ibid, art. 3(g).

50   G.A. Res 40/61, 40th sess, 108th plen mtg, [1], [6], U.N. Doc A/RES/40/61 (1985) (emphasis added).

51   See, e.g., G.A. Res 31/102, U.N. GAOR, 31st sess, 99th plen mtg, U.N. Doc A/RES/31/102 (1976); G.A. Res 34/145, U.N. GAOR, 34th sess, 105th plen mtg, U.N.

Doc A/RES/34/145 (1979); G.A. Res 38/130, U.N. GAOR, 38th sess, 101st mtg, U.N.
Doc A/RES/38/130 (1983); G.A. Res 44/29, U.N. GAOR, 44th sess, 72nd plen mtg,
U.N. Doc A/RES/44/29 (1989); G.A. Res 46/51, U.N. GAOR, 46th sess, 67th plen mtg,
U.N. Doc A/Res/46/51 (1991); G.A. Res 51/210, U.N. GAOR, 51st sess, 88th plen
mtg, U.N. Doc A/RES/51/210 (1996); G.A. Res 53/108, U.N. GAOR, 53rd sess, 83rd
plen mtg, Agenda Item 155, U.N. Doc A/RES/53/108 (1999); G.A. Res 56/160, U.N.
GAOR, 56th sess, 88th plen mtg, Agenda Item 119b, U.N. Doc A/RES/56/160 (2001)
(*'General Assembly Resolutions'*).

52   Jeffrey Addicott (2002), 'Legal and Policy Implications for a New Era: The "War On
     Terror"', 4 *Scholar: St Mary's Law Review on Minority Issues* 209, 213–14.
53   'The international conventions by and large address the form or target of the terrorist
     attack, rather than the terrorists themselves.' Leah Campbell (2000), 'Defending
     against Terrorism: A Legal Analysis of the Decision to Strike Sudan and Afghanistan',
     74 *Tulane Law Review* 1067, 1071–2.
54   Justice Rosalyn Higgins (1997), 'The General International Law of Terrorism', in
     Rosalyn Higgins and Maurice Flory (eds.), *Terrorism and International Law*, London;
     New York: Routledge, 13, 14.
55   See Louis Rene Beres (1994), 'On International Law and Nuclear Terrorism', 24
     Georgia Journal of International and Comparative Law 1, 3.
56   See Yonah Alexander (1999), 'Terrorism in the Twenty-First Century: Threats and
     Responses', 12 *DePaul Business Law Journal* 59, 92–4.
57   *US Department of Defense.*
58   *Judicial Administration*, 28 CFR § 0.85.
59   *Foreign Relations and Intercourse*, 22 USC § 2656f(d).
60   *US Department of Justice.*
61   See, e.g., Harry Henderson (2001), *Global Terrorism: The Complete Reference Guide*,
     New York: Checkmark Books, 1–30; David Long (1990), *The Anatomy of Terrorism*,
     New York: Free Press; Toronto: Collier Macmillan Canada; New York: Maxwell
     Macmillan International, 1–13; Ken Booth and Tim Dunne (2002), 'Worlds in
     Collision' in Ken Booth and Tim Dunne (eds), *Worlds in Collision: Terror and the
     Future of Global Order*, London: Palgrave Macmillan, 8.
62   International Law Association, *Draft Single Convention on the Legal Control of
     International Terrorism as contained in International Law Association, Report of the
     Fifty-Ninth Conference*, art. 1(j), 497–504 (1982).
63   Addicott, 216.
64   James Terry (1986), 'Countering State-Sponsored Terrorism: A Law-Policy Analysis',
     36 *Naval Law Review* 159, 161.
65   Ibid.
66   In defining state-sponsored terrorism, Cline and Alexander sum up this category thus:

     The deliberate employment of violence or the threat of use of violence by sovereign
     states (or sub-national groups encouraged or assisted by sovereign states) to attain
     strategic and political objectives by acts in violation of law intended to create
     overwhelming fear in a target population larger than the civilian or military victims
     attacked or threatened.

     Senate Subcommittee on Security and Terrorism, 99th Cong, 1st sess, *Report on State-
     Sponsored Terrorism* (1985), 40.
67   See, e.g., Long, 105–114; John Murphy (1989), *State Support of International
     Terrorism: Legal, Political and Economic Dimensions*, Boulder, Colo.; London:
     Westview Press; Mansell Pub., 31–44.
68   *Definition of Aggression*, G.A. Res 3314, U.N. GAOR, 29th Sess, 2319th plen mtg,
     Annex, Supp No 31, U.N. Doc A/RES/3314 (1974) 142.

69   Richard Lillich and John Paxman (1976), 'State Responsibility for Injuries to Aliens
      Occasioned by Terrorist Activities', 26 *American University Law Review* 217, 221.
70   The ILC is a body established by the UN General Assembly under G.A. Res 174(II),
      U.N. GAOR, 123rd plen mtg, 105 (1947) to make recommendations for the
      codification of customary international law.
71   See International Law Commission, *Draft Articles on Responsibility of States for
      Internationally Wrongful Acts as contained in the International Law Commission,
      Report of the International Law Commission on the Work of its Fifty-Third Session*,
      U.N. GAOR, 53rd sess, Supp No 10, 44–5, U.N. Doc A/56/10 (2001) ('*Draft
      Articles*').
72   Ibid., 45.
73   Luigi Condorelli (1989), 'The Imputability to States of Acts of International
      Terrorism', 19 *Israel Yearbook on Human Rights* 233, 239 (citations omitted).
74   *Draft Articles on Responsibility of States,* 45.
75   Scott Malzahn (2002), 'State Sponsorship and Support of International Terrorism:
      Customary Norms of State Responsibility', 26 *Hastings International and
      Comparative Law Review* 83, 98.
76   U.N. Doc. A/C.6/L.850 (1972). For a brief discussion see Geoffrey Levitt (1989), 'The
      International Legal Response to Terrorism: A Reevaluation', 60 *University of Colorado
      Law Review* 533, 537.
77   Levitt.
78   Douglas Kash (1993), 'Abductions of Terrorists in International Airspace and on the
      High Seas', 8 *Florida Journal of International Law* 65, 75–76.
79   Charles W. Kegley, Jr., (1990), *International Terrorism: Characteristics, Causes,
      Controls*, New York, NY: St. Martin's, 12 (statement of Christopher C. Joyner); see also
      Brian M. Jenkins (1985), *International Terrorism: The Other World War*, Santa
      Monica, CA: Rand (stating that the problem of defining international terrorism has led
      to the cliché 'one man's terrorist is another man's freedom fighter').
80   Raimo, 1482–83.
81   Kash, 'Abductions of Terrorists', 73.
82   G.A. Res. 2625, U.N. GAOR, 25th Sess., Supp. No. 28, at 121, U.N. Doc. A/8028
      (1970).
83   U.N. Doc. A/C.6/L.850 (1972).
84   Kash, 'Abductions of Terrorists', supra note 78, at 74–75.
85   *Tokyo Convention.*
86   *Hague Convention.*
87   *Montreal Convention.*
88   *Convention on the Prevention and Punishment of Crimes Against Internationally
      Protected Persons*, opened for signature 14 December 1973, 28 UST 1974, 13 ILM 41
      (Protection of Diplomats Convention).
89   *Convention Against the Taking of Hostages*, S.EXEC.DOC. N, 96th Cong, 2d Sess
      (1980), 18 I.L.M. 1456 (entered into force 6 January 1985) (Hostage Taking
      Convention).
90   *Hostage Taking Convention.*
91   More recently, in 1997 the General Assembly adopted the *International
      Convention for the Suppression of Terrorist Bombings*, 9 January 1998, 37 I.L.M.
      251 creating a regime of universal jurisdiction over the unlawful and intentional
      use of explosives and other lethal devices in, into or against various defined public
      places with intent to kill or cause serious bodily injury, or with intent to cause
      extensive destruction of the public place. For background on this convention, see
      Alex Obote-Odora (1999), 'Defining International Terrorism', (March) 6 *Murdoch
      University Electronic Journal of Electronic Law* 8, 59-72 online at http://0-

pandora.nla.gov.au.newcutter.newcastle.edu.au:80/parchive/2001/Z2001-Feb-26/www.murdoch.edu.au/elaw/issues/v6n1/obote-odora61.txt.

92   Organization of American States, *Convention on Terrorism*, done 2 February 1971, 27 U.S.T. 3949 O.A.S.T.S. 37.

93   Ibid., art. 5.

94   U.N. Doc. A/CONF.121/L.12/Rev.1 (1985).

95   Levitt, 539.

96   G.A. Res. 40/61, U.N. GAOR, Supp. No. 53, at 301, U.N. Doc. A/40/53 (1985).

97   Kash, 'Abductions of Terrorists', 76.

98   Daphne Doran Lincoff (1985), *Annual Review of United Nations Affairs*, New York: New York University Press, 180.

99   Ibid., 181

100   Ibid., 182.

101   Ibid., 183.

102   Ibid., 180.

103   Ibid.

104   Ibid.

105   See Christopher L. Blakesley (1988), 'Jurisdictional Issues and Conflicts of Jurisdiction', in Bassiouni, *Legal Responses To International Terrorism*, 139-40 (defining the universality principle, the protective principle, and the passive personality principle).

106   See *Black's Law Dictionary* (6th ed. 1990), St. Paul, Minn.: West Group, 1396 (defining 'sovereignty' as 'the supreme, absolute, and uncontrollable power by which any independent state is governed; supreme political authority; the supreme will').

107   See Blakesley, 'Jurisdictional Issues and Conflicts of Jurisdiction', 164–72 (defining and applying the protective principle to international terrorism).

108   *Restatement (Third) of Foreign Relations Law* (1987) S 402 cmt. f [hereinafter *Foreign Relations Restatement*].

109   Christopher L. Blakesley (1987), 'Jurisdiction as Legal Protection Against Terrorism', 19 *Connecticut law Review* 895, 933.

110   Ibid.

111   132 Cong. Rec. S1382–88 (daily ed. Feb. 19, 1986).

112   Kash, 'Abductions of Terrorists', 80.

113   Note (1974), 'Extraterritorial Jurisdiction and Jurisdiction Following Forcible Abduction: A New Israeli Precedent in International Law', 72 *Michigan Law Review* 1087, 1088 n.5.

114   See Blakesley, 'Jurisdictional Issues and Conflicts of Jurisdiction', 172–78.

115   *Foreign Relations Restatement*, supra note 108, S 402 cmt. g.

116   Kash, 'Abductions of Terrorists', 81; *Foreign Relations Restatement*, at S 402 cmt. g.

117   741 F.2d 1312 (11th Cir. 1984), cert. denied, 471 U.S. 1137 (1985).

118   Ibid., 1316.

119   18 U.S.C.S 1203 (West 1984).

120   Ibid., S 1203(b)(1)(A).

121   See Blakesley, 'Jurisdictional Issues and Conflicts of Jurisdiction', 139–40.

122   *Foreign Relations Restatement*, S 404.

123   Travalio and Altenburg, 142.

124   *Demanjuk v Petrovsky*, 776 F.2d 571, 581–82 (6th Cir. 1985).

125   Blakesley, 'Jurisdiction as Legal Protection', 915.

126   For example, in the 1984 US case *Tel-Oren v. Libyan Arab Republic*, a US court ruled that terrorism did not constitute a violation of the law of nations. (726 F.2d 774, 795 (D.C. Cir 1984), cert. denied, 470 U.S. 1003 (1985)).

127   Ibid., 795–96.

128   Sofaer, 'The Sixth Annual Waldemar A. Solf Lecture', 106–107.
129   A similar situation occurred during the Iranian hostage crisis of 1979, when militant students, with the acquiescence of the Iranian government, seized the United States Embassy and 43 hostages in Tehran. The International Court of Justice held that the seizure violated two treaties on consular relations, but did not refer to the Hostage Convention. See *United States Diplomatic and Consular Staff in Tehran* (US v Iran), 1980 ICJ 3 (May 24).
130   Ibid., at 85; D. Cameron Findlay (1988), 'Abducting Terrorists Overseas for Trial in the United States: Issues of International and Domestic Law', 23 *Texas Journal of International Law* 1, 50.
131   M. Cherif Bassiouni (1974), *International Extradition and World Public Order*, Leyden: Sijthoff ; Dobbs Ferry, NY: Oceana, 124.
132   Andrew Wolfenson (1989–90), 'The U.S. Courts and the Treatment of Suspects Abducted Abroad Under International Law', 13 *Fordham International Law Journal* 705, 707.
133   Cf. the assertion by Kash that abductions have a degree of acceptance under international law. Kash, 'Abductions of Terrorists', 82. The author disagrees with the assertion. Recognition of a given fact is one thing, acceptance another.
134   The Declaration on Principles of International Law Concerning Friendly Relations and Cooperation among States in Accordance with the Charter of the United Nations provides, in part, that a state has a duty to 'refrain from organizing, instigating, assisting or participating in ... terrorist acts in another state. ...' G.A. Res. 2625, U.N. GAOR, Supp. No. 28, at 121, U.N. Doc. A/2028 (1970); see also Findlay, 23; Michael Sorenson, *Manual of Public International Law*, London, Melbourne [etc.]: Macmillan; New York: St. Martin's, 559.
135   Sofaer, 'The Sixth Annual Waldemar A. Solf Lecture', 111. See also O'Higgins (1960), 'Unlawful Seizure and Irregular Extradiction', 36 *British Yearbook on International Law* 279, 281–82; Max Planck Institute for Comparative Pub. Law and International Law (1985), 8 *Encyclopaedia of Public International Law* 357; Dickinson (1934), 'Jurisdiction Following Seizure or Arrest in Violation of International Law', 28 *American Journal of International Law* 231; Morgenstern (1952), 'Jurisdiction in Seizures Effected in Violation of International Law', 29 *British Yearbook on International Law* 265; Bassiouni (1973), 'Unlawful Seizures and Irregular Rendition Devices as Alternatives to Extradition', 7 *Vanderbilt Journal of Transnational Law* 25.
136   Gross, 'Thwarting Terrorist Acts', 234.
137   Ibid., 238–239.
138   Travalio and Altenburg, 113.
139   Sofaer, 'The Sixth Annual Waldemar A. Solf Lecture', 91.
140   Address Before the Park Avenue Synagogue, 25 October 1984, reprinted in *Dep't of State Bull.* 12, 16 (Dec. 1984) [hereinafter Park Avenue Synagogue Address].
141   Sofaer, 'The Sixth Annual Waldemar A. Solf Lecture', 92.
142   Ibid.
143   See 144 Cong. Rec. S2989, SS3002–3 (daily ed. 1 April 1998) (statement of Senator Domenici) (emphasizing that the international terrorist threat is not the same as in the past and depicts warlike qualities).
144   Ibid.
145   See *Black's Law Dictionary,* (6th ed. 1990), 1583 (defining 'war' as 'hostile contention by means of armed forces, carried on between nations, states, or rulers, or between citizens in the same nation or state').
146   Timothy F. Malloy, 'Military Responses to Terrorism', 81 *American Society International Law Proceedings* 109, 287, 299 (asserting that the military should destroy terrorist planning and training facilities in nations harbouring those terrorists).

147 Ibid.
148 Ibid., 287. (arguing that the use of military action against terrorism as a form of low intensity warfare would be more effective and beneficial in long-term deterrence, short-term prevention and punishment than political, diplomatic, economic and legal responses).
149 Elizabeth R. P. Bowen, Note (1987), 'Jurisdiction over Terrorists Who Take Hostages: Efforts to Stop Terror Violence against U.S. Citizens', 2 *American University Journal of International Law and Policy* 153, 159.
150 Ibid., 59 (citing Begin, 'Freedom Fighters and Terrorists', in B. Netanyahu ed., (1979) *International Terrorism: Challenge and Response: Proceedings of the Jerusalem Conference on International Terrorism* 39–46).
151 Bowen, 159 n. 26.
152 Ibid., 160 n. 28.
153 Basic Principles of the Legal Status of Combatants Struggling Against Colonial and Alien Domination and Racist Regimes, G.A. Res. 3103, U.N. GAOR, Supp. No. 30, at 142, U.N. Doc. A/9030 (1973).
154 Definition of Aggression, G.A. Res. 3314, 28 U.N. GAOR, Supp. No. 30A, at 142, U.N. Doc. A/9030/Add.1 (1974).
155 Kash, 'Abductions of Terrorists', 73.
156 Alberto R. Coll, (1987), 'The Legal and Moral Adequacy of Military Responses to Terrorism', 81 *American Society of International Law Proceedings* 297, 297–298.
157 Ibid., 298.
158 See *Protocol Additional to The Geneva Conventions of 1949 (relating to the Protection of Victims of International Armed Conflict)*, [hereinafter Additional Protocol I] 8 June, 1977, 1125 U.N.T.S. 3.
159 Gross, 'Thwarting Terrorist Acts', 206.
160 See *Geneva Convention Relative to the Protection of Civilian Persons in Time of War*, opened for signature, 12 August 1949, 75 U.N.T.S. 287, art. 43, para. 1.
161 Ibid.
162 Ibid.
163 Ibid.
164 Ibid.
165 Gross, 'Thwarting Terrorist Acts', 202.
166 See Judith Gail Gardam (1993), *Non-Combatants' Immunity as a Norm of International Humanitarian Law*, Dordrecht; Boston: M. Nijhoff Publishers; Norwell, MA, 100–106; see also Heather A. Wilson (1988), *International Law and the Use of Force by National Liberation Movements,* Oxford [Oxfordshire]: Clarendon Press; New York: Oxford University Press.
167 Gross, 'Thwarting Terrorist Acts', 202.
168 *Protocol Additional to the Geneva Conventions of 12 August 1949, and relating to the Protection of Victims of Non-International Armed Conflicts* (Protocol II), Geneva, 10 June 1977, Article 1 sets out the threshold of the material field of application of the rules to non-regular forces. See generally Peter Rowe (1995), 'Liability for "War Crimes" During a Non-International Armed Conflict', (XXXIV (1–4) *Revue De Droit Militaire et de Droit de la Guerre* 149.
169 Gross, 'Thwarting Terrorist Acts', 203.
170 See Christopher C. Burris (1997), 'Re-Examining the Prisoner of War Status of PLO Fedayeen', 22 *North Carolina Journal of International Law and Commercial Regulation* 943, 975–976. See also Gregory M. Travalio (2000), 'Terrorism, International Law, and the Use of Military Force', 18 *Wisconsin International Law Journal* 145, 176, 190.
171 Antigoni Axenidou (1987), 'Should the Law of War Apply to Terrorists?', 79 *American Society of International Law Proceedings* 109 (containing panel discussion).

172 Ibid.

173 Gross, 'Thwarting Terrorist Acts', 206.

174 Ibid., at 207.

175 See H.C. 561/75, *Motti Ashkenazi v. Minister of Defense et al.*, 30(3) P.D. 309.

176 However this rule has never been understood to preclude military attacks on individual soldiers or officers, subject to normal legal requirements. 'It does not, however, preclude attacks on individual soldiers or officers of the enemy whether in the zone of hostilities, occupied territory, or elsewhere. Attacks on individual officers have been authorized and their legality has been accepted without significant controversy.' Sofaer, 'The Sixth Annual Waldemar A. Solf Lecture', 120.

177 See Jami Melissa Jackson (1999), 'The Legality of Assassination of Independent Terrorist Leaders: An Examination of National and International Implications', 24 *North Carolina Journal of International Law and Commercial Regulation* 669, 671–672.

178 *Regulations annexed to Hague Convention (IV) Respecting the Laws and Customs of War on Land*, 18 October 1907, art. 23, § II, ch. 1, 36 Stat 2227, reprinted in Dietrich Schindler and Jiri Toman (eds) (3rd revised ed.) (1988), *The Laws of Armed Conflicts: A Collection of Conventions, Resolutions, and other Documents*, Dordrecht, Netherlands: Nijhoff; Geneva: Henry Dunant Institute; Norwell, MA, 63. Paragraph 31 of the US Army Field Manual 27–10 provides in this regard that:

> (Article 23b, Hague Regulations, 1907) is construed as prohibiting assassination, proscription, or outlawry of an enemy, or putting a price upon an enemy's head, as well as offering a reward for an enemy 'dead or alive'.

179 See Additional Protocol 1, supra note 158, art. 37. This prohibition is also reflected in national proclamations and directives for example: Executive Order 12333, issued by the then US President Reagan in 1981, states that '[n]o person employed or acting on behalf of the US Government shall engage in, or conspire to engage in assassination'. (Executive Order No. 12333, 3 C.R.F. § 2.11, at 200, 213 (1982)) This order, which remains in effect and is binding on all executive branch personnel, is derived from a virtually identical provision issued by the then US President Ford in 1976. (Executive Order No. 11905, 3 C.F.R. § 5(g), at 90, 101 (1977). The only substantive change in the prohibition since that date is that the earlier version prohibited 'political' assassination; the word 'political' was deleted from the order by President Carter in 1978. Exec. Order No. 12036, 3 C.F.R. § 2–305, at 112, 129 (1979).)

180 See McConnel (1969), *The History of Assassination*, Nashville, Aurora Publishers, 12.

181 See Jackson, 686–687.

182 Gross, 'Thwarting Terrorist Acts', 224.

183 Ibid., at 229–230.

184 See James P. Rowles (1987), 'The Legal and Moral Adequacy of Military Responses to Terrorism: Substantive and Procedural Constraints in International Law', *American Society of International Law, Proceedings of the 81st Annual Meeting*, 307, 310.

185 Mention and discussion of this incident is to be found in Chapter 3 of the book.

186 This will be discussed at length in Chapters 4 and 5.

187 G. A. Res. No 2625, U.N. Doc No A/8018 (1970).

188 *Corfu Channel Case*. See also International Law Commission, Draft Articles on Responsibility of States for Internationally Wrongful Acts, U.N. Doc No A/CN.4/L.602/Rev.1 (2001) [hereinafter Draft Articles on Responsibility].

189 Sofaer, 'The Sixth Annual Waldemar A. Solf Lecture', 98.

190 See, e.g., Oscar Schachter (1989), 'The Extra-Territorial Use of Force Against Terrorist Bases', 11 *Houston Journal of International Law* 309, 312.

191 This policy of so-called 'active defence' found strong formal articulation in the National Security Strategy document, issued by President George Bush Jr in September 2002. (President George W. Bush, The National Security Strategy of the United States of America, 15–16 (17 September 2002) online at http:// www.whitehouse.gov/nsc/nss.pdf; *A.P. Newswires*, 20 September 2002, available at *Westlaw*, Newswires); see also Sofaer, 'The Sixth Annual Waldemar A. Solf Lecture', 95.

192 See Erickson, 142–43.

193 Thomas M. Franck (2001), 'The Institute for Global Legal Studies Inaugural Colloquium: The UN and the Protection of Human Rights: When if Ever May States Deploy Military Force without Prior Security Council Authorization?' 5 *Washington University Journal of Law and Policy* 57, 57–58.

Chapter 3

The Cold War Era:
Terrorist Action and Reaction

Introduction

Under the UN Charter, the response of a targeted state is predicated on principles of self-defence, and these are in turn based on what the international community regards as the 'inherent' right of national security and the attendant duty to protect one's citizens from terrorist attacks.[1] The key sticking point though is that, historically, rules on the lawful use of force have developed within a framework of state-to-state relationships. Doubt exists concerning their applicability in the terrorist arena.

Legally and conceptually, there is little dispute concerning the right to exercise self-defence. The difficulty lies in whether terrorist attacks fall within the conditions which justify the use of military force as laid down in the UN Charter. The underlying purpose of Article 2(4), to regulate aggressive behaviour between states, is identical to that of its precursor in the Covenant of the League of Nations. Article 12 of the Covenant stated that League members were obligated not 'to resort to war'.[2] The drafters of the UN Charter wished to ensure that the legal niceties of a conflict's status did not preclude cognizance by the international body. Thus, in drafting Article 2(4) the term 'war' was replaced by the phrase 'threat or use of force'. The wording was interpreted as prohibiting a broad range of hostile activities including not only 'war' and other equally destructive conflicts, but also applications of force of a lesser intensity or magnitude.[3]

As noted in Chapter 2, the UN has had a chequered history in dealing with terrorism. In the face of the apparent inability of the Security Council to control the spread of international terrorism during the Cold War era, several states (particularly the US and Israel) sought to circumvent the provisions of the UN Charter or to stretch them, arguing that they would legitimately use military force to counter terrorism. Though international law does not require states to endure repeated attacks without taking defensive action, the notion of use of force as a countermeasure against terrorism sits uneasily within the UN regime on the use of force. In any case state response has often been bogged down in a conceptual quagmire with the use of reprisal, retaliation, self-defence and anticipatory self-defence frequently mentioned in the same breath. The difficulty is that some of these concepts are by and of themselves unsettled concepts within the UN Charter framework.

This chapter seeks to provide a summation of state practice especially focusing on the US and Israel, states that have taken the lead in using both lethal and non-lethal military force in reaction to terrorist actions. Additionally the US shift in policy and its position as a superpower is of importance in setting the trend in this area. Under discussion are the uncertainties regarding the use of both lethal and non-lethal military force against terrorism. It will be readily apparent that in those instances when terrorism was used as a weapon in the Cold War era, the UN and the world community frequently condemned any attempt to co-opt use of military force as a recognized countermeasure, but every now and then seemed hesitant to do so.

Use of Military to Counter Terrorism: Putting Life into the Scarecrow

'Ever since David Ben Gurion ... proclaimed the state of Israel in a dusty hall in Tel Aviv'[4] more than five decades ago, a cycle of continuous violence was to become part and parcel of the Jewish state, orchestrated through a variety of means but chiefly through terrorism. These circumstances are at the heart of Israel's lead in the co-option of military force as a counter-terrorism measure.

As early as 1968, the attacks on an El Al plane in Athens (in 1968) and subsequently Zurich seven weeks later presented both Israel and the international community with a legal dilemma. Israel's policy crystallized into one of retaliation, a move that is, however, ringed with the murky issues of what were legitimate uses of force in the Israeli/ Palestinian stand-off. These prickly matters continue to dominate the socio-political and legal landscape both regionally and internationally. Increased attacks on American citizens and interests around the world would soon embroil the US and the international community in further difficult questions of law and policy.

In July 1976, the Israeli hostage rescue at Entebbe in the aftermath of the hijacking of Air France Flight 139 focused attention on the capabilities of elite forces trained for anti-terrorist operations and marked the opening salvo in the use of military force to counter terrorism. About three years later, on 4 November 1979, a mob of Iranians seized the US embassy in Tehran, taking a large group of employees hostage, sparking the Iranian hostage crisis.

Five months later, the impotence of diplomatic efforts led the Carter administration to order a rescue effort by helicopter, but the mission had to be aborted. In 1981, following the release of the hostages, US President Reagan stated: 'Let the terrorists be aware that when the rules of international behaviour are violated, *our policy will be one of swift and effective retribution.*'[5] The Reagan administration was sending initial indications that a hard line, conceivably involving the use of military force, would be taken with terrorists in the future.

Two years after Reagan's pugnacious proclamation, on 18 April 1983, 63 people, including the CIA's Middle East director, were killed, and 120 people injured in a 400-pound suicide truck-bomb attack on the US embassy in Beirut, Lebanon. The Islamic Jihad claimed responsibility.[6] Six months later, on 23 October 1983, in another terrorist attack, a large Mercedes truck exploded with such a terrific force that the building housing the headquarters of the Eighth US Marine Battalion in Lebanon was instantly reduced to rubble, with the loss of 241 US Marines, most of them still sleeping in their cots at the time of the suicide mission. This was the highest single day death toll for the Americans since 246 died throughout Vietnam at the start of the Tet offensive on 13 January 1968. The bombing precipitated renewed debate whether US military forces were adequately prepared to deal with terrorism and whether the United States would use force either in anticipation of, or in response to, terrorism.

The bombing of the Marine headquarters in Beirut triggered a reshaping of US thinking on the issue of terrorism. The Long Commission, constituted under the auspices of the US Department of Defense to enquire into the matter, in commenting upon the devastating attack on the US Marine Headquarters in Beirut, concluded:

[S]tate sponsored terrorism is an important part of the spectrum of warfare and ... adequate response to this increasing threat requires an active national policy which seeks to deter attack or reduce its effectiveness. The Commission further concludes that this policy needs to be supported by political and diplomatic actions and by a wide range of timely military response capabilities.[7]

New Frontiers on the Use of Force: The Reagan and Shultz Doctrines

By the early 1980s, international terrorism was increasingly regarded as a calculated means to destabilize the West. A series of suicide bombings and other terrorist activities directed mostly against American diplomatic and military targets in the Middle East was focusing attention on the rising threat of state-sponsored terrorism. Various renegade foreign regimes were becoming actively involved in sponsoring or commissioning terrorism. With international terrorism coming of age, it was becoming a type of covert or surrogate warfare, whereby weaker states could confront larger, more powerful rivals without the risk of retribution.

In the 1980s, terrorist violence had increased dramatically, with the number of terrorist incidents reaching an all-time high in 1985.[8] Worldwide, half of these attacks were directed at only ten countries, with the United States the victim in one-third of these incidents.[9] Further, with rare exception, they were carried out by state-supported groups.[10] Between 1976 and 1986, terrorists targeted US installations or officials abroad on an average of one every seventeen days.[11]

Despite definitional concerns, and fundamental issues concerning the kind of responses the United States could lawfully take within the rubric of international law, the United States, tired of so many attacks against its interests and citizens, chose to embrace military force against terrorist-inspired political violence. In opting to use force, the position was that it was necessary to accept some risks but ensure that every terrorist success did not fail to attract the military might of the US.[12] Deterrence was to be premised on terrorists fearing a forceful response from the victim state.

On 3 April 1984, in the aftermath of the Long Commission's recommendations, President Reagan signed the National Security Decision Directive (NSDD 138) which assigned responsibility for developing strategies for countering terrorism and made clear that, while use of all the non-military options will be made, the US must also be prepared to respond within the parameters set by the law of armed conflict. Defense Department official Noel Koch explained that the NSDD 'represent[ed] a quantum leap in countering terrorism, from the reactive mode to recognition that proactive steps [were] needed'.[13] Significantly, the document incorporated some key elements: the United States has a responsibility to take protective measures whenever there is evidence that terrorism is about to be committed against US interests; the threat of terrorism constitutes a form of aggression and justifies acts in lawful self-defence.[14] The ground had been formally laid for the 'Reagan Doctrine' of swift, effective retribution.

NSDD 138 and the subsequent remarks of then US Secretary of State George Shultz that same day signalled that as far as the executive branch was concerned, the debate over whether military force was within or without the range of counter-terrorism measures was over. Henceforth, the United States would use military force in both pre-emptive and retaliatory scenarios. Although Shultz had initially advocated only 'an active defence' against terrorists,[15] growing frustration over the inability of the United States to effectively counter the accelerating frequency and violence of terrorist attacks prompted him to re-evaluate his views on the nature of appropriate responses to international terrorism.

In late 1984, at the Park Avenue Synagogue in New York City, George Shultz asserted that 'the United States must be ready to use military force to fight terrorism and retaliate for terrorist attacks even before all the facts are known'.[16] This was to be the outline of what later became known as the 'Shultz Doctrine', a corollary of the 'Reagan Doctrine'. Shultz predicted that the increased terrorist attacks against strategic US interests around the world in the years ahead would necessitate a willingness to combat it using military force.[17] This signalled that an active policy of response by armed force to terrorist attacks would be followed by the United States. In the same speech Shultz claimed a broad right on behalf of the United States to use force against terrorist threats abroad, including a policy of pre-emptive strikes in foreign countries.[18]

> Although arguably effective and temporarily satisfying, the important concern was whether a policy of armed response was wise in view of its probable violation of international law. The US ran the risk of incurring massive condemnation which would accompany a policy of systematic use of armed force against terrorist attacks and the possibility of being branded an international outlaw.[19]

Even as the Reagan and Shultz Doctrines were jellying, Israeli action was actively providing a practical manifestation of the tenets underlying these doctrines with regular use of military force to counter terrorism outside its territory, in Lebanon, Syria and Tunisia, throughout the 1980s. The US position that '[a]s a matter of policy, retaliation against terrorist attacks is a legitimate response and an expression of self-defence'[20] was practically expressed in 1985 by Israel. On 1 October 1985, six F-15 Israeli fighter-bombers unleashed a barrage of bombs on the headquarters of the Palestine Liberation Organization in a suburb of Tunis, the capital of Tunisia, responding to alleged terrorist attacks.[21] Israeli Defence Minister, Yitzhak Rabin seemed to be almost echoing Reagan and Shultz when he stated: 'We decided the time was right to deliver a blow to the headquarters of those who make the decisions, plan and carry out terrorist activities.'[22] The UN Security Council was swift to vigorously condemn the act of armed aggression perpetrated by Israel against Tunisian territory in flagrant violation of the Charter of the UN, international law and norms of conduct.[23] Three days after the attack, a single session of the Security Council adopted Resolution 573 (with only one abstention by the United States), which condemned the Israeli attack; demanded that Israel 'refrain from perpetrating such acts of aggression or from threatening to do so'; urged member states to 'dissuade Israel from resorting to such acts'; and supported Tunisia's right to reparations.[24]

The international community in general condemned the Israeli Tunis raid as an act of aggression and a violation of Tunisia's sovereignty and territorial integrity.[25] Israel's argument of self-defence against terrorism was dismissed.[26] The attack and subsequent US support for the Israeli action in the face of vitriolic condemnation by most countries was symptomatic of a revolution in policy that the US was undertaking.

Prior to this the United States usually abstained from the string of condemnations which followed every Israeli action debated in the Security Council. Eventually the condemnation would stop altogether as the United States began to veto consideration of those resolutions. Change in US reaction was not necessarily just the result of a new, hawkish conservative administration, but rather the targeting of US citizens and interests by state-sponsored terrorists. US Ambassador Vernon Walters explanation of the US abstention in the Security Council Resolution that condemned Israel's bombing in Tunis is instructive:

> We, ... recognize and strongly support the principle that a state subjected to continuing terrorist attacks may respond with appropriate use of force to defend against further attacks. This is an aspect of the inherent right of self-defence recognized in the United Nations Charter.[27]

Two months after the Israeli counter-terrorist attacks, the frustration with the international regime on the use of force in countering terrorism was captured clearly by Shultz's outburst:

> It is absurd to argue that international law prohibits us from capturing terrorists in international waters or airspace; from attacking them on the soil of other nations, even for the purpose of rescuing hostages; or from using force against states that support, train, and harbour terrorists or guerrillas. International law requires no such result.[28]

With these words, Secretary of State George Shultz further fleshed out the 'Shultz Doctrine' and its highly controversial position advocating the use of military force, not only against terrorists, but also against states that support, train or harbour terrorists.[29] The 'Shultz Doctrine' was formally announced on 15 January 1986, in the Secretary's speech on terrorism at the National Defense University. In that speech, the Secretary added: 'A nation attacked by terrorists is permitted to use force to prevent or pre-empt future attacks, to seize terrorists, or to rescue its citizens, when no other means is available.'[30] This is so, Shultz said, even though others have 'asserted that military action to retaliate or pre-empt terrorism is contrary to international law'.[31]

Shortly after Shultz's speech on terrorism at the National Defense University, the Vice President's Task Force on Combating Terrorism found that terrorism had become another means of conducting foreign affairs. It went on to note that terrorists are agents whose association a state can easily deny. It summed up thus: 'Use of terrorism by the country entails few risks, and constitutes strong-arm, low-budget foreign policy.'[32] This statement echoed the Reagan administration's concerns over new and unconventional challenges to US foreign policy in critical areas of the world. It was evident that this threat of low-intensity conflict raised a host of new legal, political, military and moral questions.

However, it was not long before the US demonstrated that it was not overly concerned with the complex legal, political, military and moral questions that its new policy engendered and that the Reagan and Shultz Doctrines were not hollow rhetoric. On 5 April 1986, Le Belle discotheque in West Germany, a popular hang-out for off-duty American servicemen, was bombed leaving two Americans dead and 154 persons injured.[33] US intelligence indicated Libya sponsored this terrorist attack[34] and was about to order additional attacks against US personnel and facilities throughout Europe.[35] President Reagan responded to this threat by ordering the bombing of military targets in Tripoli and Benghazi, Libya on 15 April 1986.[36]

Immediately following the air strike, President Reagan informed the American people of the attack on Libya. President Reagan stated that the United States had carried out the air strikes against 'terrorist centres' and military bases in response to Colonel Muammar Qadhafi's actions, which had conducted a 'reign of terror' against the United States.[37] He cited the existence of proof of direct Libyan involvement in the bombing[38] and solid evidence about other attacks Qadhafi had planned against the United States' installations and diplomats and even American tourists.[39] Based on this information, he carried out what he described as a 'pre-emptive action' designed to cause Colonel Qadhafi to 'alter his criminal behaviour'.[40]

> Although President Reagan cited self-defence under Article 51 of the UN Charter as the legal basis for the air strike, his explanation implicitly included retaliation as an additional justification. In describing the attack, the White House statement said: '[i]t's our hope that action will pre-empt and discourage Libyan attacks against innocent civilians in the future.' In deciding to use military force against Libya, deterrence certainly was a major, if not the primary, consideration. President Reagan further emphasized this position, stating: 'I warned that there should be no place on earth where terrorists can rest and train and practice their skills. I meant it. I said that we would act with others if possible and alone if necessary to ensure that terrorists have no sanctuary anywhere.'[41]

Reagan's statement had found support in Vice President George Bush Sr's comments a month prior to the Libyan raid when he stated that American policy in combating terrorism would be one of a willingness to 'retaliate'.[42]

On the regional and international scene, the attack was met with wide condemnation.[43] The United States received criticism for waiting ten days before striking Libya and additionally for failing to respond proportionally to the attacks or to so-called 'imminent' attacks by striking Libyan bombers and training facilities, targets that did not seem directly related to 'imminent' threats or attacks.

> Greece called the air strike 'set[ting] dynamite to peace,' and Italy stated that it was 'provoking explosive reactions of fanaticism.' While France vetoed the Security Council

resolution along with the United States and the United Kingdom, it did call the air strikes 'reprisals that itself revives the chain of violence.' Still other members of the international community denounced the raid, including foreign ministers of the Movement of Non-Aligned Nations ...[44]

The views of the rest of the Security Council regarding the customary international law of self-defence did not follow the American viewpoint but the US seemed determined to co-opt the use of military force against terrorism within the infirm concept of anticipatory self-defence.

The Tripoli bombing was far from a one-off event; it was part of a crystallizing US policy. In the aftermath of the bombing of Pan American Flight 103 over Lockerbie Scotland on 21 December 1988,[45] President Reagan ordered an inquiry into the circumstances of the Flight 103 disaster. He further directed that a comprehensive report be prepared, intended to be 'a study and appraisal of practices and policy options with respect to preventing terrorist acts involving aviation'.[46] Among the recommendations of the President's Commission were active measures – pre-emptive or retaliatory, direct or covert – against a series of targets in countries well known to have engaged in state-sponsored terrorism.[47] These recommendations reinforced the vitality of the Reagan and Shultz Doctrines as part of US policy. The US was keen to continue to employ pre-emptive strikes. It was, however, not until the end of the Cold War that opportunity was to present itself much more clearly in the aftermath of September 11.

A Legal Quagmire: Use of Force as a Counter-terrorism Measure

Given that US (and Israeli) officials alternately spoke of military actions to counter terrorism in terms of self-defence, retaliation and reprisal, which of these, if any, provide a basis for military action under international law? The difference between the two forms of self-help lies in their purpose. The use of force in self-defence is permissible for the purpose of protecting the security of the state and its essential rights, in particular the rights of territorial integrity and political independence, upon which that security depends. In contrast, reprisals are punitive in character; they seek to impose retribution for the harm done, or to compel a satisfactory settlement of a dispute created by the initial illegal act, or to compel the delinquent state to abide by the law in the future. But coming after the event, and when the harm has already been inflicted, reprisals cannot be characterized as a means of protection.

The legal difficulties that the concepts present was manifest in the aftermath of the articulation of the 'Shultz Doctrine'. Worldwide opposition to the doctrine was swift in coming. Surprisingly, some senior officials in the US State Department expressed reservations.[48] More importantly, US Secretary of Defense Casper Weinberger, in charge of the machinery that would be tasked with effecting the doctrine, opposed responsive military strikes that needlessly 'kill women and children'.[49] Additionally, Robert Oakley, ambassador-at-large for counter-terrorism, opined that the President's Commission on Terrorism had recommended that the United States not use military force to retaliate against states supporting terrorists.[50]

International and domestic opposition in the US was owing to a number of difficult issues raised by the doctrine which Professor Jordan J. Paust identified succinctly:

> ... [I]s the responding coercion still a use of force in self-defence against an armed 'attack'? Is the responding coercion primarily pre-emptive, retaliatory, or for the purpose of imposing sanctions against a violation of international law? And if among the latter, are any of these forms of responsive coercion ever permissible?[51]

Reacting to the unpalatability of the 'Shultz Doctrine' under international law, Professor Paust noted that 'the predominant expectation is that merely pre-emptive and retaliatory reprisal actions as such are impermissible. For this reason, implementation of the "Shultz Doctrine" by the use of pre-emptive or retaliatory reprisal forms of force would place the United States in violation of international law and must be opposed'.[52]

Self-defence

The right of self-defence as codified in Article 51 of the Charter provides: 'Nothing in the present Charter shall impair the inherent right of individual or collective self-defence if an armed attack occurs against a Member of the United Nations ...'[53] The use of the word 'inherent' in the text of Article 51 suggests that self-defence is broader than the immediate Charter parameters. During the drafting of the Kellogg-Briand Treaty, for example, the United States expressed its views as follows:

> There is nothing in the American draft of an anti-war treaty which restricts or impairs in any way the right of self-defence. That right is inherent in every sovereign state and is implicit in every treaty. *Every nation is free at all times and regardless of treaty provisions to defend its territory from attack or invasion and it alone is competent to decide whether circumstances require recourse to war in self-defence.*[54] [Emphasis added]

Because self-defence is an inherent right, its contours have been shaped by custom and are subject to customary interpretation. Although the drafters of Article 51 may not have anticipated its use in protecting states from the effects of terrorist violence, customary international law has long recognized the need for flexible application. Secretary of State Shultz emphasized this point when he said: 'The UN Charter is not a suicide pact. The law is a weapon on our side and it is up to us to use it to its maximum extent ... There should be no confusion about the status of nations that sponsor terrorism against Americans and American property.'[55]

The final clause of Article 2(4) of the Charter seems to support this interpretation and forbids the threat or use of force 'in any other manner inconsistent with the Purposes of the UN'.[56] Significantly the matter is whether there is recognition of the right to counter the imminent threat of unlawful coercion as well as an actual attack within the UN Charter framework. This comprehensive conception of permissible or defensive coercion, honouring appropriate response to threats of an imminent nature, may be grounded within the ambit of customary international law.

The precise contours of the co-existence of customary law and Charter law is still a topic of significant debate, despite the forceful pronouncements of the

International Court of Justice (ICJ) in the *Nicaragua Case* that alluded to a separate existence. Of further significance is the ICJ's observation in its judgment in the *Nicaragua Case* that covert military action by a state could be classified as an armed attack if it was of sufficient gravity.[57] In any case, the UN General Assembly included certain types of terrorist activity committed by states in its definition of aggression in 1974,[58] seemingly suggesting that terrorist acts by a state can constitute an armed attack and thereby justify a military response.

Of particular note is the fact that the ICJ in the *Nicaragua Case* laid down a gravity requirement in the definition of armed attack based on a scale and effect test. The Court held that 'the prohibition of armed attacks may apply to the sending by a state of armed bands to the territory of another state, if such operation because of its scale and effects, would have been classified as an armed attack rather than a mere frontier accident had it been carried out by regular armed forces'.[59] In support of the ICJ's finding in the *Nicaragua Case* that actions by insurgents may fall within the understanding of the term 'armed attack', Professor C. Greenwood notes that: 'It would be a strange formalism that regarded the right to take military action against those who caused or threatened such actions as dependent upon whether or not their acts could be imputed to a state.'[60] Carrying this argument further, Professor Greenwood observes that:

Nothing in the language of Article 39 or the rest of the Charter suggests that only threats emanating from States can fall within its scope. In recent years, the Security Council has had no hesitation in treating acts of international terrorism, whether or not 'State-sponsored', as threats to the peace for the purposes of Chapter VII of the Charter.[61]

The scale and effect test seems to carry the implication that the factual circumstances relating to the victim and the issue of the gravity of the act against a backdrop of a terrorist attack may trigger the application of Article 51 of the UN Charter, thus loosening a strict and literal interpretation that ties Article 51 to armed attacks by statal entities. In the event of the use of force coming into play, the requirement of proportionality is linked to necessity. Professors McDougal and Feliciano define the rule as follows:

Proportionality in coercion constitutes a requirement that responding coercion be limited in intensity and magnitude to what is reasonably necessary promptly to secure the permissible objectives of self-defence. For present purposes, these objectives may be most comprehensively generalized as the conserving of important values by compelling the opposing participant to terminate the condition which necessitates responsive coercion.[62]

This definition simply requires a rational relationship between the intensity of the attack and the intensity of the response. Although the relationship need not approach precision, a nation subjected to an isolated state-sponsored terrorist attack on one of its citizens is not entitled to unleash lethal military force on the offender-nation. This in any case is tied to a logical interpretation of Article 51. 'The requirement of necessity in self-defence means that it is not sufficient that force is used after an armed attack, it must be necessary to repel that attack. The use of force in response to an armed attack that is over and done with does not meet that requirement and looks more like a reprisal.'[63]

Anticipatory Self-defence

The doctrine of anticipatory or pre-emptive self-defence, as developed historically, is applicable only when there is a clear and imminent danger of attack. The key issue concerns the elapsed time between the state-sponsored terrorist attack and the identification of the state responsible. Admittedly, there must be some temporal relationship between a terrorist act and the lawful defensive response. Nevertheless, it would be unreasonable to preclude the victim of terrorism from redress, based upon a doctrinaire determination that the threat is no longer imminent, when the terrorist state's own actions preclude immediate identification. The means used for pre-emptive response must be strictly limited to those required for the elimination of the danger, and must be reasonably proportional to that objective. But Charter law seems to expressly preclude the concept. Self-defence can only be in response to an armed attack, not a threatened attack.

Since the founding of the UN, anticipatory self-defence has never been recognized as a legitimate use of force under customary international law. The traditional understanding seems to leave no room for anticipatory self-defence. In keeping with the constrained time requirement, an anticipatory action is not self-defence because of the failure of the required 'armed attack' precondition. The charged international climate of the Cold War provided for the prudence of not resurrecting anticipatory self-defence as a recognized concept within the UN Charter regime so as to erase the preclusion of unilateral recourse to armed force. After all, as Professor Schachter observes: '[t]he absence of binding judicial or other third-party determinations relating to the use of force adds to the apprehension that a more permissive rule of self-defence will open the way to further disregard of the limits on force.'[64]

Paradoxically though, it was in the Cold War era that the threat of nuclear Armageddon offered ground for arguing that the law of self-defence ought to move away from the requirement of an actual armed attack[65] and suggestions that the traditional immediacy requirement for self-defence be modified to require imminence. In the post-Cold War era, nuclear Armageddon would soon be replaced by the spectre of terrorists and states armed with weapons of mass destruction, as will be discussed in Chapters 4 and 5 of the book.

Reprisal

The concept of reprisal has engendered considerable confusion. Part of the reason is that reprisals share many of the attributes of an expanded form of 'anticipatory' self-defence which many authorities and governments argue is precluded by Article 51 of the UN Charter.[66] Because of this similarity, discussion must inevitably be devoted to the interrelationship between the various forms of forcible self-help. The term is often used imprecisely; actions may be labelled 'reprisals' or 'retaliation' when, in fact, the proper characterization should be self-defence, and vice versa. Reprisal may be defined as an otherwise illegal act of self-help to coerce an action (for example, cessation of the offending action) or obtain redress (reparation) for a prior wrong under international law. Retaliation (retribution) differs from reprisal in that its sole purpose is to inflict punishment on the offender for a past wrong.

Coercion is not its intent; and it seeks nothing beyond the satisfaction of imposing a measured response for some prior transgression.

One feature which distinguishes reprisals from acts of anticipatory self-defence is the time in which the response is taken. Purely defensive actions will typically be closely related in time to the hostile act, whether threatened or in progress.[67] By contrast, reprisals are normally carried out after peaceful efforts are made to obtain redress or to prevent recurrences of the offending act. Consequently, a reprisal is typically undertaken after a longer period of time than the act of self-defence. Critics of the practice of reprisal frequently cite this fact as one of their chief complaints.[68] Often overlooked, however, is the continuing nature of some transgressions, such as terrorism. In the words of Michael F. Lohr:

> Under customary law, the reprisal is not authorised by any previous authoritative community decision; neither is it an act of self-defence as its aim is not directly to repel the blow of the delinquent state's preceding act. Its purpose is to coerce the state subject to the reprisal to change its policy and bring it into line with the requirements of international law. This function of law enforcement qualifies the reprisal as a sanction under international law. Finally, the reprisal must respect the conditions and limits laid down in international law for justifiable recourse to reprisals, that is, peaceful attempts of redress have been tried and failed, and proportionality in responding is observed.[69]

Professor Oscar Schachter argues that the existence of international law on the use of force is not the determining factor in a state's choice to use force, nor should it be developed with that intention.[70] Rather, a goal of international law on the use of force is to be one of the factors which must be consulted before any such decision is taken. What this amounted to, in the bipolar world prior to the fall of the Soviet Union, is that the 'law' was defined negatively as what one state can get away with.

As noted above, military actions by the US against terrorist-supporting states elicited varying responses from the international community and the United Nations. In the case of the 1986 raid on Libya, the US was largely condemned. The UN General Assembly adopted a resolution condemning the United States for the attack by a vote of 79 to 28, with 33 abstentions.[71] The then UN Secretary-General (Javier Perez de Cuellar) stated that the United States action violated international law.[72] A Security Council resolution echoing the General Assembly sentiment was vetoed by the United States, the United Kingdom and France, but France did call the air strikes 'reprisals that itself revives the chain of violence'.[73]

Summing-up The incidents of military force mentioned in this chapter were wrapped up in the rhetoric of self-defence and retaliation, leading to the observation that although the general view is that reprisals are illegal, that does not mean that states have not engaged in them. 'For example, the 1986 bombing of Libya is cited as a peacetime reprisal and not an act of self-defence. Therefore, while writers state emphatically that reprisals are illegal, state practice continues to resort to them on occasion, cloaking them in terms of self-defence while remaining careful to comply with *Naulilaa* criteria.'[74] In support to this contention, Professor C. Gray, in a survey of US (and Israeli) military action, believes that the two states 'tr[ied] to stretch the meaning of Article 51' in those cases.[75] She goes further to note that:

Even if the [American and Israeli] actions were aimed at those actually responsible for the terrorist attacks, and even if the response could be accepted as proportionate, it is difficult to see how the use of force was necessary, given that the attacks on the nationals had already taken place.[76]

Professor Gray concludes that the military actions were unlawful reprisals to punish, not acts of self-defence. Her observations are supported by Bilder and O'Connell, who note that:

Gray's approach to the use of force against terrorism is basically sound. The lawful use of armed force on the territory of another state must either meet the elements of lawful self-defence or have Security Council authorization. Force in self-defence is lawful if it is a response to an armed attack, against a responsible party, proportionate to the threat posed, and necessary for the purpose of defence.[77]

Use of Non-lethal Military Force: Justice by Stealth?

Operation Goldenrod

On 11 June 1985, Fawaz Yunis and four other terrorists boarded Royal Jordanian Airlines Flight 402 armed with hand grenades and automatic weapons. While the plane was on the ground in Beirut, Lebanon,[78] Yunis took control of the cockpit and forced the pilot to take off immediately.[79] The others tied up Jordanian air marshalls and held the passengers hostage. The hostages included two American citizens.[80]

Subsequently, an American investigation led to Yunis, and 'Operation Goldenrod' was put into effect.[81] Undercover FBI agents lured Yunis on to a yacht in the eastern Mediterranean Sea with promises of a drug deal.[82] He was arrested and transferred to a US Navy ship where he was interrogated for several days.[83] After arriving in Washington DC, Yunis was arraigned on charges of conspiracy, hostage taking and aircraft damage.[84] A grand jury added additional aircraft damage counts and a charge of air piracy.[85] Under the Hostage Taking Act,[86] since two of the passengers were US citizens, the United States was able to assert jurisdiction as 'the offender or the person seized or detained (was) a national of the United States'.[87] The court permitted the United States to assert jurisdiction by relying on the universal and passive personality principles of international law jurisdiction.[88]

Yunis argued that the manner of his apprehension violated the case of *US v Toscanino*.[89] The case involved an individual who was tricked by Uruguayan officials, acting under the instructions of US DEA agents, into leaving his Montevideo home, knocked unconscious, gagged and bound. He eventually found himself in New York via Brazil. In *Toscanino*, the US court noted the US government's duty under international law to refrain from kidnapping a criminal defendant from within the borders of another nation and remanded the case for a hearing in the district court to determine the international law claims.

In response to Yunis' challenge that the government violated *Toscanino*, the court held that, while the government's conduct was neither 'picture perfect' nor 'a model for law enforcement behavior', the 'discomfort and surprise' to which the appellant was subjected did not render his waiver of his Fifth and Sixth Amendment rights invalid.[90] In any case, a key factor in the *Toscanino* case had been the existence of formal extradition procedures leading to the conclusion by the court that the personal rights of the defendant had been infringed (significantly despite this finding, the court did not divest its jurisdiction over *Toscanino*). Commenting on the international law duty of states to prosecute or to extradite hijackers in the case of Yunis, District Judge Barrington Parker observed that nations cannot be permitted to seize terrorists anywhere in the world in an unregulated manner. Governments must act in accordance with international law and domestic statutes. However, he noted that where a state such as Lebanon is 'incapable or unwilling . . . [to] enforce its obligations under the [Montreal] Convention', or when a government 'harbors international terrorists or is unable to enforce international law, it is left to the world community to respond and prosecute the alleged terrorists'.[91]

The Achille Lauro Incident   On 7 October 1985, Palestinian terrorists hijacked the Italian cruise ship *Achille Lauro* while it was sailing the Mediterranean Sea with more than 400 people on board.[92] The hijackers demanded the release of 50 Palestinian prisoners held by Israel.[93] It was announced the following day that the terrorists were members of the Palestine Liberation Front, who commandeered the ship after it left Alexandria, Egypt. The hijacking lasted two days, during which time a disabled American was murdered and thrown overboard.[94] The hijackers surrendered to a representative of the Palestine Liberation Organization and were guaranteed safe conduct out of Egypt to an undisclosed location.[95] US intelligence picked up this information as well as the identity and flight plan of the aircraft.

As the terrorists were being flown out of Egypt in an Egyptian airliner with Egyptian security men aboard, American naval forces intercepted the plane and forced it to land in Italy at a joint Italian-NATO airbase.[96] Initial reports claimed that the plane was originally headed for Tunis and then Athens, but that the respective governments had denied landing rights.[97] When the plane landed in Italy, it was immediately surrounded by American commandos. The commandos, in turn, were surrounded by Italian soldiers.[98]

After a tense stand-off between US and Italian forces, the Italians seized the hijackers along with Abbas (the PLO representative) and took them into custody, pursuant to an agreement reached by the American and Italian governments.[99] The Italians brought criminal charges against the terrorists but refused, due to lack of evidence, American requests to hold Abbas for an investigation.[100] The day after American arrest warrants were issued for Abbas and the four hijackers, Abbas was allowed to leave Italy aboard a Yugoslavian jet.[101] Two weeks after Abbas left Italy, an Italian magistrate charged Abbas with murder, kidnapping, hijacking and transportation of arms and explosives.[102] The following July, the hijackers were convicted of various offenses relating to the Achille Lauro incident, and Abbas was tried in absentia, convicted, and given a life sentence for masterminding the hijacking.[103]

Reacting to this incident, international law expert Andreas Lowenfeld asserts: 'we did not violate anybody's air space, we didn't hurt anybody, and so I think we didn't violate international law.'[104] While intercepting an Egyptian airliner might in itself be a violation of international law, the breach of international law by Egypt in not taking the terrorists into custody and either extraditing or prosecuting them, according to Lowenfeld, prompted America's justifiable response to a 'worse breach' by Egypt.[105] Many of these same arguments can apply to Italy, Yugoslavia, South Yemen and Iraq for their assistance in helping Abbas avoid extradition and escape justice. The fact that only America wanted to prosecute all of the terrorists, including Abbas, suggests that the other nations had motives other than seeking justice for all of the participants involved in the hijacking.

The 'Wings of Law': Israel   On 4 February 1986, Israeli warplanes intercepted a Libyan executive jet over the Mediterranean Sea just east of Cyprus and 70 miles from the Israeli coast.[106] Israel had hoped to find on board senior leaders of the Popular Front for the Liberation of Palestine as well as two leading Palestine terrorist organizers.[107] Embarrassingly though, after an intense search lasting several hours, none of the Israeli targets were found on board.[108] The plane was then permitted to continue on to Damascus.

Then Israeli Defence Minister Yitzhak Rabin, commenting on the interception of the Libyan jet, remarked that 'one must show initiative. One must dare even if sometimes the entire goal is not achieved'.[109] Terrorists will, as a result, be afraid to travel. By restricting their movements, their influence will be restricted as well. Not knowing where and when abductors will come for them will no doubt impede the terrorists' effectiveness. Then US Ambassador to the UN Vernon Walters weighed in on Israel's side, noting that: '[W]e must be clear that terrorist violence – and not the response to terrorist violence – is the cause of the cycle of violence which tragically mars ... the entire world.'[110]

Israel's dilemma in dealing with terrorism was summed up by Abba Eban, chairman of the Foreign Affairs and Defence Committees in the Israeli Parliament.

> There is nothing that stands more in contradiction to the law than terrorism. But terrorism hides behind the wings of the law. What determines the international reaction is the success or lack of success. If that person were on the plane, the free world would hail our action. Since the effort failed, I assume there will be criticism on the grounds of the need to respect the law.[111]

Like the United States interception of the Egyptian airplane, Israel's action was neither piracy or hijacking. It was not piracy because the action was not carried out by a 'private ship or aircraft' and it was not done for 'private ends'.[112] The action was also not a hijacking because the international conventions dealing with this offence pertain only to acts undertaken on board aircraft.[113] In order for Israel to claim that the interception was an act of self-defence, it would require that possible future acts of the terrorists sought could be properly attributable to Libya.[114] Additionally, the peril created by further terrorism must be not only grave but imminent.[115]

On the face of it, the interception of a state's aircraft (more so a civilian one) in peacetime by another is inconsistent with international law. It is proximate to a use of force which violates its territorial integrity. The dilemma, however, is increased when the intercept is done in international airspace as this technically seems to undercut the argument of a 'threat or use of force against the territorial integrity or political independence of any state' within the meaning of Article 2(4) of the United Nations Charter.[116]

A Unique Solution, Uncertain Legal Ground

Self-defence as a justification   Argument can be made that the American and Israeli actions violated Article 2(3) of the United Nations Charter, which prohibits behaviour that jeopardizes international peace and security. From a practical perspective, the Israeli action, like the American interception, can be categorized as a 'surgical' operation where only the terrorists, not the civilians, are targeted. From a legal perspective, one school of thought, led by Professor Derek Bowett, asserts that the customary right of self-defence allows a state to use force not only to defend against an armed attack by another state, but also to protect the lives or property of nationals or to ensure a state's political independence against non-military threats.[117] Based on this view, Professor Kash (in relation to the Israeli action) posits:

> The [Israeli] interception can be explained as not only an action to ensure justified punishment, but also to preempt future terrorist actions against Israeli citizens and property. It can be assumed that, because of the past history of these terrorist groups (for which Israel was targeting their leaders), they will strike again ... – [and indeed did so.][118]

Notwithstanding the practical and legal rationalization of the actions, it is to be borne in mind that the UN Charter introduced to international politics a radically new notion: a general prohibition on the unilateral resort to force by states. The American and Israeli actions sit uneasily within the UN Charter regime on the use of force which spells out only two exceptions – self-defence and Security Council authorization. Thus it would appear that Article 2(4) of the Charter which prohibits the use of force or threat of force against the territorial integrity or political independence of any state, or in any manner inconsistent with the purposes of the United Nations, is violated by such adventures. The troubling question is if it takes such a 'surgical' action to prevent an attack, is it logical that these types of interceptions be considered an act of self-defence?

State responsibility as a justification   The second ground on which the actions can find legal traction is based on Andreas Lowenfeld's argument above in relation to the *Achille Lauro* incident: that the abducting state can show complicity by the territorial state. 'Evidently when a nation permits an official government jet to ferry terrorists to a safe location, that nation is acting with, if not for, the terrorists.'[119]

Under international law, once a government has notice that its territory is being used for the preparation of hostile acts in or against another state, it must take effective steps to prevent those acts in order to satisfy its duty under international law.[120] This would appear then to provide reasonable grounds for the assertion that sending agents into a state's territory, specifically targeting an individual who, like a terrorist, is a criminal, does not violate the territorial integrity or political independence of the state.[121]

In any case the actions of espionage or law enforcement agents within a nation's territory, though attracting strong condemnation, have never been considered a use of force under international law.[122] This would appear then to provide reasonable grounds for the assertion by Professor Derek Bowett that sending agents into a state's territory, specifically targeting an individual who, like a terrorist, is a criminal, does not violate the territorial integrity or political independence of the state.[123] Bowett's position finds support in Abraham D. Sofaer's postulation that: '... a state may cross the border of another state in order to capture a terrorist, and this act will not necessarily be considered a violation of that state's sovereignty.'[124]

The Ker-Frisbie Doctrine   No doubt territorial integrity is not the only principle of international law that deserves protection. Attendant to the right of territorial integrity is the obligation on all states to control persons within their borders to ensure that they do not utilize their territory as a base for criminal activity. This lends weight to Sofaer's observation that:

> ... territorial integrity is not entitled to absolute deference in international law, and [US] national defense requires that [the US] claim the right to act within the territory of other states in appropriate circumstances, however infrequently we may choose for prudential reasons to exercise it.[125]

Sofaer's observation is reflected in practice by American courts which have 'developed what is known as the Ker-Frisbie doctrine, which holds that a forcible abduction neither offends due process nor requires a court to free a suspect seized in violation of international law'.[126] Therefore, a court need not divest itself of *in personam* jurisdiction over a defendant based on the method by which the defendant was arrested and brought before the court.[127]

American law enforcement officials, relying on statutes making terrorist attacks on Americans overseas federal crimes, like to refer to abductions as 'arrests'.

> The availability of a US law on which to base the issuance of a warrant may provide law enforcement personnel with the authority to act under US law; it provides no authority, however, to act under either international law or the law of the state whose territorial sovereignty is breached. To be acceptable under international law an abduction must satisfy far more exacting standards than the mere availability of an arrest warrant issued by the state responsible for the action.[128]

In a bid to tone down the vitriolic tenor of condemnation from the international community regarding infringement of territorial integrity, the US generally has sought to orchestrate abductions in international airspace and in international waters. Further, in a bid to address the inevitable outrage that abductions attract, US courts have held that they would lose its jurisdiction only if the methods of abduction were 'deliberate, unnecessary and (an) unreasonable invasion of the accused's constitutional rights'.[129] Additionally, the courts have held that in order for a court to surrender its jurisdiction, the agents' conduct must be of a 'most shocking and outrageous character', a classification limited to 'torture, brutality and similar outrageous conduct'.[130]

According to then US Secretary of State George Shultz: '[I]t is impossible to argue that international law prohibits [the US] from capturing terrorists in international waters or airspace, [or] from attacking them on the soil of other nations. ... A nation attacked by terrorists is permitted to use force ... to seize terrorists or rescue its citizens when no other means is available.'[131] In a spirited defence of the US position, Abraham D. Sofaer asserts that:

The principle of territorial integrity is a major – and proper – legal constraint to taking actions against terrorists or States that support terrorism. World-class terrorists need bases in which to live and work, to train, to store their weapons, to make their bombs, and to hold hostages. The States in which they locate are almost invariably unable or unwilling to extradite them. An extradition request in such cases will do nothing more than reveal that we know their location, an advantage that would thereby be squandered. The only possible remedies against such terrorists often would require infringement of the territorial integrity of the State in which they are located.[132]

The book now turns to discuss the use of lethal military force. The use of military force ranges from so called 'surgical strikes' targeting individuals and terrorist facilities to large-scale military campaigns.

Summing-up The author concludes these complex arguments by noting that seizures of suspected terrorists overseas arguably constitute a serious breach of the territorial sovereignty of another nation and a violation of international law.[133] This is in light of the fact that sovereignty is one of the most fundamental attributes of international law.[134] Under international law, the government of one country cannot conduct activities in the territory of another country unless acting with the consent of that nation.[135]

Abducting terrorists in another country's territory by unauthorized law enforcement agents infringes upon a nation's sovereignty and breaches international law.[136] This generally creates fertile ground for adverse reciprocal treatment among nations. The consequences of infringing on the sovereignty of another nation may increase tension between states and weaken the fight against overseas terrorism through the use of international law.[137]

Conclusion

The use of military force to combat terrorists is an appealing option because it means striking a blow against individuals, factions, and even states that have taken violent and often ruthless action in pursuit of their political goals. Forceful responses from victimized nations against terrorists or states sponsoring terrorism for the purpose of deterring further terrorism should more properly be termed 'reprisals', rather than 'self-defence'. The concept of self-defence has been enlisted in uses of military force even where it is rather clear that the action is a reprisal. The UN has condemned as reprisals those defensive actions that greatly exceeded the provocation.[138] Lack of honesty by states in distinguishing between self-defence and reprisals, however, ensures that no real debate can be undertaken by the UN in acknowledging and setting criteria for actions such as peacetime reprisals in countering terrorism.

It is the linkage between the terrorist and the sponsoring state that is crucial to providing governments with the justification for a response against that state and with the ability to capitalize on the response in terms of deterrence. Unfortunately these linkages are never publicly established. Understandably it would lead to compromising the intelligence assets which states are averse to in the interests of national security. However, military action is frequently shrouded in a jumble of half-truths that raises scepticism among scholars and the international community not helped by a confusing mish-mash of legal justifications.

'International law tries mightily to limit the ability of nation-states to use military force against one another. While it has not successfully eliminated international military conflict, states nonetheless strive to couch military actions in terms justifiable under international law.'[139] The end result is that the illusion of self-defence was (and still is) used and misused, preventing the evolution of any meaningful state practice.

With the end of the Cold War, acts generally described as 'terrorism' proliferated in frequency and severity. The rise of globalization and decolonization, and the increasing accessibility and availability of weapons and technology was quickly enabling well-financed and organized terrorist organizations to transform themselves into global outfits with greater reach and lethality.[140] Globalization and technology was quickly enhancing the capabilities of the outfits. The appeal of terrorism as a low-cost, relatively low-risk, activity with possibilities of high yield in terms of publicity, weakening of the victim or infliction of harm achieved new dimensions.[141]

With less confrontation and more cooperation between states in the post-Cold War era, terrorism soon gained the recognition that Cold War ideological and political squabbles prevented it from gaining – a pernicious and underestimated threat to international peace and security. The terrorist attacks of September 11 revealed the breadth and ambition of international terrorism. It also raised a host of issues and problems. The attacks and subsequent actions engaged the international legal framework as well as political and strategic processes in a manner never seen before. The attacks are a turning point to a new world order but that order is as yet unclear as the fear of American hegemony and the threats posed to international law jostle for position. The book now turns to analyse this event and the manner in which it seems to have made and unmade the international regime on the use of force, in Chapters 4 and 5.

Notes

1   See generally 'UN Secretary General Affirms US Rights to Self-Defence', October 2001, online at http://usinfo.state.gov/topical/pol/terror/01100903.html (visited November 2002).

2   See *The Covenant of the League of Nations*, incorporated in the *Treaty of Peace Between the Allied and Associated Powers and Germany, Peace Treaty of Versailles*, concluded at Versailles, 28 June 1919, 2 Bevans 43, art 12. This terminology, however, left unmentioned hostilities which, although violent, could not be considered war.

3   M. McDougal and F. Feliciano (1961), *Law and Minimum World Public Order: The Legal Regulation of International Coercion*, New Haven: Yale University Press, 142–43.

4   Aryeh Avneri (1970), *The War of Attrition*, Jerusalem, Madim Books, 12.

5   *New York Times*, 3 February 1981, B 13, col. 3 (emphasis added).

6   'Beirut Memorial Brochure', 4 February 2004, online at http://www.beirut-memorial.org/history/embassy.html.

7   Report of DoD Commission on Beirut International Airport Terrorist Act of 23 October 1983, at 129, 20 December 1983, reprinted in (1983) *American Foreign Policy Document* 122 at 349, col. 2.

8   *Vice President's Task Force on Combating Terrorism, Public Report*, (February 1986, Vol 2, 4).
9   Ibid.
10 See N. Livingstone and T. Arnold (1985), 'The Rise of State Sponsored Terrorism', in N. Livingstone and T. Arnold, (eds) *Fighting Back*, New York: Simon and Schuster, 11–24.
11 James Terry (1986), 'Countering State-Sponsored Terrorism: A Law-Policy Analysis', 36 *Naval Law Review* 159, 163. Writing in 1986, Colonel James P. Terry observed that between 1966 and 1986 as many US diplomats had died at the hands of terrorists as were killed in the previous two centuries.
12 Brian M. Jenkins (1985), 'The US Response to Terrorism: A Policy Dilemma', (April), *Armed Forces Journal of International Law* 44.
13 'Preemptive Anti-Terrorist Raids Allowed', *Washington Post*, 16 April 1984, at A-19, Col 4 (City ed). The National Security Decision Directive remains classified.
14 R. McFarlane, 'Terrorism and the Future of Free Society', Speech Delivered at the Defence Strategy Forum, National Strategic Information Centre, Washington DC (15 March 1985).
15 'Shultz urges "Active" Drive on Terrorism', *Washington Post*, 25 June 1984.
16 Address by Secretary of State George Shultz, 'Terrorism and The Modern World', The Scherr Lecture, at the Park Avenue Synagogue, New York, 25 October 1984, at 23, reported in *New York Times*, 26 October 1984, at 12.
17 'Address before the Park Avenue Synagogue', 25 October 1984, reprinted in *Department of State Bulletin* 12, 16, December 1984, (Park Avenue Synagogue Address).
18 Ibid.
19 Ernest Evans (1979), *Calling a Truce to Terror: The American Response to International Terrorism*, Westport, Conn.: Greenwood Press, 97–99.
20 See 'US Supports Attack, Jordan and Egypt Vow to Press for Peace', *New York Times*, 2 October 1985 at A9, Col. 1. US Ambassador Walters supported the Israeli justification for the attack in spite of the abstention:

> My Government could not support the draft resolution disproportionately placing all blame for this latest round of the rising spiral of violence in the Middle East onto only one set of shoulders, while not also holding at fault those responsible for the terrorist acts which provoked it ... We speak of a pattern of violence, but we must be clear: it is terrorism that is the cause of this pattern, not responses to terrorist attacks ... [W]e recognize and strongly support the principle that a state subjected to continuing terrorist attacks may respond with appropriate use of force to defend itself against further attacks. This is an aspect of the inherent right of self-defence recognized in the *UN Charter*. We support this principle regardless of attacker, and regardless of victim.

    40 U.N. SCOR (2615th mtg.) at 111–12, UN Doc S/PV.2615 (1985).
21 The Israeli attack by six F-15 fighter-bombers apparently left 70 men, women and children dead and more than 100 Tunisians and Palestinians wounded. See 'Cycle of Terrorism Will Continue With Retaliatory Strikes', *Houston Post*, 2 January 1986 at 2B, Col 1.
22 'Israel Calls Bombing a Warning to Terrorists', *New York Times*, 2 October 1985, at A8, Col. 1.
23 U.N. Doc. S/RES/573 (4 October 1985) (vote: 14-0-1) reprinted in 24 I.L.M. 1740–41, November 1986, extract reprinted in (1986) 80 *American Journal of International Law* 166.
24 S.C. Res 573, 40 U.N. SCOR, Res & Decs at 23, U.N. Doc S/INF/41 (1985); see also 40 U.N. SCOR (2615th mtg) at 108, U.N. Doc S/PV.2615 (1985).

25   However, the US supported the attack. See 'US Supports Attack, Jordan and Egypt Vow to Press for Peace', *New York Times*, 2 October 1985 at A9, Col 1; statement of support by US Ambassador to the U.N. Vernon Walters in the Security Council, 40 U.N. SCOR (2615th mtg.) at 111–12, U.N. Doc S/PV.2615 (1985).

26   40 U.N. SCOR (2615th mtg.) U.N. Doc S/PV.2615 (1985) 5. See, e.g., ibid., 5 (remarks by Ambassador Ononaiye (Nigeria/UN Africa Group)); ibid., 12–13 (Golob (Yugoslavia)); ibid., 23–26 (Kusumaatmadja (Indonesia)); ibid., 31 (Chamorro Mora (Nicaragua)); ibid., 53–55 (Wasiuddin (Bangladesh)); ibid., 58 (Shihabi (Saudi Arabia)); ibid., 63 (Zarif (Afghanistan)); ibid., 68 (Le Kim Chung (Vietnam)).

27   'US Mission to the UN Press Release No. 106 (85)', 4 October 1985, extract reprinted in (1986) 80 *American Journal of International Law* 166, 167.

28   'Statement of Secretary of State George Shultz', (15 January 1986). See 'Shultz Urges Limited Attack on Terrorists', *Houston Chronicle*, 16 January 1986 at 6, Col. 3; 'Shultz Supports Armed Reprisals', *New York Times*, 16 January 1986, at A1, Col. 5. The entire speech is reprinted in 25 *International Legal Materials* 204, January 1986. For quoted language, see ibid., at 206.

29   See 'Abraham Sofaer – State's Legal Adviser Deals with Policy, Then the Law', *Washington Post*, 10 March 1986 at A13, Col. 1.

30   Shultz Supports Armed Reprisals', *New York Times*, 16 January 1986, at A1, Col 5. The entire speech is reprinted in 25 I.L.M. 204, January 1986.

31   Ibid. For earlier remarks concerning the need for pre-emptive strikes, see, e.g., *New York Times*, 26 October 1984 at A12, Col. 2. Analyzed in Richard Falk (1985), 'The Decline of Normative Restraint in International Relations', 10 *Yale Journal of International Law* 263, 265-66.

32   Vice President's Task Force on Combating Terrorism, Public Report 2, February 1986, (Public Report).

33   *New York Times*, 6 April 1986, at A1, Col. 6.

34   (1986) 86 *Department State Bulletin 2111*, June, at 8.

35   *New York Times*, 16 April 1986, at A18, Col. 1.

36   Ibid., Col. 5. See also 86 *Department State Bulletin*.

37   *New York Times*, 15 April 1986 at A1, Col. 6.

38   US Ambassador to the UN Vernon Walters cited the exchange of diplomatic cables between the Libyan Embassy in East Berlin and Tripoli as the evidence to which President Reagan had referred. (1986) 86 *Department State Bulletin* 2111 at 8, June.

39   *New York Times*, 16 April 1986 at A17, Col. 5. US officials later explained that Libyan agents had planned a daylight machine gun and grenade attack on an American visa office in Paris.

40   'Speech by Ronald Reagan, International Terrorism', (1986) *US Dep't of St. Bureau of Pub. Affairs Spec. Rep. No. 24*, 1.

41   Philip A. Seymour (1990), 'The Legitimacy of Peacetime Reprisal as a Tool against State-Sponsored Terrorism', 39 *Naval Law Review* 221, 223.

42   Ibid.

43   William V. Shannon (1987), 'Thatcher's Reservations', *The Boston Globe*, at A21 (10 June) ('[Thatcher] had strong doubts about the raid ... Her doubts arose from her strong devotion to the concept of international law. Thatcher has a law degree, and part of her strongly held creed is that lawfulness by nations as well as individuals is one of the hallmarks of civilized behaviour.'); see also Statement of Sir John Thompson, 41 U.N. SCOR, 41st Sess, 2679th mtg, at 27, U.N. Doc S/PV.2679 (1986) (Prime Minister Thatcher primarily concerned with proportionality).

44   Michael J. Kelly (2003), 'Time Warp to 1945 – Resurrection of the Reprisal and Anticipatory Self-Defence Doctrines in International Law', 13 *Journal of Transnational Law Policy* 1, 17.

45   *Newsweek*, 2 January 1989, at 14–23.

46   *Executive Order No 12*, 686 (1989).

47   *Report of the President's Commission on Aviation Security and Terrorism*, 15 May 1990 at 125.

48   See, e.g., 'Abraham Sofaer – State's Legal Adviser Deals with Policy, Then the Law', *Washington Post*, at A13, Col. 1 (10 March 1986).

49   See 'Task Force Supports US Policy on Global Terrorism, Official Says', *Houston Post*, at A13, Col. 3 (2 March 1986).

50   Ibid., Col 3–4.

51   Jordan J. Paust (1986), 'Responding Lawfully to International Terrorism: the Use of Force Abroad', 8 *Whittier Law Review* 711, 716.

52   Ibid., 719.

53   *UN Charter*, art. 51.

54   M. Whiteman (1965), *Digest of International Law*, Vol 5, § 25, 971-72.

55   G. Shultz (1986), 'Low Intensity Warfare: The Challenge of Ambiguity', *US Department of State Current Policy No. 783*, 3 (January).

56   *UN Charter,* art. 2(4).

57   *Military and Paramilitary Activities* (Nicaragua v US), 1986 I.C.J. 14 (June 27). 102-103.

58   G.A. Res 1334, U.N. GAOR, 29th Sess, Supp No 31, U.N. Doc A/9631 (1974) (G.A. Res 1334). Article 3 lists a series of acts that are to be considered as aggression and includes, in sub-paragraph (g), 'the sending by or on behalf of a state of armed bands, irregulars or mercenaries which carry out acts of armed force against another state of such gravity as to amount to the acts listed [earlier in the paragraph].'

59   See I.C.J. Reports 1986, para 195.

60   Christopher Greenwood (2003), 'International Law and the Preemptive Use of Military Force: Afghanistan, Al Qaida and Iraq', 4 *San Diego International Law Journal* 7, 17.

61   Ibid., 2.

62   M. McDougal and F. Feliciano (1961), *Law and Minimum World Public Order*, 242.

63   Greenwood, 23.

64   Oscar Schachter (1991), *International Law in Theory and Practice*, Dordrecht; Boston: M. Nijhoff Publishers, 145 (*Developments In International Law Series*, Vol 13).

65   See, e.g., 'President Kennedy, Radio and Television Report to the American People on the Soviet Arms Build-up in Cuba', 22 October 1962, 12 November 2003, online at http://www.jfklibrary.org/j102262.htm ('We no longer live in a world where the actual firing of weapons represents an efficient challenge to a nation's security to constitute maximum peril.'); see also Beth Polebaum (1984), 'National Self-Defence in International Law: An Emerging Standard for a Nuclear Age', 59 *New York University Review* 187, 203 n. 102 (referencing Alford (1966), 'The Legality of American Military Involvement in Viet Nam: A Broader Perspective', 75 *Yale Law Journal* 1109, 1113 (1966) (arguing that 'armed attack' should be understood to include processes as well as specific events)).

66   *UN Charter*, art. 51. See also Baker (1987), 'Terrorism and the Inherent Right of Self-Defence (A Call to Amend Article 51 of the United Nations Charter', 10 *Houston Journal of International Law* 25.

67   Julius Stone (1958), *Aggression and World Order; A Critique of United Nations Theories of Aggression*, Berkeley, University of California Press, 245.

68   See generally Comment (1972), 'Reprisals and Self-Defence: The Customary Law', 66 *American Journal of Interantional Law* 586.

69   Michael Lohr (1985), 'Legal Analysis of U.S. Military Responses to State-Sponsored International Terrorism', 34 *Naval Law Review* 1, 31–32.

70   See, e.g., Oscar Schachter (1984), 'The Right of States to Use Armed Force', 82 *Michigan Law Review* 1620.

71	G.A. Res 41/38, U.N. GAOR, 41st Sess, Supp No. 53, at 34, U.N. Doc A/41/53 (1986).
72	Michael Ratner and Jules Lobel (1993), 'Bombing Baghdad, Revisited; Lawful Self-Defence or Unlawful Reprisal?', *Connecticut Law Tribune*, at 24 (19 July).
73	Gregory Francis Intoccia (1987), 'American Bombing of Libya: An International Legal Analysis', 19 *Case Western Reserve Journal of International Law* 177, 187 (quoting Robert A. Manning (1986), 'Little Fallout for NATO Expected; In Western Europe, Strains Among Friends', *US News & World Republican*, at 24–25 (28 April)).
74	Greenwood, 13.
75	Christine Gray (2002), *International Law and the Use of Force*, Oxford; New York: Oxford University Press, 118.
76	Ibid.
77	Richard B. Bilder and Mary Ellen O'Connell (2003), Book Review, 'International Law and the Use of Force', 97 *American Journal of International Law* 446, 450.
78	*United States v Yunis*, 924 F 2d 1086, 1089 (DC Cir 1991).
79	Ibid.
80	Ibid.
81	Ibid.
82	Ibid.
83	Ibid.
84	Ibid.
85	Ibid.
86	18 USC S 1203 (West 1984).
87	18 USC S 1203 (b)(1)(A) (West 1984).
88	*United States v Yunis*, 924 F.2d at 1091.
89	*United States v Toscanino*, 500 F 2d 267, 275 (2d Cir.) reh'g denied, 504 F 2d 1380 (1974).
90	*United States v Yunis*, 895 F2d 953, 969 (DC Cir 1988).
91	*United States v Yunis*, 681 F. Supp 896, 906–07 (DDC 1988).
92	John Tagliabue (1985), 'Ship Carrying 400 Seized', *New York Times*, at A1 (9 October).
93	Tagliabue, ibid.; Judith Miller (1985), 'Hijackers Yield Ship in Egypt', *New York Times*, at A1 (10 October).
94	Judith Miller (1985), 'Hijackers Yield Ship in Egypt', *New York Times*, A1 (10 October).
95	Ibid.
96	18 USC S 1203 (West 1984).
97	Ibid.
98	Jill Smolowe (1985), 'Piecing Together the Drama', *Time*, 31 (28 October).
99	Ross Laver (1985), 'Striking Back', *Maclean's*, at 36 (21 October).
100	John Tagliabue (1985), 'Italians Attempt to Reassure U.S.', *New York Times*, A1 (14 October).
101	Loren Jenkins (1985), 'PLO Leader Slips from U.S. Grasp in Italy', *Washington Post*, A1 (13 October).
102	'Court in Italy Issues Warrant for Abul Abbas', *Los Angeles Times*, 27 October 1985, 8.
103	Loren Jenkins (1986), '11 Hijackers Sentenced in Genoa Court', *Washington Post*, A1 (11 July).
104	Stuart Taylor Jr. (1985), 'Capture of Hijackers: Plane Diversion Raises Legal Issues', *New York Times*, A11 (11 October).
105	Ibid.
106	Thomas L. Friedman (1986), 'Israelis Intercept a Libyan Civil Jet and then Let It Go', *New York Times*, A1 (5 February).
107	Henry Kamm (1986), 'Rabin Defends Air Interception: Vows More "Unconventional" Acts', *New York Times*, A10 (6 February).

108   Friedman, 'Israelis Intercept a Libyan Civil Jet'.

109   Kamm, 'Rabin Defends Air Interception'.

110   'U.S. Vetoes Anti-Israeli Move', *New York Times*, 7 February 1986, A6.

111   Kamm, 'Rabin Defends Air Interception'.

112   George M. Borkowski (1986), 'Recent Developments – Use of Force: Interception of Aircraft', 27 *Harvard International Law Journal* 761, 765; see also Convention on the High Seas, done 29 April 1958, 13 U.S.T. 2312, 450 U.N.T.S. 82 (hereinafter High Seas Convention)

113   George M. Borkowski (1986), 'Recent Developments – Use of Force: Interception of Aircraft', 27 *Harvard International Law Journal* 761, 765; see also *Convention on Offences and Certain Other Acts Committed on Board Aircraft* (Tokyo Convention), opened for signature 14 September 1963, 704 U.N.T.S. 219.

114   Borkowski, ibid., 769, 770; see also *Report of the International Law Commission on the Work of Its Thirty-first Session*, U.N. Doc. A/34/10/Corr.1 (1975), reprinted in (1979) 1 *Year Book of the International Law Commission* 87–136 (hereinafter Draft Articles).

115   Borkowski, ibid., 770; see Draft Articles.

116   Douglas Kash (1993), 'Abductions of Terrorists in International Airspace and on the High Seas', 8 *Florida Journal of International Law* 65, 84.

117   D. Cameron Findlay (1988), 'Abducting Terrorists Overseas for Trial in the United States: Issues of International and Domestic Law', 23 *Texas International Law Journal* 1, 30.

118   Kash, 'Abductions of Terrorists', 93.

119   Ibid., 85.

120   Findlay, 23; The Declaration on Principles of International Law Concerning Friendly Relations and Cooperation among States in Accordance with the Charter of the United Nations provides, in part, that a state has a duty to 'refrain from organizing, instigating, assisting or participating in ... terrorist acts in another state ...' G.A. Res. 2625, U.N. GAOR, Supp. No. 28, at 121, U.N. Doc. A/2028 (1970).

121   Derek Bowett (1958), *Self Defence in International Law*, New York, NY: Praeger, 55; See also Ian Brownlie (1963) *International Law and the Use of Force by States*, Oxford: Clarendon Press, 361.

122   See Brownlie, ibid., 56 where Professor Brownlie argues that actions specifically directed against individuals within the territory of a state do not violate the territorial integrity or political independence of that state.

123   Bowett, *Self Defence in International Law*, 55; see also Brownlie, *International Law and the Use of Force by States*, 361.

124   Kash, 'Abductions of Terrorists', at 79.

125   Sofaer, 'The Sixth Annual Waldemar A. Solf Lecture', 106.

126   Kash, 'Abductions of Terrorists', 82–83; see also Findlay, 47.

127   Findlay, ibid., 46.

128   Sofaer, 'The Sixth Annual Waldemar A. Solf Lecture', 106, 110.

129   *United States v Toscanino*, 5000 F 2d 267, 267 (2d Cir.), reh'g denied, 504 F.2d 1380 (1974).

130   *United Nations ex rel. Julio Juventino v Gengler* 510 F.2d 62, 65 (2d Cir.), cert. denied, 421 U.S. 1001 (1975).

131   Terry Richard Kane (1987), 'Prosecuting International Terrorists in the United States Courts: Gaining the Jurisdictional Threshold', 12 *Yale Journal of International Law* 294, 339–40.

132   Sofaer, 'The Sixth Annual Waldemar A. Solf Lecture', 106.

133   See FBI Authority to Seize Suspects Abroad: Hearings Before the Subcommittee on Civil and Constitutional Rights of the House Committee on the Judiciary, 103d Cong. 16, 23, 31 (1989) [hereinafter FBI Authority to Seize Suspects Abroad].

134   Ibid., 31 (describing sovereignty as 'one of the most fundamental attributes of international law').

135   See *Restatement (Third) of Foreign Relations Law* (1987), sec. 432 cmt. b (1987) (explaining the infringement of sovereignty).

136   See *Foreign Relations Restatement*, sec. 432(2) (1987) (requiring consent for a state's law enforcement officers to conduct activities within another state).

137   See Bryan F. MacPherson (1998), 'Building an International Criminal Court for the 21st Century', 13 *Connecticut Journal of International Law* 21–23 (identifying negative implications of sovereignty infringement under international law through the use of self-help); see also Malloy, 317 (asserting that countries' failure to abide by existing international laws weakens the fight against terrorism abroad).

138   See the Security Council's discussion in 36 U.N. SCOR (2285–2288 mtgs.), U.N. Docs S/VP 2285–88 (1981).

139   Christopher Clarke Posteraro (2002), 'Intervention in Iraq: Towards A Doctrine of Anticipatory Counter-Terrorism, Counter-Proliferation Intervention', 15 *Florida Journal of International Law* 151, 155. See also generally Louis Henkin (1991), *The Use of Force: Law and US Policy, In Right v Might*, New York: Council on Foreign Relations, 39-40.

140   In relation to the rise of terrorism, see Peter Chalk (1996), W*est European Terrorism and Counter-Terrorism: The Evolving Dynamic,* New York: St. Martin's Press (specifically chapters 2 and 4); Sunga, Lyal S., *The Emerging System of International Criminal Law: Developments in Codification and Implementation* (Martinus Nijhoff, The Hague, The Netherlands).

141   Paul Wilkinson (1994), 'Terrorist Targets and Tactics: New Risk to World Order', in Alison Jamiesone (ed.), *Terrorism and Drug Trafficking in the 1990s,* Aldershot, UK; Brookfield, VT: Dartmouth, 181.

Chapter 4

Jumping the Gun – An Old Problem as a Solution for New Threats? Afghanistan, Iraq and Beyond

Introduction

The horrors of September 11 and the events that unfolded that tragic day presented a terrible day in history. Global terrorism had finally come of age. The clandestine Al-Qaeda terrorist network demonstrated that transnational terrorism represented 'the most pernicious and underestimated threat to international peace and security in the post-Cold War world'.[1]

The attacks against the US changed the context of UN activities. After September 11, the Security Council weighed in on the matter and quickly became the locus of action.[2] Resolution 1368, passed a day after the attacks, unequivocally condemned the terrorist attacks of September 11, calling on all states to 'work together urgently to bring to justice the perpetrators, organizers and sponsors'[3] of the attacks, and reaffirmed the inherent right of self-defence in accordance with Article 51 of the UN Charter. 'Given the circumstances, this affirmation was significant: it implied that the attacks triggered the right even if, at the time of adoption, the UN Security Council knew almost nothing about who or what had launched them.'[4]

The shift in the law is evident when one considers that in 1985, the international response to military strikes made by Israel against Tunisia was strongly condemnatory. So much so that the Security Council in Resolution 573[5] condemned the air attack on PLO headquarters as an 'act of armed aggression ... in flagrant violation of the Charter of the United Nations, international law and norms of conduct'.[6] This was despite Israel's argument that Tunisia's acts of harbouring, supplying and assisting non-state actors who they claimed committed terrorist acts in Israel should be sufficient to attribute the acts of those non-state actors to it.[7] The fact that Resolution 573 condemned Israel's attack as contrary to the UN Charter implied that no justification based on self-defence was found. The claim of self-defence was subsequently also rejected by states as justification for the US bombing of Tripoli (in response to a terrorist bomb in a Berlin nightclub) and the 1993 bombing of the Iraqi Secret Service (after an assassination attempt was made on former US President George Bush Sr in Kuwait).[8]

It is significant though that, in 1992, a watershed of sorts was marked when the Security Council characterized as a threat to international peace and security Libyan support for terrorism. In Resolution 748, the Security Council imposed economic sanctions on Libya for its continuing involvement with terrorist activities and for its refusal to extradite two Libyan nationals alleged to have been involved in the 1988 bombing of Pan Am Flight 103 over Lockerbie, Scotland. The Council affirmed that:

> In accordance with Article 2, paragraph 4 of the Charter of the United Nations, every State has a duty to refrain from organizing, instigating, assisting or participating in terrorist acts in another State or acquiescing in organized activities within its territory directed toward the commission of such acts, when such acts involve a threat or use of force.[9]

In characterizing Libyan action as a threat to international peace and security, it would seem that the door to possible use of military force had been opened. After all Article 1(1) gives, as the first purpose of the United Nations, the centrality of maintaining international peace and security, and to that end: to take effective collective measures for the prevention and removal of threats to the peace, and for the suppression of acts of aggression or other breaches of the peace, and to bring about by peaceful means, and in conformity with the principles of justice and international law, adjustment or settlement of international disputes or situations which might lead to a breach of the peace. In the words of Professor Christopher Greenwood:

> These provisions make clear the importance, in the legal order embodied in the Charter, of maintaining international peace but also the readiness to use force to combat aggression and to prevent threats to the peace from materializing into acts of aggression or breaches of the peace – the Charter is about keeping the peace not about pacifism.[10]

The Security Council's express recognition of terrorism as a threat to international peace and security in Resolution 748 was taken a step further in the aftermath of September 11. The Security Council's resolutions on Afghanistan not only condemn the terrorist acts, they also explicitly mention the right of individual and collective self-defence. In a further sign that military force could be a countermeasure against terrorism, the subsequent military strikes did not attract any condemnation.[11] In fact the military action against Afghanistan, targeting the recalcitrant Taliban regime in a bid to destroy Al-Qaeda's refuge, was largely welcomed and supported.

It was not long, however, before the support and cooperation the US had enjoyed in launching 'Operation Enduring Freedom' in Afghanistan began to fizzle away. Emboldened by international support (and cooperation) during its military campaign in Afghanistan, the US adopted an even bolder and far-sweeping agenda; it would target rogue states through military action. International anxiety was quickly stoked when US President George Bush Jr elaborated on his administration's strategy to focus on terrorist groups of global reach as well as states that were complicit in one way or another in supporting international terrorism.[12] This would involve delicate national-driven policy judgments that would complicate the rather tenuous regime on the use of force. If the military operation in Afghanistan marked a potential for the transformation of the international system on the use of force, that transformation suffered a major hit in March 2002, when the United States indicated that it was planning military actions against Iraq. A large section of the international community (including some major states) protested. The

Arab League adopted the most radical standpoint when it stated that such an action would be an act of aggression.[13]

This chapter discusses the technicalities and complexities of the so called 'Bush Doctrine' of hot pre-emption or pre-emptive strikes against states alleged or proved to sponsor terrorism. As the US proceeds with its 'War on Terror', US policymakers are yet again thrust into the murky waters surrounding the international legal norms relating to the doctrine of self-defence.

Proactive Counter-terrorism Policy

In 1993, following the discovery of an Iraqi plot to assassinate former President George Bush Sr on a visit to Kuwait, then US President Bill Clinton ordered the US Navy to launch 23 cruise missiles in retaliation against Iraqi intelligence targets within Iraq, including the headquarters of the Iraqi intelligence service. The attack came after the capture of several key people involved in the plot by Kuwaiti authorities, and an analysis of the bomb.[14] The attack came after those involved in the plot in Kuwait had been arrested and former President George Bush Sr had completed his planned visit, suggesting that the plot had been effectively thwarted prior to the cruise missile strikes. Nevertheless, the justification presented to Congress by the President was that the action was within the right of self-defence under Article 51.[15]

In contrast to previous widespread condemnation from the international community, most states either supported or did not object to the 1993 cruise missile attack on Baghdad in response to the foiled Iraqi assassination attempt on former President Bush Sr. However, most of the Arab world expressed regret regarding the attack.[16] In response to the American presentation before the UN Security Council, the representatives of other member states either expressed support for the US action or refrained from criticizing it; only China questioned the attack.[17] The General Assembly took no action.

The next significant case of American action to counter terrorism through military action came in 1998. 'On 7 August 1998, the US embassies in Kenya and Tanzania were bombed. At least 252 people died (including 12 US citizens) and more than 5,000 were injured.'[18] The attacks on the US embassies in East Africa were characterized by the Security Council as a threat to international peace and security,[19] although there was no clear indication of state involvement in the incidents. Secretary of State Madeleine Albright pledged that the US would use all means at its disposal to track down and punish those responsible.[20]

On 20 August 1998 the US responded by launching 79 Tomahawk cruise missiles[21] from US warships, directed at an Osama bin Laden-bankrolled Al-Qaeda terrorist training camp in Afghanistan and a Sudanese pharmaceutical plant[22] that the Administration suspected was producing chemical weapons components with Osama bin Laden's funding.[23] The use of military force was distinguished not only by its scale but by the nature of its target: 'a stateless confederation of terrorist groups, without strict hierarchy, government or territory.'[24]

International reaction to the 1998 US cruise missile strikes against terrorist targets in Afghanistan and Sudan in response to the US embassy bombings in East

Africa was mixed, with the most intense criticism focused on the Sudan attack. Western European nations supported the US actions to varying degrees, while the Russian President Boris Yeltsin declared that he was 'outraged' by the 'indecent' behaviour of the United States.[25] China issued an ambiguous statement condemning terrorism, and Japan said it 'understood America's resolute attitude towards terrorism'.[26]

The American justification for their military action was based on both reprisal and anticipatory self-defence.[27] In his address to the nation, Clinton told the American people that the strikes against the 'terrorist-related facilities in Afghanistan and Sudan' were necessary because of the 'imminent threat they presented to [US] national security'.[28] In a report sent to Congress, the President Clinton claimed the strikes were justified under the 'inherent right of self-defence consistent with Article 51', and at the same time were intended to 'prevent and deter additional attacks'.[29]

Thus the Clinton administration, like the Reagan administration before it, justified its response to the terrorist strikes by claiming self-defence. Moreover, President Clinton invoked the traditional *Caroline* requirements of imminence, necessity and proportionality, claiming that all three had been met.[30] Indeed, when Bill Richardson, the then US Ambassador to the United Nations, wrote the letter notifying the UN Security Council of the US missile attacks on Afghanistan and Sudan, he clearly laid out the US arguments in support of the attacks in the familiar language of self-defence.[31] Clinton's Secretary of Defense, William S. Cohen, went further by warning terrorist organizations that the US would not limit itself to 'passive defence' when faced with choosing either to 'fight or fold in pathetic cowardice'.[32] Significantly, Cohen stated that in cases where proof of state-sponsored terrorism is found, the US would respond and retaliate as swiftly as possible, a restatement of American policy that stretched back to the Reagan era.[33]

Many of the same critiques of the Reagan administration's bombing of Libya also apply to the Clinton administration's cruise missile attacks in Afghanistan and Sudan, leading many observers to conclude that the cruise missile attacks violated the rules of international law.[34] 'The care with which ... President [Clinton] and US officials characterized the justification for the missile attacks show[ed] their concern that the actions of the US could be perceived as a violation of international law.'[35] This, however, proved insufficient to ward off criticism. In characterizing the cruise missile strikes as more like a 'retaliation rather than legitimate self-defence'[36] critics took issue with the fact that the targets of the attacks in both Afghanistan and Sudan had no direct link to any 'imminent' attack against the US.[37] In any case the attacks seemed to clearly violate the requirement of proportionality.

In Leah Campbell's observation, far more likely than not, the destruction of the terrorist training camps in Afghanistan, and the levelling of the pharmaceutical plant in Sudan, did not meet the proportionality requirement regulating uses of force in self-defence.[38] Thus no matter how the Clinton administration chose to justify the attacks – whether as retaliation or as self-defence – the equation simply did not add up to an acceptable use of force under international law.[39] The legitimacy of the strikes was doubtful at best and outrightly illegitimate at worst.

The most significant aspect of the bombings was that it was the 'first time the US had given such primary and public prominence to the pre-emptive, not just retaliatory, nature and motive of a military strike against a terrorist organization or network. For the first time the US had unreservedly acknowledged a pre-emptive military strike against a terrorist organization or network.'[40] The writing was on the wall. US policymakers were setting a new direction in counter-terrorism – a more proactive and global counter-terrorism policy, less constrained when targeting terrorists, their bases, or infrastructure.

Then US Defense Secretary William S. Cohen, in words similar to those of then National Security Adviser Sandy Berger, characterized the response as 'the long term, fundamental way in which the US intends to combat the forces of terror' noting that the US would not simply play passive defence. Then US Secretary of State Madeleine Albright stressed that the US was involved in a long-term struggle which she predicted was war of the future. National Security Adviser Sandy Berger was also vocal, noting that states would not be expected to fight this new enemy simply in defence but had to be prepared to go on the offensive.[41]

In a warning to terrorist groups who may seek weapons of mass destruction, President Clinton, in his 21 August 1998 statement from Martha's Vineyard, gave as one of four reasons for ordering the attacks efforts by the Al-Qaeda terrorist network to acquire chemical weapons and other dangerous weapons.[42] The Clinton administration had not only declared war on terror[43] but also laid down the framework which the Bush administration would take to the next level in the aftermath of September 11.

September 11, 2001: Crossing the Rubicon

In a coordinated operation whose breadth and audacity stunned the world, terrorists believed to be part of the Al-Qaeda network carried out the worst terrorist attack in modern times, targeting the symbols of US supremacy leaving about 3000 people dead.[44] The day after the attacks, the UN Security Council tersely stated that: 'The magnitude of [the] acts goes beyond terrorism as we have known it so far … We therefore think that new definitions, terms and strategies have to be developed for the new realities.'[45] On the same day, the UN General Assembly, at its first plenary meeting of the year, adopted Resolution 56/1 without a vote, urgently calling for international cooperation to prevent and eradicate acts of terrorism, stressing that those responsible for aiding, supporting or harbouring the perpetrators, organizers and sponsors of such acts would be held accountable.[46]

On 20 September 2001, nine days after the September 11 terrorist attacks, President Bush pledged: 'Our war on terror begins with Al-Qaeda, but it does not end there. It will not end until every terrorist group of global reach has been found, stopped and defeated.'[47] The UN Security Council agreed with President Bush on the urgent need to fight terrorism and cooperate in that endeavour to successfully purge the world of international terrorists.[48] In addition, every major regional organization, including the Arab League, agreed that the September 11 hijackings and attacks on the World Trade Center and Pentagon were acts of terrorism in violation of international law.[49]

Amidst a swell of international support, the US quickly identified the Al-Qaeda terrorist network, with the support of the Taliban government, as the perpetrators of the September 11 terrorist attacks.[50] This was coupled with a recognition that the modern threat to US power and security rises not from one particular organization, but from the growing threat of international terrorism, particularly terrorism that enjoys active or tacit state support.[51] 'Operation Enduring Freedom' in Afghanistan signalled a renewed determination on the part of the US to combat international terrorism and states that sponsor it and laid fertile ground for debate on the strategic or legal approach that states should adopt in responding to such threats.

Strategically, the US military action against terrorism was based on the 'Reagan Doctrine' of swift and effective retribution against terrorist organizations that strike US interests[52] as well as the 'Shultz Doctrine' of active military engagement of terrorists and states that sponsor or support them. Though legally, the US justified 'Operation Enduring Freedom' under the established doctrine of self-defence,[53] talk from Washington was articulating pre-emptive self-defence. Essentially, the US did not consider military action against Afghanistan as a formal war against the state but pre-emption of further attacks by terrorists based in that state.

As the US moved against Afghanistan, the highest levels of military, legal and diplomatic policymakers in Washington began debating how the US should confront states that sponsor terrorism and proliferate weapons of mass destruction. The immediate focus of that debate centred on US policy towards Iraq. Soon after the military action in Afghanistan, the 2002 State of the Union address – the so-called 'Axis of Evil' speech – provoked heated reaction with its strong overtones of unilateral military action by the US against countries that support terror and an intimation of expansion of the scope of military operations beyond Afghanistan, without indication that such an expanded theatre of operations would depend on Security Council approval.[54]

The 'Bush Doctrine'

Though the genesis of the 'Bush Doctrine' can be traced to the immediate aftermath of the September 11 attacks,[55] it was five months after the 'Axis of Evil' speech that the US President delivered the fullest exposition of the doctrine in a speech at West Point on 1 June 2002.[56] Warning that the US faced 'a threat with no precedent' through the proliferation of weapons of mass destruction and the emergence of global terrorism, Bush stated that the traditional strategies of deterrence and containment were no longer sufficient. Because of the new threats that the US faces, he claimed that a proper understanding of the right of self-defence would now extend to authorizing pre-emptive attacks against potential aggressors, cutting them off before they are able to launch strikes against the US that might be devastating in their scale and scope. Under these circumstances, he concluded 'If we wait for threats to fully materialize, we will have waited too long.'[57]

Expounding on the strategic aspect of the doctrine, President Bush stated that there was a need to '... take the battle to the enemy, disrupt his plans, and confront the worst threats before they emerge'.[58] In the same address, he went on to tell the future US military officers at West Point that: 'The military must be ready to strike at a moment's notice in any dark corner of the world. All nations that decide for aggression and terror will pay a price.'[59] That doctrine carried an explicit warning for Iraq and other states that pursue weapons of mass destruction: if a hostile regime also pursues the acquisition or development of chemical, biological or nuclear weapons, the decisive use of anticipatory military force to end that regime is a legitimate response.

Iraq was particularly prominent on the list of places where military intervention was envisioned.[60] The first step was achieved when the US and United Kingdom successfully encouraged the UN Security Council to pass Resolution 1441,[61] which gave Iraq a final opportunity to comply with its disarmament obligations through weapons inspections. Resolution 1441, however, made no mention of military force and, pursuant to the French proposal, it specified that in the event of Iraqi non-compliance, the Security Council would reconvene to consider what action to take in response. It did not conform to the favoured American approach of an automatic military attack at the first instance of Iraqi non-compliance. As noted by Allison Ehlert:

> In his statement upon the passage of the resolution, US Ambassador to the UN John Negroponte confirmed that the resolution contained no 'hidden triggers' or 'automaticity' to use force; the United States had indeed agreed to return to the Security Council for a second debate in the event of Iraqi non-compliance. This was the vital American assurance that the French, Russians, and others were looking for, and that therefore made Resolution 1441 a reality.[62]

Despite its recourse to the Security Council, the US position quickly crystallized as one of armed intervention justifiable on the basis of pre-emptive or anticipatory self-defence, and hence providing a green light to proceed independently of Security Council approval.[63] US national security strategy was adamant in its commitment not to hesitate to act alone, and increasingly chafed at UN control over the use of force against rogue states that present perceived security threats.[64] The end game of this debate was cemented by President George Bush Jr when he announced that 'the policy of [his] government [was] the removal of Saddam [Hussein]'.[65]

President Bush spent months making a case for waging war against Iraq with a confusing jumble of arguments that were long on rhetoric and short on substance. His favourite arguments, however, were invocation of a sweeping new foreign policy based on the right of the US to pre-emptive self-defence, the need to punish Iraq for not complying with the Security Council resolutions to which it agreed in exchange for an end to the Gulf War of 1990, and the need for massive retaliation. President Bush seemed unsure of the exact contours of his doctrine tying up pre-emptive strikes with retaliation (this, the author avers, falls under the rubric of peacetime reprisal).

> Deterrence – *the promise of massive retaliation against nations* – means nothing against shadowy terrorist networks with no nation or citizen to defend ... Containment is not possible when unbalanced dictators with weapons of mass destruction can deliver those weapons or missiles or secretly provide them to terrorist allies ... *If we wait for threats to fully materialize, we will have waited for too long* ... In the world we have entered, the only path to safety is the path of action. And this nation will act.[66] [Emphasis added]

Though the more modest but controversial argument of retaliation may have been the strongest, nonetheless his doctrine was articulated more firmly in favour of anticipatory self-defence three months later. The National Security Strategy document, issued by President Bush in September 2002, asserted that:

For centuries, international law recognized that nations need not suffer an attack before they can lawfully take action to defend themselves against forces that present an imminent danger of attack. Legal scholars and international jurists often conditioned the legitimacy of pre-emption on the existence of an imminent threat – most often a visible mobilization of armies, navies, and air forces preparing to attack …

The US has long maintained the option of pre-emptive actions to counter a sufficient threat to our national security. *The greater the threat, the greater is the risk of inaction – and the more compelling the case for taking anticipatory action to defend ourselves, even if uncertainty remains as to the time and place of the enemy's attack.* To forestall or prevent such hostile acts by our adversaries, the US will, if necessary, act pre-emptively.[67] [Emphasis added]

Despite the delicate nature of US post-September 11 security strategy, it had Iraq firmly in its sights. The US and her allies continued to put forward what even then was regarded as faulty intelligence (now proven to be so)[68] in an attempt to link Iraq to the September 11 attacks notwithstanding the fact that UN inspectors had so far been unable to find significant evidence of an illegal weapons programme, with the arguable exception of ballistic missiles that slightly exceeded UN-mandated restrictions,[69] a violation equivalent to 'driving 36 mph in a 30 mph limit'.[70] 'No convincing evidence [was] shared with an American and world public clearly primed to receive it, including during Secretary of State Colin Powell's February 5, 2003 presentation to the Security Council.'[71]

Surprisingly, months earlier Powell had gone as far as to admit that he was unaware of any 'smoking gun' linking Iraq to September 11.[72] At least he was being honest from the outset, considering that President Bush and other senior US government officials were to sheepishly admit months later after the war in Iraq was officially over what most states suspected all along – there was no link between Iraq and the September 11 attacks.[73]

Before the war though, despite international and domestic scepticism, the hawkish Bush administration was economical on truth, having decided that the tragic events of September 11 had altered the context of the US-Iraq confrontation.[74] The resulting US shift to an aggressive Iraq policy forced it to advance rather dubious legal justifications for a full-scale invasion of Iraq, relying on the new, multifaceted 'Bush Doctrine', that advocates pre-emptive or preventive strikes against terrorists, states that support terrorists, and hostile states possessing weapons of mass destruction.

Chafing impatiently at the slow pace of the UN weapons inspection process, the US rashly assumed evidence of Iraqi involvement with terrorist activity and of persisting Iraqi capacity for weapons of mass destruction.[75] Regardless of the existence of Iraqi connections to the September 11 attacks, the US, citing Iraq's capacity to use weapons of mass destruction, asserted that self-defence legitimized the anticipatory intervention against Iraq.[76] Self-defence, it was suggested, also fuels the need for internal 'regime change' in Iraq and US support of such change.[77]

Without waiting for the UN Security Council to declare Iraq in breach of Security Council Resolution 1441, thus a threat to international peace and security for which the Council could then explicitly authorize military intervention,[78] the US and its allies proceeded with military action against Iraq premised on pre-emptive or anticipatory self-defence. Against a background of loud protests, even from some of its traditional allies, the US launched military action in March 2003. Its vastly technologically superior army waged a highly organized technical war that impressed an otherwise angry international community, drove Saddam Hussein out of power, and occupied the country. The war against Iraq was to be the defining moment in the evolution of the 'Bush Doctrine' marking a growing coherence and confidence in the strategy of 'offensive defence'.

In March 2003, when Australia, the UK and the US reported to the Security Council on the legal justifications for using force against Iraq,[79] all three offered justifications within the accepted law, although the US also included a reference to pre-empting future threats. This course of action, viewed in the background of the more reasoned arguments by the US, extends self-defence to a pre-emptive or anticipatory form. Although the legality of anticipatory self-defence is to be assessed in its own right, such legality may be facilitated by the changes to self-defence prompted by the September 11 attacks.

In this regard, state practice may have gradually set the tone for the legitimacy of anticipatory self-defence. That progression in state practice to support the operationalization of such self-defence through the use of force against Iraq was effectively stifled with the unilateral decision by the US that seemed to justify unilateral enforcement powers to any state strong enough to use them. What was particularly worrying was that the US was 'much less demanding in terms of the factual predicate required to justify a strike on Iraq'.[80] The US stance and argument would ultimately invest all states with a unilateral right both to determine a threat to international peace and to take action against the threat.

In sum, the circumstances surrounding US intervention in Iraq differed fundamentally from those in Afghanistan. The US did not conclusively prove that Al-Qaeda maintained Iraqi training bases or that it received financial, logistic or military support from the Iraqi Government. The strategic and legal calculus for action in Iraq did not compare to that which motivated US action in Afghanistan in late 2001. What was different with the military action in Afghanistan, as opposed to the military action in Iraq, was that the September 11 attacks drew favourable response to the use of force, with America's right of self-defence being mentioned in the same breath as terrorist attacks, but it is worth noting that the Security Council avoided speaking of 'armed attack' as required by Article 51 of the UN Charter, using instead the notion of 'terrorist attack' without expressly linking this notion to Article 51 which is mentioned in a separate paragraph.[81]

Anchoring the Attacks on Afghanistan and Iraq

Afghanistan

The US connected the Taliban regime to Al-Qaeda on the grounds that it harboured Osama bin Laden and his organization, refused to deliver bin Laden to requesting states and that the Taliban increased their responsibility for Al-Qaeda's actions after the fact by endorsing the September 11 attacks.[82] Before the US even attacked Afghanistan, the UN Security Council affirmed that the September 11 attacks gave rise to a right of self-defence.[83] Passed by the Council the day after the attacks, Resolution 1368 condemned the attacks and recognized 'the inherent right of individual or collective self-defence in accordance with the Charter'.[84]

Resolution 1373, passed seventeen days later, reaffirmed the right of self-defence in the context of the September 11 attacks and went on to reaffirm 'the need to combat by all means, in accordance with the Charter of the United Nations, threats to international peace and security caused by terrorist acts'.[85] Moreover, the Security Council's subsequent characterization of those acts as 'armed attacks' was echoed by other international bodies.[86] Thus, the US enjoyed strong support from the Security Council before it had to articulate the actual case for its actions in Afghanistan and despite the possibility that existing restrictions on the right of self-defence precluded a lawful exercise of that right under the circumstances.[87] Professor Christopher Greenwood opines that:

> The international reaction to the events of September 11, 2001 confirms the commonsense view that the concept of armed attack is not limited to state acts. The UN Security Council, in its resolutions 1368 and 1373 (2001), adopted in the immediate aftermath of the attacks, expressly recognized the right of self-defence in terms that could only mean it considered that terrorist attacks constituted armed attacks for the purposes of Article 51 of the Charter, since it was already likely, when these resolutions were adopted, that the attacks were the work of a terrorist organization rather than a state.[88]

Professor Jack M. Beard notes that: 'The unprecedented response of the UN Security Council and the international community in general to the September 11 terrorist attacks on the United States provides a stark contrast to the reaction to the raid on Libya [in 1986].'[89] He concludes by asserting: 'Assessing a number of factual and legal distinctions between the circumstances surrounding the September 11 attacks and previous terrorist attacks giving rise to the use of force by the United States helps to demonstrate the propriety of the most recent exercise of self-defence under Article 51 and customary international law.'[90]

The positive sentiments above are based on the willingness of states and the UN Security Council to invoke and affirm the right of self-defence in response to the September 11 terrorist attacks on the United States in sharp contrast to previous terrorist attacks.

> Before the September 11 terrorist attacks, the UN Security Council had never approved a resolution explicitly invoking and reaffirming the inherent right of individual and collective self-defence in response to a particular terrorist attack ... The Council's unprecedented willingness to invoke and reaffirm self-defence under Article 51 in response to the September 11 terrorist attacks is an important act and, for some states, helped legitimize the US military response as a legal use of force.[91]

'Operation Enduring Freedom' commenced on 7 October 2001 with a mix of air strikes from land-based bombers, carrier-based jetfighters and cruise missiles. The initial military objectives of 'Operation Enduring Freedom' included the destruction of terrorist training camps and infrastructure within Afghanistan, the capture of Al-

Qaeda leaders, and the cessation of terrorist activities in Afghanistan.[92] US Secretary of Defense Donald Rumsfeld stated that US objectives included making it clear to Taliban leaders that the harbouring of terrorists is unacceptable, acquiring intelligence on Al-Qaeda and Taliban resources and preventing the use of Afghanistan as a safe haven for terrorists.[93] By 20 October 2001, US and coalition forces had destroyed virtually all Taliban air defences. By mid-March 2002, the Taliban had been removed from power and the Al-Qaeda network in Afghanistan had been destroyed.

Operations in Afghanistan involved significant contributions from the international community. By 2002 the coalition had grown to more than 68 nations, with 27 nations having representatives at the US Central Command (CENTCOM) headquarters. Wide support for the US action as well as the fact that the action was given firm footing by Security Council resolutions led many to believe that the UN Charter regime on the use of force was visibly enrolled in change. Professor Frederic L. Kirgis optimistically observes:

> The US [] relied on its right of self-defence in using military force to respond to the September 11 attacks. Other governments have not challenged the right of the US to do so ... Because customary international law is often developed through a process of official assertions and acquiescences, the absence of challenge to the US asserted right of self-defence could be taken to indicate acquiescence in an expansion of the right to include defence against governments that harbour or support organized terrorist groups that commit armed attacks in other countries.[94]

The view by Professor Kirgis is shared by a number of commentators who note the international community's wide support for US actions post-September 11,[95] including the observation that states' acceptance of US actions would in effect condone the use of anticipatory self-defence to fight international terrorism. Despite these positives, the US military's targeting and toppling of the ruling Taliban who had harboured Al-Qaeda raised many questions about whether the US responded proportionately to the September 11 attacks. As Michael C. Bonafede observes: 'The right to self-defence under international law is not a blank cheque to destroy one's enemy; indeed, self-defence is limited by the requirements of an armed attack, necessity, immediacy, and proportionality.'[96]

The sticking point though is that there has never been any authoritative definition of what is and what is not a proportional state response to a terrorist attack.[97] Nonetheless, self-defence seems to imply that the mechanism only lasts as long as it takes the victim of the attack to address the immediate threat to that self-preservation. Bonafede laments:

> ... in the wake of the deadliest terrorist strikes in US history, the Bush Administration is filling this void with its own rules and ideas about what is proportional and appropriate. According to the Bush Administration, the US – like no other nation in the modern era – has a clear and justified mandate to use whatever means it deems necessary to combat and defeat all forms of international terrorism.[98]

In any case, '[I]f the Bush Administration is correct – that the only way to address and defeat international terrorism is to engage it wherever it is found – then that mission is far beyond the scope of any response to an attack that any nation has ever attempted during peacetime'.[99] A significant number of international legal scholars and diplomats would most likely conclude that the US response which went beyond Al-Qaeda to encompass toppling the Taliban and secure regime change violates the doctrine of proportionality. The conclusion could be reached even if one applied an expanded view of the current international rules regulating the right to self-defence.

> While statements of support for America's right of self-defence were numerous and impressive, the unprecedented types of assistance that states were willing to offer the United States provide another important and powerful representation of state practice affirming the right of self-defence in this case. Aware of the political and international legal significance of a state making its territory and airspace available for US and coalition military operations against Afghanistan, states nonetheless made numerous offers of such assistance to the United States.[100]

The actions of the UN Security Council and the decisive, widespread and unprecedented actions and statements by states supporting the US right of self-defence against the September 11 terrorist attacks seem to offer compelling evidence of the international community's assessment of the applicability of Article 51 of the UN Charter to America's new war on terror. Nonetheless it should be noted that these state actions occurred against vastly different factual and legal backgrounds from previous terrorist attacks that resulted in more widely criticized uses of force by the United States against terrorist-supporting states.

The emerging alteration of the right of self-defence in a post-September 11 world was soon put to a more severe test when the US administration, buoyed by the support it had enjoyed in 'Operation Enduring Freedom', emphasized the need for pre-emptive strikes and sought to extend its military adventures. Iraq was soon in its sights; however, unlike Al-Qaeda and the Taliban in Afghanistan, Iraq did not bear responsibility for a recent terrorist attack against the US.[101] The absence of such an attack limited the application of any new rule of international law to Iraq. The US, however, chose to sweep aside this significant difference and would soon be squandering away the legal and political capital it had gained in the action against Afghanistan, when it invaded Iraq on a mish-mash of justifications that were generally met with international scepticism.

Iraq

The terrorist attacks of September 11 and the US military response in Afghanistan against the Al-Qaeda terrorist organization and the Taliban militia that harboured it, led to a sharper focus on the Iraq problem. In the pre-September 11 environment, the Saddam Hussein regime in Iraq was regarded as a source of irritation and annoyance and did not feature prominently on the list of US responses to terrorism. Iraq was seen more as a standard state-to-state threat than as a state sponsor of terrorism.[102] However, the magnitude of the threat of the September 11 attacks altered the equation dramatically. The possibility of collusion between a rogue, troublesome nation with potential access to WMDs and terrorists was sufficient to send pulses racing in Washington. Iraq was soon identified as another prime target for an armed attack by the US.[103] As President Bush said in his January 2002 State of the Union address:

> States like these, and their terrorist allies, constitute an axis of evil, arming to threaten the peace of the world. By seeking weapons of mass destruction, these regimes pose a grave and growing danger. They could provide these arms to terrorists, giving them the means to match their hatred. They could attack our allies or attempt to blackmail the US. In any of these cases, the price of indifference would be catastrophic.[104]

The result was the Bush administration's obsession with depicting Iraq as both a traditional threat and a major terrorist threat. In the words of Patrick McLain:

> The resulting US shift to an aggressive Iraq policy [] forced the US to advance legal justifications for a full-scale invasion of Iraq; justifications that place great strain on the coherence of the general prohibition on the use of force. To justify its policy toward Iraq and other hostile states, the Bush Administration [] developed a new, multifaceted strategic doctrine, known as the 'Bush Doctrine,' that advocates pre-emptive or preventive strikes against terrorists, states that support terrorists, and hostile states possessing WMD.[105]

About six months after routing Al-Qaeda fighters and toppling the Taliban from power, on 12 September 2002, President Bush challenged the UN to address the threat posed by Iraq as highlighted by its continuing defiance of the Security Council.[106] President Bush sought to portray the 'War on Terror' as a broad campaign against all terrorist groups of global reach and states that support or harbour them, not just those responsible for the September 11 attack.[107] About seven weeks later, on 8 November 2002, the Security Council unanimously approved Resolution 1441 to address 'the threat Iraq's non-compliance with Council resolutions and proliferation of weapons of mass destruction and long-range missiles poses to international peace and security'.[108] The resolution deplored the absence of international inspections in Iraq since December 1998 and Iraq's continued failure to renounce international terrorism and cease the repression of its civilian population, and gave Iraq 'a final opportunity to comply with its disarmament obligations under relevant resolutions of the Council'.[109] It reminded Iraq that the Security Council has repeatedly warned that 'serious consequences' would result from the continued violation of its obligations.[110]

The US maintained a hard line, voicing repeatedly that unilateral action remained an option despite the passage of Resolution 1441 by the Security Council.[111] Though the US chose to channel its Iraq policy through the Security Council, it was increasingly clear that international law was not going to stand in the way of US policy.[112] This hard line stand by the US is not surprising considering that one of the pillars of the 'Bush Doctrine' was that the possession of WMDs by unaccountable, unfriendly, despotic governments was itself a threat that must be countered. In his haste to force the hand of the Security Council, the US President deliberately blurred the distinction between the threat posed directly by Iraq and the threat posed by terrorists that might or might not strike at the US.[113] The Bush administration sought to draw a link to Iraq's involvement in terrorism and links with Al-Qaeda in order to make their possible collusion a compelling threat requiring pre-emptive US action:

We know that Iraq and al Qaeda have had high-level contacts that go back a decade. Some al Qaeda leaders who fled Afghanistan went to Iraq... We've learned that Iraq has trained al Qaeda members in bomb making and poisons and deadly gases. And we know that after September the 11th, Saddam Hussein's regime gleefully celebrated the terrorist attacks on America.[114]

After months of impatience, dodgy intelligence dossiers and large doses of international disapproval, on 19 March 2003, at the head of an *ad hoc* force from the 'coalition of the willing' the US invaded Iraq. The forces rapidly advanced through the desert, racing towards Baghdad in a military campaign dominated by smart weaponry. Even the sullen international community was impressed as the Iraq armed forces were quickly subdued and the regime of Saddam Hussein toppled. On 1 May 2003, an overconfident President Bush announced that major combat operations in Iraq had ended, but as time was to show the headaches were just beginning for the coalition.

Relating to the legality of the US-led military action, John Yoo argues that:

International law permitted the use of force against Iraq on two independent grounds. First, the Security Council authorized military action against Iraq to implement the terms of the cease-fire that suspended the hostilities of the 1991 Gulf War. Due to Iraq's material breaches of the cease-fire, established principles of international law – both treaty and armistice law – permitted the US to suspend its terms and to use force to compel Iraqi compliance. Such a use of force was consistent with US practice both with regard to Iraq and with regard to treaties and cease-fires. Second, international law permitted the use of force against Iraq in anticipatory self-defence because of the threat posed by an Iraq armed with WMD and in potential cooperation with international terrorist organizations.[115]

But the factual and legal grounds are not as straightforward as Yoo's assertion seems to suggest. To begin with, it should be noted that the military action in Iraq led many other leading nations (primarily France, Germany and Russia) and many international scholars to argue that international law did not justify the war in Iraq. This argument is not without merit. The justifications for the Iraq war, however, pose a legal minefield considering that the factual and legal setting leading up to the Iraq war were rather complicated, since two independent sources of law were invoked by the US and its allies as the basis of the authority to use force in Iraq: UN Security Council resolutions and the right to self-defence.[116]

Though at the outbreak of the 2003 conflict Iraq was reluctantly complying with its disarmament obligations, the international community was largely opposed to any military action pending compelling evidence of Iraq's possession of WMDs, the primary US reason for seeking to launch a military campaign. The largely sceptical international community is perhaps being proven right. At the time of this writing, many months after the conclusion of the war in Iraq, coalition forces continue to search for WMD sites, sites which the world was led to believe the coalition forces would have no trouble unearthing. In any case the economy of truth regarding both Iraqi WMDs and its active support of Al-Qaeda is enough to show that the US was spoiling for a fight whatever the facts or lack of them.

Murky Legal Waters: The Use of Force as a Counter-terrorism Measure in Light of the UN Charter

As the system of collective security has been of little practical significance, international legal practice since 1945, contrary to the intentions of the authors of the Charter, continues to be determined by the unilateral use of force by states. Yet in this respect the Charter provides in Article 51 for an exclusive regulation, allowing individual states the threat or use of force only under the conditions stipulated there.[117] The right of self-defence laid down in Article 51 of the UN Charter, being the only exception to the prohibition of force of practical significance, is therefore the pivotal point upon which disputes concerning the lawfulness of the use of force in inter-state relations usually concentrate.

Article 51 of the UN Charter is generally taken as an authoritative definition of the right of self-defence. However, it has proved to be a battleground for scholars and states alike with regard to whether it subsumes customary international law and extinguishes the concept of anticipatory self-defence or whether it simply codifies a right that continues to exist with all its attendant doctrines under customary international law. The key question thus becomes one of interpretation. Under customary international law, the right of self-defence is judged by the standard first set out in the 1837 case of *The Caroline*[118] which established the right of a state to take necessary and proportional actions in anticipation of a hostile threat. Based on the *Caroline* incident, the preconditions for anticipatory self-defence are 'necessity', 'proportionality' and 'imminence'.[119]

This section undertakes an analysis of the use of force with particular relation to post-September 11 military action. It is arguable that the right to self-defence is visibly enrolled in a process of change. Many of the strict requirements of the *Nicaragua Case* in the definition of the notion of armed attack appear to have been overturned or opened to challenge. However, there are serious risks in broadening the ambit of permissible uses of force since this will lead to uncertainty and indeterminacy of the limits of unilateral use of force.

Anticipatory Self-defence

Customary International Law: Alive or Dead?   Customary international law has long recognized that no requirement exists for states to 'absorb the first hit'. The doctrine of anticipatory or pre-emptive self-defence, as developed historically, is applicable only when there is a clear and imminent danger of attack. The key issue concerns the elapsed time between the terrorist attack and the identification of the state responsible. Admittedly, there must be some temporal relationship between a terrorist act and the lawful defensive response. Nevertheless, it would be unreasonable to preclude the victim of terrorism from redress, based upon a doctrinaire determination that the threat is no longer imminent, when the terrorist state's own actions preclude immediate identification. The means used for pre-emptive response must be strictly limited to those required for the elimination of the danger, and must be reasonably proportional to that objective. But Charter law seems to expressly preclude the concept. Self-defence can only be in response to an armed attack, not a threatened attack.

In the aftermath of the September 11 attacks and the general support and cooperation that the US received in the military campaign against the Taliban regime in Afghanistan, the US began to capitalize on this goodwill, arguing that it was legally justified in exercising a right of anticipatory self-defence to attack hostile 'rogue' states and states that harbour terrorists, even if the US had not been attacked. This stance is premised on the argument that the UN Charter is not a suicide pact. In any case, the International Court of Justice considered this proposition in its 1996 *Advisory Opinion on the Legality of the Threat or Use of Nuclear Weapons*, noting that it would not lose sight of the fundamental right of every state to survival, and thus its right to resort to self-defence, in accordance with Article 51 of the Charter, when its survival is at stake.[120]

The September 11 terrorist attacks influenced the US to fast-track its mindset. No longer was terrorism merely a sporadic series of pinpricks, but in view of the possibility of WMDs ending up in the hands of terrorists from rogue states, terrorism could inflict catastrophic destruction[121] and thus posed a threat to the security and survival of the US. This stance is strongly captured in the National Security Strategy document released about five months before the Iraqi invasion started, as mentioned above, in which the US appealed to customary international law, noting that it was justified under customary international law to defend itself against an imminent danger of attack.[122]

It can be said that in the *Nicaragua Case*, the International Court of Justice identified the need to supplement the Charter provisions with customary international law;[123] the problem though is whether anticipatory self-defence is recognized considering that the UN Charter discounts the notion. But the matter is not that simple in view of the split between the 'restrictionist' and 'counter-restrictionist' views of anticipatory self-defence which was evaluated in Chapter 1.

A significant number of scholars argue that the UN Charter precludes any right of anticipatory self-defence.[124] This argument relies on a restrictive reading of Article 51 of the UN Charter. As discussed in Chapter 1, 'these writers assert that this language, at least by implication, precludes the use of force in anticipation of an attack or other event triggering the right of self-defence. The basis for the argument is that, once recognized, a right to anticipatory self-defence is potentially very difficult to define or limit, and bad faith or an error in judgment could easily lead to unnecessary conflict'.[125]

> It is contended that the right to respond with force in self-defence, even to a triggering act that has already occurred, is temporally limited. As the *Caroline* incident indicates, the customary right of self-defence appears to require immediate action. Otherwise, there is a strong argument that the use of force is nothing more than a reprisal, which, while permitted under limited circumstances by customary international law, is widely agreed to have been outlawed by the United Nations Charter.[126]

Restrictionists further state that an armed attack is the exclusive circumstance in which the use of armed force is sanctioned under Article 51.[127] This further provides grounds for precluding any right of anticipatory self-defence.[128] These writers assert that the language of Article 51, at least by implication, precludes the use of force in anticipation of an attack or other event triggering the right of self-defence.[129] In the same vein, these legal scholars argue that the right of anticipatory self-defence expressed by the *Caroline* incident was overridden by the specific language of the UN Charter. In this view, Article 51 fashions a new and more restrictive statement on self-defence, one that relies on the literal qualification of a prior 'armed attack'. In fact, one commentator has gone so far as to state that 'the leading opinion among scholars' is that the right of self-defence in Article 51 does not extend beyond armed attack.[130] This is backed up by the ICJ's observation in the *Nicaragua Case* where the world court clearly stated that the right of self-defence under Article 51 only accrues in the event of an armed attack.[131]

This narrowly technical interpretation perhaps seems to ignore that international law cannot compel any state to wait until it absorbs a devastating or even lethal first strike before acting to protect itself. Strategic circumstances and the consequences of strategic surprise have changed a great deal since the *Caroline* incident. Today, in an age of chemical/biological/nuclear weaponry, the time available to a vulnerable state could be notably very short.

Though it is contended that the 'armed attack' requirement in Article 51 of the UN Charter seems to supersede any pre-existing right of anticipatory action, Israel and the US have been particularly notorious in seeking to rely upon the concept of anticipatory self-defence on numerous occasions, with a generally negative response from the international community. International opinion on this issue was never clearer than when Israel attacked an Iraqi nuclear reactor at Osirak in 1981, leaving it in a pile of ruins.[132] Notwithstanding near universal condemnation, five years after the bombing of the Osirak nuclear reactor, the US, which had joined the chorus of condemnation, bombed Libya after a suspected (subsequently proven) Libyan government agent planted a bomb in a Berlin disco which killed an American serviceman in 1986.[133] The then US President Ronald Reagan called the action 'pre-emptive' on the grounds there was already a pattern of Libyan terrorist actions.[134]

About a decade later, in 1998, after terrorist attacks on US embassies in Kenya and Tanzania, the US fired cruise missiles on the al-Shifa pharmaceutical plant in Sudan. The then US President Bill Clinton argued that it was making chemical and biological weapons for Osama bin Laden, who was assumed (subsequently proven) to be behind the embassy bombings. Clinton said there was 'compelling evidence' that the Al-Qaeda terrorist network was planning to mount further attacks against Americans, and he was therefore entitled to act.[135] Nonetheless, the international community was uneasy with the legal framework advanced. But, apart from a few Western governments which approved or kept quiet, most states condemned the Reagan and Clinton air strikes. They did not accept them as legitimate self-defence under the UN Charter. Even the contentious grounds of anticipatory self-defence and reprisals provided unsure footing. This is not surprising: in an eloquent observation on the former ground, Professor Christine Gray notes:

[T]he actual invocation of the right to anticipatory self-defence in practice is rare. States clearly prefer to rely on self-defence in response to an armed attack if they possibly can. In practice they prefer to take a wide view of armed attack rather than openly claim anticipatory self- defence. It is only where no conceivable case can be made for this that they resort to anticipatory self-defence. This reluctance expressly to invoke anticipatory self-defence is in itself a clear indication of the doubtful status of this justification for the use of force. States take care to try to secure the widest possible support; they do not invoke a doctrine that they know will be unacceptable to the vast majority of states.[136]

Weapons of Mass Destruction: A New Calculus   Some scholars believe that a right of truly anticipatory self-defence has emerged outside of Article 51 in light of the availability of weapons of mass destruction.[137] Professor Thomas Franck accounts for the emergence of a viable doctrine of anticipatory self-defence through 'the transformation of weaponry to instruments of overwhelming and instant destruction. These [weapons bring] into question the conditionality of Article 51, which limits states' exercise of the right of self-defence to the aftermath of an armed attack. Inevitably, first-strike capabilities begat a doctrine of "anticipatory self-defence".'[138] Professor C. Greenwood weighs in with the observation that in a nuclear age, it is the potentially devastating consequences of prohibiting self-defence unless an armed attack has already occurred that leads one to prefer the interpretation permitting anticipatory self-defence. He argues further that:

> ... this view accords better with State practice and with the realities of modern military conditions than with the more restrictive interpretation of Article 51, which would confine the right of self-defence to cases in which an armed attack had already occurred – although it has to be said that, as a matter of simple construction of the words alone, another conclusion might be reached.[139]

The positions by Franck and Greenwood are supported by Professor Michael Glennon who eloquently lays out five factual contemporary realities that the UN Charter drafters did not have the benefit of more than half a century ago when drafting the document. He begins by noting that 21st century security needs are different from those imagined at the founding of the United Nations and then sets out the following five factual realties:

1. The intended safeguard against unlawful threats of force – a vigilant and muscular Security Council – has yet to materialize and remains unfulfilled.
2. Modern methods of intelligence collection, such as satellite imagery and communications intercepts, now make it unnecessary to sit out an actual armed attack to await convincing proof of a state's hostile intent.
3. The advent of weapons of mass destruction and their availability to international terrorists means that the first blow can be devastating – far more devastating than the pinprick attacks on which the old rules were premised.
4. Terrorist organizations 'of global reach' were unknown when Article 51 was drafted. They have however flourished owing to large 'war chests' facilitating development and stockpiling of weaponry, acquisition of state of the art communications equipment and safe training camps. All this requires a sanctuary, which only states can provide – and which only states can take away.
5. The danger of catalytic war erupting from the use of pre-emptive force was easily understood in the Cold War but decreased considerably with the end of the Cold War thus making less sense to today, when safe-haven states and terrorist organizations are not themselves possessed of pre-emptive capabilities.[140]

The arguments above are particularly strong when one considers that shortly after the birth of the UN Charter, the Atomic Energy Commission suggested in its First

Report in December 1946 that preparation for atomic warfare in breach of a multilateral treaty or convention would, in view of the appalling power of the weapon, have to be treated as an 'armed attack' within Article 51 of the UN Charter.[141]

> More specifically, the AEC made the following recommendations to the Security Council about the control of nuclear energy and nuclear weapons: 'The development and use of atomic energy are not essentially matters of domestic concern of the individual nations, but rather have predominantly international implications and repercussions.'[142]

The impact of WMDs on the modern self-defence doctrine appears to be the basis on which some commentators have concluded that a doctrine permitting certain anticipatory self-defence actions is available for states to utilize.[143] Truly anticipatory self-defence would permit the use of force '[i]f a state has developed the capability of inflicting substantial harm upon another, indicated explicitly or implicitly its willingness or intent to do so, and to all appearances is waiting only for the opportunity to strike'.[144]

It cannot be supposed that the inviolability of territory is so sacrosanct as to mean that a state may harbour within its territory the most blatant preparation for an assault upon another state's independence with impunity; the inviolability of territory is subject to the use of that territory in a manner which does not involve a threat to the rights of other states.[145] Supporting this position further is the argument that there is no requirement under the literal letter of Article 51 that a foreign government itself directly undertake the attack to which a state responds. Thus anticipatory self-defence against even the harbouring of terrorists by Iraq may give rise to legitimate, legal justification for an anticipatory US military intervention.

The US saw the use of military action to remove the threat of chemical, biological and nuclear proliferation in Iraq as a strategic imperative arguing rather strongly that the risk of inaction in the face of such a threat is intolerable. The decision to attack was done over the loud objections of other major powers and many international scholars who were worried by the effect of failure by the US to secure a Security Council mandate. Perhaps the answers to the headstrong stance by the US (the world's sole superpower) lie in C.C. Posteraro's observation that:

> Legality becomes clear once [a] doctrine has become 'authoritative state practice.' The authoritativeness of a rule is determined by examining 'official and unofficial communications by decision-making elites.' ... State practice is the measure of control a given doctrine exerts on state behaviour. Put simply, 'the rule is controlling if international actors comply with the rule.' ... Justice need not operate through statutes, charters or custom. The NATO intervention in Kosovo proved this to much of the world ... State practice is, in the long term, the ultimate arbiter of what international law is. It is a consequence of this fact that more powerful states will exert the greatest influence on the development of international law, and the US should not hesitate to take the lead in practicing the legitimate doctrine of anticipatory counter-terrorism, counter-proliferation intervention.[146]

Prickly Legal Matters: Gauging the Benchmarks   Any claims to anticipatory self-defence are still fundamentally based on the concept of self-defence. Therefore, it is still restricted by a number of threshold requirements including imminence, necessity and proportionality.[147] Based on a critical analysis of 'Operation Enduring Freedom' against the benchmarks of 'necessity', 'proportionality' and 'imminence', Professor Greenwood notes that:

> The pre-emptive action that the United States and its allies took against Al-Qaida in Afghanistan was, therefore, a lawful exercise of the right of self-defence. It would, however, be a mistake to assume that self-defence would cover every military action that the United States or an ally might want to take against Al-Qaida (or other terrorist groups) in other countries. The use of force in Afghanistan fell within the concept of self-defence because the threat from Al-Qaida was imminent and because Afghanistan was quite openly affording sanctuary to large numbers of Al-Qaida personnel. These considerations will not necessarily be present in every case.[148]

There are of course debates as to whether 'Operation Enduring Freedom' met the benchmark of proportionality, not helped by the US subsequently espousing a doctrine of 'regime change' in relation to rogue states which the US is keen to put out of business, especially when they seek to develop or acquire WMDs.

When we juxtapose 'Operation Enduring Freedom' against 'Operation Iraqi Freedom', significant legal questions are left open. While the US can make a case for the necessity of intervening against Iraq, it has a much more difficult time satisfying the proportionality and imminency requirements, since it indicated long before the military action that it would undertake the extraordinarily broad intervention at a time and place of its choosing, thus effectively jettisoning the proportionality and imminency requirements.[149]

Even allowing for creativity and alluding to the doctrine of 'necessity' as a justification for US intervention in Iraq by stretching it to encompass the broad threat posed by the Hussein regime, necessity, however, paradigmatically has been restricted to cases more limited in nature, brief in duration and restricted in responsive means required. Furthermore, necessity constitutes a 'ground for precluding the wrongfulness' of otherwise illegal conduct.[150] In a critical observation of US motives, Professor Michael J. Kelly notes:

> Unilaterally, the United States articulated its right to act pre-emptively to eliminate the threat posed by a potentially nuclear-armed Iraq. However, because the existence of an imminent threat could not be established, when the President brought the old anticipatory self-defence doctrine back to life, he eliminated that threshold and replaced it with the showing of only an 'emerging' threat.[151]

'The war in Iraq presents a new form of (preventive) self-defence which does not come within the ambit of the traditional concepts of Chapter VII or Article 51, but derives some legitimacy from the interplay between collective security and self-defence.'[152] Professor Kelly avers that in the absence of a link between Iraq and Al-Qaeda, the US sought to shop around for a doctrine that would legitimize an attack on Baghdad. Considering that a plain reading of Article 51 disallows striking Iraq absent an armed attack, the Bush administration returned to 'the legal history books and pull[ed] out another disused doctrine to justify [its] unilateral military action ... The one that seems to fit best, albeit imperfectly, is the doctrine of anticipatory self-defence'.[153]

In essence the US, though in various degrees relying on the concept of anticipatory self-defence, sought to water down the standard in as far as it is understood in customary international law. Leaving the UN Charter to one side for the moment, there is no such basis in international law of the doctrine of 'pre-emption' encompassing a right to respond to threats that might materialize at some time in the future. The test is clear – imminence which connotes immediacy.

A broad right of anticipatory self-defence premised on a new standard of 'emerging threat' would introduce dangerous uncertainties relating to the determination of potential threats justifying pre-emptive action. With this determination being state-based, the probability of opportunistic interventions justified as anticipatory self-defence will rise. After all the reality is that only states with the military muscle will be able to make use of this avenue and unilateral action will inevitably be coloured by national interest considerations. The development of such a right will likely prompt potential targets into striking first, to use rather than lose their biological, chemical and nuclear weapons.

A. Unilateral Threat Assessment   As a matter of principle and policy, anticipatory self-defence is open to a number of objections. It involves a determination of the certainty of attack which is extremely difficult to make and necessitates an attempt to ascertain the intention of a government. This process may lead to a serious conflict if there is a mistaken assessment of a situation. Furthermore, even if a state is preparing an attack, it still has a *locus poenitentiae* prior to launching its forces against the territory of the intended victim. Nor is the state which considers itself to be the object of military preparations forced to remain supine, but may take all necessary precaution before commencing attack.

B. Proportionality   Another consideration which is usually ignored is the effect of the proportionality rule on the problem. It is possible that in a very limited number of situations force might be a reaction proportionate to the danger, where there is unequivocal evidence of an intention to launch a devastating attack almost immediately. However, in the great majority of cases, to commit a state to an actual conflict when there is only circumstantial evidence of impending attack would be to act in a manner which disregards the requirement of proportionality. To permit anticipatory action may well be to accept a right which is wider than that of self-defence and akin to that of self-preservation. It is true that states must be accorded the right to decide on defensive necessity in the first instance, but in making this *ex parte* decision they should be inhibited by a rule which is related to facts which have objective characteristics and not to mere estimates of intention.[154]

C. Armed Attack Nexus   Carsten Stahn notes that: 'The legal response to the September 11, 2001, attacks [was] unusual. In unprecedented moves, both NATO and the Organization of American States qualified the September 11 attacks as "armed attacks" against the United States, justifying the exercise of self-defence. Russia and China, which had often opposed the use of military force against terrorist acts, displayed support for America's self-defence response – Operation Enduring Freedom.'[155]

The scale of the September 11 attacks was one of the main factors guiding NATO and the Security Council in their qualification of the acts as armed attacks. Moreover, the requirement of gravity under Article 51 has received another dimension in the context of terrorism.

The fundamental shortcoming of reliance on a literal reading of Article 51 to support US action against Iraq is self-evident – self-defence is justified only when there has been an armed attack. However, as noted above, the counter argument is that the nature of weapons of mass destruction is such that the international community could not wait to be the victim of Iraqi-sponsored chemical, biological or nuclear terrorism, otherwise then the notion of self-defence loses any practical meaning.

In favourable response to this assertion, it can be said that the Webster formula (discussed in Chapter 1) confined justifiable anticipatory self-defence to circumstances 'in which the necessity of that self-defence is instant, overwhelming, and leaving no choice of means, and no moment for deliberation'.[156] This recognized standard setting out a method of evaluating claims of self-defence when an armed attack has not yet occurred is, however, restrictive in relation to weapons of mass destruction.[157] Though in view of the facts of the *Caroline* incident and the requirements of the *Caroline* case, only a very narrow category of acts of anticipatory self-defence could be permissible, nonetheless, the restrictive nature of the doctrines of immediacy, necessity and proportionality limited the US flexibility in crafting a military response that would neutralize the Iraqi threat.

It is submitted that there is considerable justification for the conclusion that the right of self-defence, individual or collective, which has received general acceptance has a content identical with the right expressed in Article 51 of the Charter. Professor Jordan J. Paust, however, argues against the position that Article 2(4) prohibits every form of armed coercion with the exception of the permitted instances in the UN Charter, restrictively read. He opines that:

> Article 2(4) of the United Nations Charter does not prohibit every form of armed coercion. The first portion prohibits merely the threat or use of force directed against the territorial integrity or political independence of another state. It is certainly arguable, for example, that armed force used to pre-empt or retaliate against terrorist acts as such or to impose sanctions against a violator of international law is not a use of force directed against the territorial integrity or political independence of another state. The question remains, however, whether or not such uses of force are proscribed under the remaining clause – that prohibiting the threat or use of force 'in any other manner inconsistent with the Purposes of the United Nations'.[158]

Responding to the argument centred on the qualitative uses of force under Article 2(4), Stahn states:

> Some have claimed that forcible responses to terrorism are permissible because they do not violate the qualitative threshold of Article 2(4). The use of limited, temporary force to eliminate a terrorist threat, so goes the argument, does not violate the territorial integrity or independence of a state in which the terrorists are located and is therefore consistent with the Charter. This argument has been rightly criticized. To create an exception to the prohibition of the use of force because of the motive or consequences of the intervention

would deprive Article 2(4) of much of its intended effect. Whatever the merit of an exception to Article 2(4) may be, it is becoming increasingly redundant under an emerging right to self-defence against terrorist attacks.[159]

Certain international legal scholars 'believe that state sponsorship and support of international terrorists constitutes a use of force contemplated by Article 2(4)'.[160] State practice also supports the view that terrorist bombings may constitute an armed attack justifying self-defence under Article 51. For example, the US justified its cruise missile attacks against Sudan and Afghanistan following the 1998 terrorist bombings of the US embassies in Tanzania and Kenya, as an exercise of self-defence.[161] The US has maintained the policy of considering terrorist bombings armed attacks for some time and has accordingly justified several US military actions against states that have supported terrorists.[162] In strong support of this position, C.C. Posteraro states that:

> ... the international community has increasingly agreed that terrorist bombings qualify as armed attacks for the purposes of justifying military action in self-defence. Significant evidence exists that Iraq has supported terrorist operations that target the US. Therefore, if the US can establish that Iraq harbours terrorists that have attacked the US, it can justify military action against Iraq under even a rather strict reading of Article 51. The primary drawback of relying on this justification is that the US would be required to wait until it has become the target of such an armed attack.[163]

Reprisals

It is contended that in the history of the United Nations, there have been authoritative condemnations of both pre-emptive and retaliatory reprisal actions,[164] so it seems safe to conclude that both are widely expected to be inconsistent with the purposes of the United Nations and are therefore proscribed under Article 2(4) of the Charter. From a legal viewpoint it should be recognized that characterizations of responding coercion may be conclusory. These and any number of other categorizations of violence such as 'intervention', 'interdiction', 'intercession', 'interposition' or 'retortion' should be made only after careful inquiry into the nuances of context and full realization of the legal policies at stake. Nevertheless, the predominant expectation is that merely pre-emptive and retaliatory reprisal actions as such are impermissible.

Military actions by the US against terrorist-supporting states have elicited varying responses from the international community and the United Nations. In the case of the 1986 raid on Libya, the US was largely condemned. The UN General Assembly adopted a resolution condemning the United States for the attack by a vote of 79 to 28, with 33 abstentions.[165] In contrast, the 1993 cruise missile attack on Baghdad in response to the foiled Iraqi assassination attempt on former President Bush was met with support or tacit acquiescence, although most of the Arab world expressed regret regarding the attack,[166] while reaction to the 1998 US cruise missile strikes against terrorist targets in Afghanistan and Sudan in response to the US embassy bombings in East Africa was mixed.

The same criticism that has dogged previous American uses of force against states supporting terrorists is replayed in 'Operation Iraqi Freedom' – '... the perceived lack of evidence tying the terrorists to a particular organization and tying that organization to a particular state. Some critics have argued that the US Government has shown "consistent disregard of evidentiary showings" in such previous uses of force and that it has effectively taken the position that the factual premises of these actions were unreviewable.'[167] This can be traced back to US Secretary of State Shultz's statement in 1985 that: 'We may never have the kind of evidence that can stand up in an American court of law.'[168] Obviously matters of national security and intelligence gathering mechanisms are at issue, but when flawed evidence is presented, it simply deepens the mistrust of the international community. In relation to the military action against Iraq, Professor Greenwood notes that:

> The requirement of necessity in self-defence means that it is not sufficient that force is used after an armed attack, it must be necessary to repel that attack. The use of force in response to an armed attack that is over and done with does not meet that requirement and looks more like a reprisal. The US action has therefore been criticized for constituting what some consider to have been a reprisal, rather than a genuine action in self-defence.[169]

In light of the UN Charter and in relation to military action against Iraq, C.C. Posteraro further observes that:

> [u]nless the US or an ally is a victim of an Iraqi attack, and the US response is in defence against such an attack, it cannot justify a military intervention under the letter of Article 51. Therefore, unless there is an Iraqi military offensive against the US or its allies, it is unlikely that the US will be able to make a case that military action against Iraq meets the strict requirements of Article 51. Although the US has gradually broadened its interpretation of Article 51, it has never claimed a right to act in self-defence unless an armed attack has occurred. The concept of armed attack, however, has proven rather elastic. For the US to argue that Iraq has perpetrated an armed attack, it will have to rely on less overt actions than past examples of Iraqi aggression against Iran in 1981 and Kuwait in 1990.[170]

Conclusion

Military action in Afghanistan in the aftermath of the September 11 attacks drew favourable responses to the use of force, the US right of self-defence often being mentioned in the same breath as the terrorist attacks. However, the military action in Iraq following the 'Axis of Evil' speech by US President George Bush Jr provoked strong opposition, given its definite overtones of unilateral military action by the US against countries that support terror. This was in spite of US insistence that the act was a strategic imperative in its strategy of 'offensive defence'.

The need for more dramatic targets seemed to fuel new and somewhat exaggerated emphasis on biological, chemical and nuclear weapons. Saddam Hussein's use of poison gas during the Iran-Iraq war and against Kurdish villagers in 1988 was advanced as proof that he would use such weapons against the US and her allies, even though doing so would ensure his own destruction. What is most striking about the new US policy is that it portrays weapons of mass destruction as a new problem, and unilateral action as the only way of dealing with them.

Military action against Iraq not surprisingly split the international community and inflamed the world's major powers, since it raises much debate both as a policy matter and as a legal matter. Considering that the use of armed force can only be justified under international law when used in self-defence, can the US go beyond the rhetoric and actually carry the 'War on Terror' to those rogue nations who are identified so closely as supporters and sponsors of terrorist activities, but have not actually physically engaged in an act of aggression against the US?[171]

The convergence of international terrorism and weapons of mass destruction presents a grave threat to international peace, security and prosperity by threatening the survival of entire nations. This threat multiplies exponentially when governments foster and encourage these dual scourges. What is disturbing about the US stance is the fact that an old problem in contemporary international law – anticipatory self-defence – is being touted as an appropriate vehicle in the war against international terrorism, yet the general view is that the 'armed attack' requirement in Article 51 of the UN Charter superseded any pre-existing right of anticipatory action.

The old truism, that international law is not a suicide pact, is forceful in 'an age of uniquely destructive weaponry'.[172] Nevertheless, strategically there is little precedent for a major US military offensive against a state that has not proximately used force against US interests. Legally, while a number of legitimate justifications might permit the use of force, the international legal system does not currently provide such an outlet. An appropriate international law doctrine, under which the US could execute the military campaign it launched against Iraq, does not currently exist. But that lacuna was seemingly plugged with the 'Bush Doctrine' that advocates pre-emptive strikes against rogue states and/or entities involved in terrorism. To put it in more staid phraseology, the pre-emptive strikes are premised on a right of anticipatory self-defence. The so-called 'Bush Doctrine' articulates a new rule of international law that seeks to bring to life the doctrine of anticipatory self-defence as an appropriate means through which to combat terrorism (including states that actively support terrorism or that are themselves terror states in the sense of acquiring and stockpiling weapons of mass destruction).

While the US has several legal arguments to support military intervention in Iraq, these arguments do not articulate the underlying paradigm-shift that US action against Iraq constitutes.[173] Even if the US can establish that the Hussein regime actively or tacitly supported international terrorism and acquired and stockpiled weapons of mass destruction (unlikely), the reliance on anticipatory self-defence resurrects a problem in contemporary international law on the use of force with its echoes of the supposedly obsolete right of self-preservation that fell into disuse in the early part of the 20th century with the prohibition of war and the legal demarcation of the limits of the right to self-defence. Certain pre-Charter doctrines are being revived in one form or the other, notably the concept of pre-emptive or anticipatory self-defence.

> ... there are inherent dangers in resurrecting such pre-Charter doctrines. One of the very reasons the world community decided to do away with them was to reduce legal justifications for, and thus the possibility of, unilateral military action. The pre-Charter doctrines were used erratically and unreliably prior to 1945. Now, if these doctrines are

returned to service by the world's superpower and are allowed to pass into customary practice once again, we will find ourselves in a time warp back to 1945 – a period of fear, uncertainty and suspicion; a period of global dominance by a handful of nations; a period defined by the geopolitics of raw power and militaristic influence; a period of instability devoid of collective security. Even more disturbingly, some of the re-articulated rules have been watered down to allow more latitude in unilateral action. And this time we will be returning to that world with weapons of mass destruction in our arsenals.[174]

However, Professor Michael J. Glennon disagrees with the general spirit of the statement above, noting that: '[w]aiting for an aggressor to fire the first shot may be a fitting code for television westerns, but it is unrealistic for policy-makers entrusted with the solemn responsibility of safe-guarding the well-being of their citizenry.'[175] The author agrees with the strong reality postulate underpinning Glennon's analogy, but disagrees strongly with its conclusion.

In the author's view and, of course, reality (which Glennon alludes to) whenever military action is undertaken, it is for real – real bombs, real missiles, real deaths. States should not be allowed to act based on mere apprehension backed up by dubious or unclear intelligence. Once the military action is over, it is over; it cannot be unmade by commissions of enquiries or concessions that perhaps a few facts were not quite right, but that a war was based on a belief that they were!

It is noteworthy that when Australia's prime minister suggested changing the Charter to allow pre-emptive self-defence, he was heavily criticized by members of the Association of Southeast Asian Nations and received no support from members of the European Union.[176] In addition, UN Secretary-General Kofi Annan, in remarks regarding anticipatory self-defence during the opening of the 58th session of the UN General Assembly in September 2003, warned of the dangers:

Article 51 of the Charter prescribes that all States, if attacked, retain the inherent right of self-defence. But until now it has been understood that when States go beyond that, and decide to use force to deal with broader threats to international peace and security, they need the unique legitimacy provided by the United Nations.

Now, some say this understanding is no longer tenable, since an 'armed attack' with weapons of mass destruction could be launched at any time, without warning, or by a clandestine group.

Rather than wait for that to happen, they argue, States have the right and obligation to use force pre-emptively, even on the territory of other States, and even while weapons systems that might be used to attack them are still being developed ...

Excellencies, we have come to a fork in the road. This may be a moment no less decisive than 1945 itself, when the United Nations was founded.[177]

All in all, the role of multilateral global coalitions or unilateral action in policing 'evil-doing' may be increasing and potentially supplanting what initially was designed as the role of the Security Council or the United Nations generally. If supra-national institutions weaken, then decisions regarding the use of force once again become nationalized. National decisions to use force may lead to anarchic, piecemeal, random and unilateral enforcement of the desirable shared goal of stamping out terrorism. After September 11, states simply may believe, more than before, that they are justified in acting outside the UN system.

A collective, institutional response to terrorism may be more effective than ad hoc unilateralism or narrow coalition building. It may be difficult to prevent ad hoc unilateralism from devolving into self-interested opportunism. Who defines what is an armed attack? A 'threat to the peace'? Who defines when, where, how, and why the use of force can be initiated to contain (or punish) rogue states? If the US can use extensive military force to respond to terrorism, there is no principled basis to deny others that entitlement.[178]

Commenting on an elastic understanding of self-defence as a catalyst for chaos, Professor M. Drumbl poses the following pointed questions:

Might India now be able to use force against Pakistan given suspected Pakistani links to terrorism committed in India (for example, attacks against the Indian Parliament undertaken by Kashmiri terrorists)? What about Russian activity in Chechnya, where, in the past, squashing insurrection has led to allegations of systemic human rights abuses? In the post-September 11 world order, is there broader license to use force to crush insurgency movements that may be stigmatized as terrorist? Along with Russia, a number of countries are 'now characterizing their own internal struggles as battles against terrorism.' Who will defend the world if the use of self-defence becomes opportunistic and colourable?[179]

A broad right of anticipatory self-defence would introduce dangerous uncertainties relating to the determination of potential threats justifying pre-emptive action. With this determination being state-based, the probability of opportunistic interventions justified as anticipatory self-defence will rise. After all, the reality is that only states with the military muscle will be able to make use of this avenue and unilateral action will inevitably be coloured by national interest considerations. The development of such a right will likely prompt potential targets into striking first, to use rather than lose their biological, chemical and nuclear weapons. This is not too far-fetched, as the increasing volatility in the Korean Peninsula demonstrates.

Only those who have no reason to fear military force can contemplate a world without the combined protections of the UN Charter and the customary law of the *Caroline* case. The US feels able to claim a broad right of pre-emptive action because other states do not currently have the capacity to retaliate. What President George Bush Jr fails to realize is that his actions will encourage other states to acquire the very weapons that he purports to abhor.

Notes

1   Scott M. Malzahn (2002), 'State Sponsorship and Support of International Terrorism: Customary Norms of State Responsibility', 26 *Hastings International and Comparative Law Review* 83.

2   'That the larger world could not agree on a definition of terrorism or condemnation of terrorism in all circumstances became irrelevant': Nicholas Rostow (2001), 'Before and After: The Changed UN Response to Terrorism Since September 11th', 35 *Cornell International Law Journal* 475, 481.

3   U.N. SCOR, 56th Sess, 4370th mtg, U.N. Doc S/RES.1368 (2001), para 3.

4   Rostow, 481.

5   U.N. SCOR, 40th sess, 2615th mtg, 1, U.N. Doc S/RES/573 (1985).

6   Ibid. See generally Marian Nash Leich (1986), 'Contemporary Practice of the United States Relating to International Law', 80 *American Journal of International Law* 151, 165–7, which discusses the UN Security Council's condemnation of Israel's air attack.

7   Admittedly the situation differs in exact factual circumstance to September 11, but does reflect the general stance of the international community prior to that event. The Security Council was obviously faced with a situation that profoundly differs from the previous incidents where there were limited casualties.

8   Michael Byers (2002), 'Terrorism, the Use of Force and International Law after 11 September', 51 *International and Comparative Law Quarterly* 401, 407.

9   S.C. Res 748, U.N. SCOR, 47th Sess, 3063d mtg at 52, U.N. Doc S/RES/748 (1992).

10   Christopher Greenwood (2003), 'International Law and the Pre-emptive Use of Military Force: Afghanistan, Al Qaida and Iraq', 4 *San Diego International Law Journal* 7, 10.

11   See, e.g., *The Situation in Afghanistan,* S.C. Res 1390, U.N. SCOR, 57th sess, 4452nd mtg, U.N. Doc S/RES/1390 (2002); *The Situation in Afghanistan,* S.C. Res 1401, U.N. SCOR, 57th sess, 4501st mtg, U.N. Doc S/RES/1401 (2002).

12   See Neil King Jr. and Jim Vandehei (2001), 'Defining "Global Reach" May Prove Elusive', *Wall Street Journal Europe,* available at 2001 WL-WSJE 21838298(27 September).

13   See Neil MacFarquhar (2002), 'Arabs Back Overture to Israel and Declare Support for Iraq', *New York Times,* A1 (29 March).

14   The Central Intelligence Agency and the Federal Bureau of Investigation concluded that the explosives were Iraqi-made and that Saddam's intelligence service was behind the conspiracy.

15   Bill Clinton (1993), 'Letter to Congressional Leaders on the Strike on Iraqi Intelligence Headquarters', 23 *Weekly Compilation of Presidential Documents* 12 (28 June).

16   See Stephen Robinson (1993), 'UN Support for Raid on Baghdad', *Daily Telegraph* (London), 1 (28 June); 'European Allies Are Giving Strong Backing to US Raid', *New York Times,* at A7 (28 June); 'Arab Governments Critical', *New York Times,* 28 June 1993, at A7.

17   Stanley Meisler (1993), 'UN Reaction Mild as US Explains Raid', *Los Angeles Times,* A1 (28 June).

18   Raphael F. Perl (1998), 'Terrorism: U.S. Response to Bombings in Kenya and Tanzania: A New Policy Direction?', CRS Report to Congress (updated 1 September 1998), available at http://www2.gwu.edu/~nsarchiv/NSAEBB/NSAEBB55/crs19980901.pdf.

19   S.C. Res 1189, U.N. SCOR, 53rd Sess, 3915th mtg, U.N. Doc S/RES/1189 (1998); S.C. Res 1267, U.N. SCOR, 54th Sess, 4051st mtg, U.N. Doc S/RES/1267 (1999) (S.C. Res 1267).

20   President Clinton Vows 'No Sanctuary For Terrorists', 20 August 1998, online at http://www.fas.org/man/dod-101/ops/docs/98082014_tpo.html; Brian Knowlton (2004), 'US Pledges to Retaliate if Any Nation is Responsible', *International Herald Tribune,* (20 February) online at http://www.iht.com/IHT/BK/98/bk081098.html.

21   Michael Reisman (1999), 'International Legal Responses to Terrorism', 22 *Houston Journal of International Law* 3, 47.

22   Many critics later raised doubts about the quality of the evidence relied upon by the Clinton Administration in its decision to strike the Sudanese pharmaceutical plant. For a discussion of such doubts, see Sara N. Scheideman (2000), 'Standards of Proof in Forcible Responses to Terrorism', 50 *Syracuse Law Review* 249, 257–60.

23   See Maureen F. Brennan (1999), Comment, 'Avoiding Anarchy: Bin Laden Terrorism, the US Response, and the Role of Customary International Law', 59 *Louisiana Law*

Review 1195. It should be noted that Clinton's reasons for striking Afghanistan and Sudan (in an effort to reach bin Laden) are analogous to Reagan's reasons for attacking Libya (in an effort to reach Qadhafi). As Brennan explains:

> [Though a]dmitting that the bin Laden terrorist 'network' was not sponsored by any state, Clinton outlined four reasons for the action: 1) overwhelming evidence showed bin Laden 'played the key role in the embassy bombings'; 2) his network had been responsible for past terrorist attacks against Americans; 3) officials had 'compelling information' that bin Laden was planning future attacks and 4) his organization was attempting to obtain chemical weapons. In a second statement, President Clinton carefully characterized the strikes as necessary to defend against the threat of 'imminent' and 'immediate' future attacks, and not as retribution or punishment.

Ibid., 1195–96 (quoting President William J. Clinton (1998), 'Remarks on Military Strikes against Afghanistan and Sudan', Pub. Papers 1460, 1460 (20 August)).

24   Barton Gellman and Dana Priest (1998), 'US Strikes Terrorist-Linked Sites in Afghanistan, Factory in Sudan', *Washington Post*, A01 (21 August). This article is available online at http://www.washingtonpost.com/wp-srv/inatl/longterm/eafricabombing/stories/strikes082198.htm.

25   Phil Reeves (1998), 'Outraged Yeltsin Denounces "Indecent" US Behaviour', *Independent* (London), 2 (22 August).

26   Ibid.

27   'Remarks of President Clinton on Departure for Washington DC, from Martha's Vineyard, Massachusetts', 34 *Weekly Compilation of Presidential Documents* 1642 (20 August 1998).

28   President William J. Clinton (1998), 'Address to the Nation on Military Action against Terrorist Sites in Afghanistan and Sudan', Pub. Papers 1460, 1460 (20 August).

29   'Letter to Congressional Leaders Reporting on Military Action Against Terrorist Sites in Afghanistan and Sudan', 34 *Weekly Comp. Pres. Doc* 1650 (21 August 1998).

30   Ibid.

31   Ambassador Richardson's letter to the President of the UN Security Council, dated 20 August 1998, stated in part:

> These attacks were carried out only after repeated efforts to convince the Government of Sudan and the Taliban regime in Afghanistan to shut these terrorist activities down and to cease their cooperation with the bin Laden organization. That organization has issued a series of blatant warnings that 'strikes will continue from everywhere' against American targets, and we have convincing evidence that further such attacks were in preparation from these same terrorist facilities. The US, therefore, had no choice but to use armed force to prevent these attacks from continuing. In doing so, the US has acted pursuant to the right of self-defence confirmed by Article 51 of the Charter of the United Nations. The targets struck, and the timing and method of attack used, were carefully designed to minimize risks of collateral damage to civilians and to comply with international law, including the rules of necessity and proportionality.

Reisman, 48–49 (quoting Letter from Bill Richardson, the Permanent Representative of the United States of America to the United Nations, to the President of the Security Council of the United Nations, 20 August 1998, U.N. Doc S/1998/780, available online at http://www.undp.org/missions/usa/s1998_780.pdf).

32   Scheideman, 250.

33   Knowlton.

34   See, e.g., Jules Lobel (1999), 'The Use of Force to Respond to Terrorist Attacks: The Bombing of Sudan and Afghanistan', 24 *Yale Journal of International Law* 537, 557

('[T]he August 20 missile strikes represent the assertion of imperial might and arrogance [by the United States] in opposition to international law.').

35   See Brennan, 'Comment', 1197.

36   Ibid., 1210.

37   Ibid., 1209–10 (citations omitted).

38   See Leah M. Campbell (2000), 'Defending Against Terrorism: A Legal Analysis of the Decision to Strike Sudan and Afghanistan', 74 *Tulane Law Review* 1067, 1095.

39   See ibid., 1096 ('If the purpose of the strikes was retaliatory, it contravened conventional international law. If the strikes were motivated by self-defence, it appears that the necessary elements [an armed attack, necessity, immediacy, and proportionality] were not present.').

40   Raphael F. Perl (1998), 'Terrorism: U.S. Response to Bombings in Kenya and Tanzania: A New Policy Direction?', CRS Report to Congress (updated 1 September 1998), available at http://www2.gwu.edu/~nsarchiv/NSAEBB/NSAEBB55/crs19980901.pdf.

41   Ibid.

42   'President Clinton's Statement from Martha's Vineyard announcing US military strikes against terrorist camps in Afghanistan and Sudan', *Federal Document Clearing House*, Friday, 21 August 1998, A17; 'Our Objective Was to Damage Their Capacity to Strike', 14 July 2003, online at http://www.washingtonpost.com/wp-srv/inatl/longterm/eafricabombing/keystories.htm.

43   Senior administration officials involved in planning the attacks said they signalled the start of what one called 'a real war against terrorism', emphasizing that 'this is not a one-shot deal here'. Barton Gellman and Dana Priest (1998), 'US Strikes Terrorist-Linked Sites in Afghanistan, Factory in Sudan', *Washington Post*, A01 (21 August). This article is available online at http://www.washingtonpost.com/wp-srv/inatl/longterm/eafricabombing/stories/strikes082198.htm.

44   Four commercial aircraft were hijacked, two of them were flown into the twin towers of the World Trade Center in New York City, causing both buildings to collapse a third aircraft crashed into the Pentagon building in Arlington, Virginia, which houses the headquarters of the US Department of Defense and the US armed forces the fourth aircraft crashed near Somerset, Pennsylvania. Rensselaer Lee and Raphael Perl (2002), Congressional Research Service, Order Code IB95112, *Terrorism, the Future, and US Foreign Policy* 1 (6 August).

45   Statement of Ambassador Valeriy Kuchinsky, Ukrainian Representative to the United Nations. Transcript of the 4370th meeting of the Security Council, 3, U.N. Doc S/PV.4370 (12 September 2001).

46   G.A. Res 56/1, U.N. GAOR, 56th Sess, Supp No 49, U.N. Doc A/56/49 (2001) (Resolution 56/1) 4.

47   President Bush, Address to Joint Session of Congress (20 September 2001), in US Newswire, 20 September 2001, available online at 2001 WL 21898403.

48   U.N. SCOR, 56th Sess, 4385th mtg, U.N. Doc S/RES.1373 (2001) 2.

49   The UN General Assembly condemned the attacks as illegal and criminal acts of terrorism. Resolution 56/1, above note 46. The Security Council condemned the attacks 'as a threat to international peace and security'. U.N. SCOR, 56th Sess, 4370th mtg, U.N. Doc S/RES.1368 (2001). The Northern Atlantic Treaty Organization, European Union, Organization of American States, Association of South East Asian Nations, Organization of African Unity, and Arab League also agreed that the hijacking of American passenger airliners by Al-Qaeda terrorists was criminal. Colin Powell (2001), 'A Long, Hard Campaign', *Newsweek*, 53 (15 October).

50   See President George W. Bush, Address to a Joint Session of Congress and the American People, in 37 *Weekly Compilation of Presidential Documents* 1347 (20

September 2001) ('The evidence we have gathered all points to a collection of loosely affiliated terrorist organizations known as al [sic] Qaeda').

51   The war on terror 'will not end until every terrorist group of global reach has been found, stopped and defeated. ... From this day forward, any nation that continues to harbour or support terrorism will be regarded by the US as a hostile regime'. President George W. Bush, Address to a Joint Session of Congress and the American People, ibid.

52   Ronald Crelinsten and Alex P. Schmid (1992) (eds.), *Western Responses to Terrorism; A Twenty Five Year Balance Sheet*, Aldershot, UK, Brookfield, VT: Ashgate, 307, 316. The policy described by Crelinsten and Schmid has clearly been continued by Reagan's successors. This is evident in Clinton's air strikes against Iraq for the attempted assassination of George Bush Sr and his strikes against Sudan and Afghanistan following the embassy bombings in Tanzania and Kenya.

53   For a discussion of the international legal validity of US military action 'Operation Enduring Freedom' in Afghanistan, see Jack Beard (2002), 'America's New War on Terror: The Case for Self-Defence under International Law', 25 *Harvard Journal of Law and Policy* 559, 559.

54   'The President's State of the Union Address', 29 January 2002, available online at http://www.whitehouse.gov/news/releases/2002/01/20020129-11.html.

55   Nine days after the attacks, US President George Bush announced that: '[f]rom this day forward, any nation that continues to harbour or support terrorism will be considered by the United States as a hostile regime.' President George W. Bush, Address to a Joint Session of Congress and the American People, above note 50.

56   Commencement address by President George Bush at the West Point Military Academy graduation, 1 June 2002, announcing an expansive new policy of pre-emptive military action. The speech is available online at http://www.whitehouse.gov/news/releases/2002/06/20020601-3.html.

57   Ibid.

58   Ibid.

59   Ibid.

60   Thomas Shanker and David E. Sanger (2002), 'US Envisions Blueprint on Iraq Including Big Invasion Next Year', *New York Times*, (A1 28 April) (reporting that direct military involvement is being considered after the Bush administration concluded that a coup in Iraq would be unlikely to succeed); Patrick E. Tyler (2001), 'US Again Placing Focus on Ousting Hussein', *New York Times*, at A1 (18 December) (reporting that '[t]he option of taking the war against terrorism to Iraq and Saddam Hussein has gained significant ground in recent weeks'). Although the US appeared to be seeking Security Council approval for the use of force against Iraq, it reserved the right to proceed independently in the event that such approval failed to materialize and the US deems force to be necessary in self-defence. The use of force against Iraq in the event of non-compliance with weapons inspections received support from some, but not all, US allies. See, e.g., John Ibbitson (2002), 'Bush Rallies Support for Wider War', *Globe and Mail*, Toronto, A1 (12 March) (discussing the United Kingdom's support); Julia Preston and Eric Schmitt (2002), 'US-French Split on Iraq Deepens', *New York Times*, A1 (15 October) (discussing French opposition to US action in Iraq); 'US Offers a Deal for UN Resolution on Iraq', *New York Times*, 17 October 2002, online at http://www.nytimes.com (reporting that two dozen nations refused to endorse military force if Iraq failed to comply with weapons inspections).

61   S.C. Res 1441, U.N. SCOR, 57th Sess, 4644th mtg, U.N. Doc S/Res/1441 (2002). The UN Security Council unanimously passed Resolution 1441. The resolution declared Iraq to be in material breach of its obligations under past UN mandates. It also informed Iraq it would face 'serious consequences' if it failed to cooperate. It is questionable whether it authorized a member state to unilaterally take action in the event of further non-compliance.

62   Allison Ehlert (2003), 'Iraq: At the Apex of Evil', 21 *Berkeley Journal of International Law* 731, 764–765.

63   See Oliver Moore (2001), 'US Troops Going Cave-to-Cave in Tora Bora', *Globe and Mail*, Toronto (18 December) available online at www.globeandmail.com ('Asked whether the US might need a new resolution from the United Nations Security Council to strike suspected terrorist targets outside Afghanistan, [Defence Secretary Rumsfeld] said: "Nothing is needed by way of additional authorization. Every country has the right to self-defence."') (visited 4 July 2003); Steven R. Weisman (2002), 'U.S and France Near Deal on Iraq Attack', *New York Times*, A1 (30 October) ('American officials made clear that the US would reserve the right to lead a military action against Iraq if Iraq continued to block inspections, even if the Security Council did not give its approval').

64   President George W. Bush (2002), The National Security Strategy of the United States of America, 15–16 (17 September) online at http://www.whitehouse.gov/nsc/nss.pdf; *A.P. Newswires*, 20 September 2002, online at *Westlaw*, Newswires.

65   'Allies Discuss Terrorism and the Middle East: Bush and Blair on Policy', *New York Times*, 7 April 2002, A14.

66   West Point Commencement Speech.

67   Bush's National Security Strategy.

68   Dana Priest (2002), 'US Not Claiming Iraq Link to Terror', *Washington Post*, A1 (10 September) (reporting that CIA analysts were unable to validate reports that the Iraqi government had ties to Al-Qaeda); Walter Pincus (2002), 'No Link Between Hijacker, Iraq Found, US Says', *Washington Post*, A9 (1 May); Kenneth M. Pollack (2002), *The Threatening Storm: The Case for Invading Iraqi*, xxi–xxii; John Kampfner (2003), 'Blair's Wars; "No 10 Denies Straw had War Doubts"', *The Guardian*, London, 15 September 2003 online at http://www.guardian.co.uk/uk_news/story/0,3604,1042511,00.html; Matthew Tempest (2003), 'Hoon Regrets "Misunderstanding"', *The Guardian*, London (11 September) online at http://politics.guardian.co.uk/iraq/story/ 0,12956,1039958,00.html; 'Evidence "Useless"', *The Observer*, London, 20 July 2003, online at http://observer.guardian.co.uk/international/story/ 0,6903,1002061,00.html (alleging that documents used to bolster the US' claims that Iraq presented a nuclear threat were crudely-forged documents relating to Iraqi attempts to buy uranium from Niger).

69   See generally Howard Friehl (2003), 'Evidence and Iraq', *World Editorial and Int'l L.*, (January).

70   This is in the estimation of Daniel Richardson, editor of the respected journal *Jane's Missiles and Rockets*. See 'Blair: Weapons Report Breaches UN Resolution', *The Guardian*, London, 13 February 2003 online at http://0-www.guardian.co.uk.newcutter.newcastle.cdu.au:80/Iraq/Story/0,2763,894628,00.html.

71   George E. Bisharat (2003), 'Tyranny with Justice: Alternatives to War in the Confrontation with Iraq', 7 *Journal of Gender, Race and Justice* 1, 42–43.

72   Bill Keller (2001), 'The World According to Colin Powell', *New York Times Magazine*, 63 (24 November).

73   On 17 September 2003, President Bush stated that there was no evidence that Saddam Hussein was involved in the terrorist attacks of September 11, 2001 – disputing an idea held by many Americans. This came a day after his hawkish Defense Secretary Donald Rumsfeld said he had not seen any evidence that Saddam was involved in the attacks. The National Security Adviser, in support of the Bush and Rumsfeld sentiments, said: 'We have never claimed that Saddam Hussein had either direction or control of 9/11.' 'Bush: No Evidence Saddam was involved in 9/11 Attacks', 17 September 2003, online at http://edition.cnn.com/2003/US/09/17/sprj.irq.bush.ap/index.html (visited 17 September 2003).

74 Pollack, xxi–xxii.

75 Much debate initially surrounded the credibility of the US evidence regarding Iraq's links to Al-Qaeda. The issue of the possession of weapons of mass destruction, their quantity and nature were matters of much controversy. Initially it was difficult to conclude one way or the other but the international community remained divided over the matter right up to the day of military action. See, e.g., Chris Hedges (2001), 'Defectors Cite Iraqi Training for Terrorism', *New York Times*, A1 (8 November) (providing evidence of Iraqi government camps that had trained Islamic terrorists); David E. Sanger (2002), 'Bush Sees "Urgent Duty" to Pre-empt Attack by Iraq', *New York Times*, A1 (8 October) (reporting President Bush as building a lengthy, if circumstantial, case of Saddam Hussein's ties to Al-Qaeda). Kevin J. Kelly (2003), 'Fake Iraq-Africa Link That Drove America to War', *The East African*, Nairobi (31 March), online at http://www.nationaudio.com/News/EastAfrican/current/Regional/ Regional3103200359.html, arguing that during a crucial four-month period leading up to the current war in Iraq, US and British officials falsely charged that Saddam Hussein's government had tried to buy large quantities of uranium for nuclear weapons from an African country, with President George W. Bush including this in his annual State of the Union address on 29 January 2002. The doubts and scepticism have been finally laid to rest in favour of the sceptics, by the admission of no links between the September 11 attacks and Iraq by none other than US President George Bush and senior government officials. See above note 73.

76 Traditionally, anticipatory or pre-emptive self-defence has not been favoured under international law. See Michael Byers (2002), 'Terrorism, the Use of Force and International Law after 11 September', 51 *International and Comparative Law Quarterly* 410, 402. However, the notion of pre-emptive 'counter-proliferation' forms an important part of the new US national security strategy. See Bush's National Security Strategy, above note 67.

77 The US affirmed it would provide 'lethal assistance' in the form of military training and arms to Iraqi opposition volunteers and Kurdish fighters in Iraq. Patrick E. Tyler (2002), 'US and Britain Drafting Resolution to Impose Deadline on Iraq', *New York Times*, A14 (26 September); Julia Preston and Eric Schmitt, 'US-French Split on Iraq Deepens', *New York Times*, at A1 (15 October) (reporting that the CIA has begun covert operations in the Kurdish area of northern Iraq with a view to fomenting an uprising in Iraq).

78 *UN Charter*, arts 39, 42. A plain reading of Resolution 1441, above note 61, suggests another Security Council meeting in the event of an Iraqi breach, at least to discuss the inspectors' report, at which point the use of force could be authorized. On the other hand, the use of fuzzy and ambiguous language could be read as supporting the notion that the Security Council is allowing individual states greater interpretive latitude in deciding when force can be used.

79 Letter Dated 20 March 2003 from the Permanent Representative of Australia to the United Nations Addressed to the President of the Security Council, U.N. Doc S/2003/352 (20 March 2003); Letter Dated 20 March 2003 from the Permanent Representative of the United Kingdom of Great Britain and Northern Ireland to the United Nations Addressed to the President of the Security Council, U.N. Doc S/2003/350 (21 March 2003); Letter Dated 20 March 2003 from the Permanent Representative of the United States of America to the United Nations Addressed to the President of the Security Council, U.N. Doc S/2003/351 (21 March 2003); see also Mary Ellen O'Connell (2003), 'Addendum to Armed Force in Iraq: Issues of Legality', (April) online at http:// www.asil.org/insights/insigh99al.htm.

80 Patrick McLain (2003), 'Settling the Score with Saddam: Resolution 1441 and Parallel Justifications for the Use of Force against Iraq', 13 *Duke Journal of Comparative and International Law* 233, 262.

81   See S.C. Res 1368.
82   Byers, 408–09.
83   S.C. Res 1368.
84   Ibid.
85   S.C. Res 1373.
86   Press Release, North Atlantic Council (12 September 2001), online at http://usinfo.state.gov/topical/pol/terror/01091205.htm. The Foreign Ministers of the Organization of American States, meeting in consultation, likewise invoked the 1947 Inter-American Treaty of Reciprocal Assistance in declaring that 'these terrorist attacks against the United States of America are attacks against all American States'. Twenty-fourth Meeting of Consultation of Ministers of Foreign Affairs, Terrorist Threat to the Americas, OAS Doc RC.24/Res.1/01 (21 September 2001) online at http://www.oas.org/OASpage/crisis/RC.24e.htm (visited January 2003).
87   Michael J. Glennon (2002), 'The Fog of Law: Self-Defence, Inherence, and Incoherence in Article 51 of the United Nations Charter', 25 *Harvard Journal of Law and Public Policy* 539, 542–44.
88   Greenwood, 17.
89   Jack M. Beard (2002), 'Military Action Against Terrorists Under International Law: America's New War on Terror: The Case for Self-Defence under International Law', 25 *Harvard Journal of Law and Public Policy* 559, 565.
90   Ibid.
91   Ibid.
92   As articulated by President George W. Bush in his 20 September 2002 Address to a Joint Session of Congress and his 7 October address to the country. The text of both speeches is available online at http://usinfo.state.gov.
93   In a 7 October Department of Defense Briefing. The text of both speeches can be accessed at the US government information website http://usinfo.state.gov. (visited December 2003).
94   Frederic L. Kirgis, 'The American Society of International Law (ASIL) Insights: Israel's Intensified Military Campaign Against Terrorism', 10 December 2001, online at http://www.asil.org/insights/insigh78.htm).
95   See e.g. Judith Miller (2002), 'Remarks at the Cornell International Law Journal Symposium on Terrorism: Implications of the Response to September 11, 2001' (14 February) ('The unity in the international community regarding the legal basis for US action has been quite remarkable ... [T]he overall international agreement is that the US had a proper legal basis for taking self-defensive actions ... in response to the deliberate attack[s]... in New York and Washington D.C.'); furthermore, Professor Beard states:

>   The European Union ..., along with its member states individually, pledged to support US action against terrorism. Similar views and various offers of support were made by America's Pacific allies, including Australia, New Zealand, Japan, the Philippines, and South Korea. In addition..., numerous states throughout Eastern Europe, Africa, and Asia expressed their support for the US military response to the September 11 terrorist attacks.
>   ...
>   While public opinion in the Arab and Muslim world opposed the US action against Afghanistan, several Arab states such as Bahrain, Egypt, and Jordan expressed support for the US anti-terror campaign. Other Arab states also made significant contributions to US military efforts, including Pakistan..., Saudi Arabia..., and Persian Gulf states such as Oman and Kuwait...

       Beard, 569–70 (citations omitted).

96   Michael C. Bonafede (2002), 'Here, There and Everywhere: Assessing the Proportionality Doctrine and the US Uses of Force in Response to Terrorism after the September 11 Attacks', 88 *Cornell Law Review* 155, 185.

97   See Yoram Dinstein (3rd ed. 2001), *War, Aggression and Self-Defence*, New York: Cambridge University Press, 184 ('[Proportionality] is frequently depicted as "of the essence of self- defence", although it is not always easy to establish what proportionality entails.... [As such,] the principle of proportionality must be applied with some degree of flexibility.' (citations omitted)), Judith Gail Gardam (1993), 'Proportionality and Force in International Law', 87 *American Journal of International Law* 391, 405 ('Proportionality is a complex concept to apply to particular cases and there will inevitably be differences of opinion.' (citation omitted)).

98   Bonafede, 159.

99   Ibid., 186.

100 Beard, 571.

101 Pollack, 157.

102 Paul Pillar (2001), *Terrorism and US Foreign Policy*, Washington DC: Brookings Institution Press 160.

103 See William M. Arkin (2001), 'Should Iraq be Next?', *Washington Post*, (3 December) online at http://www.washingtonpost.com/wp-dyn/nation/columns/dotmil.

104 George W. Bush, 'State of the Union Address', 29 January 2002, 38 *Weekly Compilation of Presidential Documents* 125, 135, 4 February 2002 online at http://www.whitehouse.gov/news/releases/2002/01/iraq/20020129-11.html.

105 McLain, 236.

106 George W. Bush (2002), UN General Assembly in New York City Address, 38 *Weekly Compilation of Presidential Documents* 1529 (12 September) online at http://www.whitehouse.gov/news/releases/2002/09/20020912-1.html.

107 President Bush, Address to the United Nations General Assembly, n 67. See also Wendy Ross (2001), 'Bush Says Iraq Must Permit Weapons Inspections', (26 Novemebr 26) (reporting President Bush's White House press conference on 26 November 2001) online at http:// usinfo.state.gov/topical/pol/terror/01112608.htm.

108 See S.C. Res. 1441, 1.

109 Ibid., 3.

110 Ibid., 5.

111 xi See President George W. Bush, 'Remarks by the President on the United Nations Security Council Resolution', 8 November 2002, online at http://www.whitehouse.gov/news/releases/2002/11/20021108-1.html ('The United States has agreed to discuss any material breach with the Security Council, but without jeopardizing our freedom of action to defend our country. If Iraq fails to fully comply, the United States and other nations will disarm Saddam Hussein.'); Statement by US Ambassador John Negroponte, UN Press Release SC/7564, 8 November 2002 online at http://www.un.org/News/Press/archives.htm ('The resolution contained, he said, no "hidden triggers" and no "automaticity" with the use of force. The procedure to be followed was laid out in the resolution. And one way or another, Iraq would be disarmed. If the Security Council failed to act decisively in the event of further Iraqi violation, the resolution did not constrain any Member State from acting to defend itself against the threat posed by that country, or to enforce relevant United Nations resolutions and protect world peace and security.').

112 See Michael Hirsh (2002), 'Bush and the World', *Foreign Policy*, 20 (October) ('Bush, to judge by his actions, appears to believe in a kind of unilateral civilization ... the United Nations is an afterthought, treaties are not considered binding').

113 'Terror cells and outlaw regimes building weapons of mass destruction are different faces of the same evil. Our security requires that we confront both.' See President

George W. Bush (2002), 'Remarks by the President on Iraq in Cincinnati, Ohio' (7 October) online at http://www.whitehouse.gov/news/releases/2002/10/20021007-8.html.

114   Ibid.

115   John Yoo (2003), 'International Law and the War in Iraq', 97 *American Journal of International Law* 563, 575.

116   For a discussion of the Security Council resolution tangent, see Jackson Maogoto (2003), 'Rushing to Break the Law? The Bush Doctrine of Pre-Emptive Strikes and the UN Charter on the Use of Force', 7 *University of Western Sydney Law Review* 1, 18-19.

117   Article 51 of the Charter provides:

> Nothing in the present Charter shall impair the inherent right of individual or collective self-defence if an armed attack occurs against a Member of the United Nations, until the Security Council has taken measures necessary to maintain international peace and security. Measures taken by Members in the exercise of this right of self-defence shall be immediately reported to the Security Council and shall not in anyway affect the authority and responsibility of the Security Council under the present Charter to take at any time such action as it deems necessary in order to maintain or restore international peace and security.

118   A Digest of International Law as Embodied in Diplomatic Discussions, Treaties and other International Agreements, International Awards, the Decisions of Municipal Courts, and the Writings of Jurists, Washington DC: Government Printing Office, Vol. 2, 409–14. The affair of *The Caroline* involves a US ship being used by US citizens to transport reinforcements to Canadian territory in support of insurgents battling Great Britain's rule. The case is illustrative of a state's right to undertake necessary actions in 'anticipatory' self-defence of an impending, though not necessarily imminent, hostile attack. See also *Corfu Channel* (UK v Albania) 1949 I.C.J. 4, which has been cited for the proposition that the International Court of Justice recognized a residual right to reprisal remaining in the international legal order, the UN Charter notwithstanding.

119   See Roberto Ago (1980), 'Addendum to the 8th Report on State Responsibility', *Yearbook of the International Law Commission*, Vol. 2, 52, U.N. Doc A/CN.4/318/ADD. 52, 68–69, para 119 (describing requirements frequently viewed as essential conditions for admissibility of self-defence pleas).

120   1996 I.C.J. 226, 96 (July 8).

121   See President Bush, Address to the United Nations General Assembly, above note 107 ('[I]f an emboldened regime were to supply [weapons of mass destruction] to terrorist allies, then the attacks of September 11th would be a prelude to far greater horrors').

122   The National Security Strategy.

123   *Nicaragua v United States of America*, 1986 I.C.J. 14 at 176 (27 June); Christine Gray (2000), *International Law and the Use of Force*, Oxford; New York: Oxford University Press, 154.

124   See, e.g., Yoram Dinstein (2nd ed., 1994), *War, Aggression, and Self-Defence*, Cambridge: Grotius; New York: Press Syndicate of the University of Cambridge, 184–187; Richard Erickson (1989), *Legitimate Use of Force against State Sponsored Terrorism*, Maxwell Air Force Base, Ala.: Air University Press, 136–38 and authorities cited therein.

125   Gregory M. Travalio (2000), 'Terrorism, International Law, and the Use of Military Force', 18 *Wisconsin International Law Journal* 145, 163-164.

126   Ibid.

127   See, e.g., Dinstein (2nd ed., 1994), 183 (choice of words in Article 51 is deliberately restrictive; right of self-defence is limited to armed attack).

128 See, e.g., Dinstein (2nd ed., 1994), 184–187; Erickson.

129 See Baker, 45.

130 Dinstein (2nd ed., 1994), 186. See Michael Lohr (1985), 'Legal Analysis of US Military Responses to State-Sponsored International Terrorism', 34 *Naval Law Review* 1, 18 (referring to Phillip Jessup (1948), *A Modern Law of Nations: An Introduction*, New York: Macmillan, 166 and Lassa Oppenheim, *International Law* (H. Lauterpact 7th ed.), London: Longmans 156).

131 In para. 195 of its opinion, the Court said that the exercise of the right of self-defence by a state under Article 51 'is subject to the state concerned having been the victim of an armed attack'. 1986 I.C.J. 103.

132 The United Nations Security Council condemned the Israeli attack on the Iraqi nuclear reactor in a unanimous resolution adopted on 19 June 1981. The Security Council also condemned, by a vote of 14-0, with the US abstaining, the 1985 attack by Israeli F-16s on the PLO Headquarters located in Tunisia. For an excellent discussion of the history of United Nations' responses to various Israeli anti-terrorist campaigns in Lebanon, see William V. O'Brien (1990), 'Reprisals, Deterrence and Self-Defence in Counter-terror Operations', 30 *Virginia Journal of International Law* 421, 462–63. The US appears to have accepted at least a limited doctrine of anticipatory self-defence. Its 1986 attack on Libya was, in part, justified on the basis of deterring future acts of terrorism by Libya. See Statement of Ambassadors Okun and Walters before the UN Security Council, 14–15 April 1986, reprinted in (1986) 80 *American Journal of International Law* 632–33. Former Secretary of State George Shultz stated that the US is justified in using force to pre-empt attacks by terrorists or to seize terrorists when no other means are available. See Erickson, 138. Certainly, some of the statements of government officials following the attack on Osama bin Laden and the alleged chemical weapons plant in Sudan seem to assert a broad right of anticipatory self-defence. See, e.g., Paul Richter (1998), 'US Has Right to Kill Terrorists, Officials Say', *Dallas Morning News*, (29 October).

133 See, e.g., Gregory Francis Intoccia (1987), 'American Bombing of Libya: An International Legal Analysis', 19 *Case Western Reserve Journal of International Law* 177, 190; Reisman, 33–34; Bob Woodward and Patrick E. Tyler (1986), 'Libyan Cables Intercepted and Decoded', *Washington Post*, (15 April) A1.

134 President Ronald Reagan (1986), Address on 14 April 1986, in *Washington Post*, A23 (15 April).

135 Arthur Brice (1998), 'Terror Suspect Says Now It's War, US Ready, Says Official: "We're Going to Be on the Offense as Well as Defense"', *Atlanta Journal-Constitution*, (22 August), A1.

136 Gray, 123.

137 D. Bowett (1958), *Self-Defense in International Law*, Manchester University Press, Manchester, England, 191–92; see also Erickson, 142–43.

138 Thomas M. Franck (2001), 'The Institute for Global Legal Studies Inaugural Colloquium: The UN and the Protection of Human Rights: When if Ever May States Deploy Military Force without Prior Security Council Authorization?', 5 *Washington University Journal of Law and Policy* 57, 57–58.

139 Greenwood, 15.

140 Michael Glennon (2002), 'Preempting Terrorism; The Case for Anticipatory Self-Defence', *Weekly Standard*, 24, 26 (28 January).

141 See generally Claud H. M. Waldock (1952), 'The Regulation of the Use of Force by Individual States in International Law', 2 *Recueil des Cours* 451, 496–97 (discussing Article 51 of the UN Charter). See Waldock, above note 32, at 498 (recounting the Atomic Energy Commission's suggestions to the UN Security Council).

142 Leo Van Den Hole (2003), 'Anticipatory Self-Defence Under International Law', 19 *American University International Law Review* 69, 91.

143 Erickson, 149 ('anticipatory self-defence, can be a legal justification for the use of armed force').

144 See Michael Glennon (2002), 'Self-defence and Incoherence in the UN Charter', 25 *Harvard Journal of Law and Public Policy* 552.

145 Bowett, 191-92; see also Erickson, 54.

146 Christopher Clarke Posteraro (2002), 'Intervention in Iraq: Towards A Doctrine of Anticipatory Counter-Terrorism, Counter-Proliferation Intervention', 15 *Florida Journal of International Law* 151, 211.

147 See Sean M. Condron (1999), 'Justification for Unilateral Action in Response to the Iraqi Threat: A Critical Analysis of Operation Desert Fox', 161 *Military Law Review* 115, 147. Some scholars would further limit the right of anticipatory self-defence, adding inter alia: last resort, reasonableness, and a requirement of reporting to the UN Security Council. See also Erickson, 145–50.

148 Christopher Greenwood (2003), 'International Law and the Pre-emptive use of Military Force: Afghanistan, Al Qaida and Iraq', 4 *San Diego International Law Journal* 7, 10.

149 See Condron, 151–52 (discussing the failure of 'Operation Desert Fox' to satisfy the proportionality and imminency requirement of anticipatory self-defence).

150 Cf. John-Alex Romano (1999), 'Combating Terrorism and Weapons of Mass Destruction: Reviving the Doctrine of a State of Necessity', 87 *Georgia Law Journal* 1023, 1048–1059.

151 Michael J. Kelly (2003), 'Time Warp to 1945 – Resurrection of the Reprisal and Anticipatory Self-defence Doctrines in International Law', 13 *Journal of Transnational Law Policy* 1, 2–3.

152 Carsten Stahn (2003), 'International Law Under Fire; Terrorist Acts as "Armed Attacks": The Right to Self-Defense, Article 51 (1/2) of the UN Charter, and International Terrorism', 27 *Fletcher Forum of World Affairs* 35, 40.

153 Kelly, 22.

154 Ian Brownlie (1963), *International Law and the Use of Force by States*, Oxford: Clarendon Press, 260.

155 Stahn, 35.

156 The *Caroline* incident; Beard, 585–86.

157 See Erickson, 109, 111.

158 Jordan J. Paust (1986), 'Responding Lawfully to International Terrorism: The Use of Force Abroad', 8 *Whittier Law Review* 711, 716–717.

159 Stahn, 37–38.

160 See Erickson, 109, 113.

161 See Sean D. Murphy (2002), 'Terrorism and the Concept of "Armed Attack" in Article 51 of the UN Charter', 43 *Harvard International law Journal* 49–50.

162 Louis Henkin (1991), 'The Use of Force: Law and US Policy', in *Right v Might: International Law and the Use of Force*, New York: Council on Foreign Relations, 46; see also Letter from the Acting Permanent Representative of the United States of America, to President of the UN Security Council, United Nations (14 April 1986), U.N. SCOR, 41st Sess, U.N. Doc S/17990 (1986).

163 Posteraro, 180.

164 Richard Falk (1985), 'The Decline of Normative Restraint in International Relations', 10 *Yale Journal of International Law* 265, 266. See generally, Levitt (1986), 'International Law and the US Government's Response to Terrorism', 8 *Whittier Law Review* 755.

165 G.A. Res 41/38, U.N. GAOR, 41st Sess, Supp No. 53, at 34, U.N. Doc A/41/53 (1986).

166 See Stephen Robinson (1993), 'UN Support for Raid on Baghdad', *Daily Telegraph*, 1 (28 June); 'European Allies Are Giving Strong Backing to US Raid', *New York Times*, 28 June 1993, A7; 'Arab Governments Critical', *New York Times*, 28 June 1993, A7.

167 Beard, 575.
168 George Shultz (1985), 'Terrorism and the Modern World', 7 *Terrorism* 431, 435.
169 Greenwood, 23.
170 Posteraro, 179–180.
171 Jeffrey Addicott (2002), 'Legal and Policy Implications for a New Era: The "War On Terror"', 4 *Scholar: St Mary's Law Review on Minority Issues* 209.
172 Louis R. Beres (1992), 'The Permissibility of State-Sponsored Assassination during Peace and War', 5 *Temple International and Comparative Law Journal* 231, 239.
173 Ibid., 151.
174 Greenwood, 3.
175 Glennon, Michael J. (2002), 'The Fog of Law: Self-Defence, Inherence, and Incoherence in Article 51 of the United Nations Charter', 25 *Harvard Journal of Law and Public Policy*, 539.
176 Amando Doronila (2002), 'Backlash Shocks Canberra', *Philadelphia Daily Inquirer*, (5 December), 2002 WL 103480280; 'EU Not Supportive of Australia's Proposed Asian Terrorism Action', *Asia Pulse*, 5 December 2002, 2002 WL 103864236.
177 'Adoption of Policy of Pre-emption Could Result in Proliferation of Unilateral, Lawless Use of Force, Secretary-General Tells General Assembly', U.N. Doc SG/SM/8891-GA/10157, 2003 online at http://www.un.org/News.
178 Mark Drumbl (2002), 'Victimhood in Our Neighborhood: Terrorist Crime, Taliban Guilt, and the Asymmetries of the International Legal Order', 81 *North Carolina Law Review* 1, 32–33.
179 Ibid., 25–26.

Chapter 5

Striking the Enemy's Lair: The War on Terror and State-sponsored Terrorism

Introduction

Terrorism is ambiguous: it unsettles victim states as they must search for an appropriate means of response, or determine if any response is legitimate. Because there is no cohesive enumeration of appropriate responses to terrorist acts in the international system,[1] individual states have developed internal mechanisms for dealing with terrorists through criminal laws.[2] However, as noted in Chapter 2, frequently these internal mechanisms are the result of treaty agreements[3] and the system remains weak owing to the reality that terrorists may evade capture in the same way other criminals do – by exploiting faulty extradition treaties and weaknesses in law enforcement.[4] The uncertain nature of permissible countermeasures against international terrorism within the international system means that the efficacy of domestic criminal laws is weakened in the face of transnational terrorist groups whose membership and conspiracy may spread across many borders.[5]

The challenge to states and the international community is compounded when states (actively or passively) support terrorism, thus enhancing the capabilities of terrorist organizations, as well as their ability to avoid both domestic and international enforcement regimes, paving the way for impunity. States that sponsor terrorism have a great capacity to evade responsibility. This is in light of the reality that the state-to-terrorist relationship can be protected at the discretion of a state sponsor, thereby sheltering the perpetrator from immediate coercion and other legal claims offered by victim states. Traditionally state responsibility has been the vehicle through which pressure is exerted on states sponsoring terrorism.

The lethal capabilities of terrorists demonstrated by the September 11 attacks, however, have fundamentally changed the political and legal landscape. The tragic events of September 11 prompted the international community to examine international terrorism anew. The magnitude of the acts went beyond terrorism as it was known, and statements from various capitals around the world pointed to a need to develop new strategies to confront a new reality. The US response (with the active support of the international community) was to launch a broad assault on Al-Qaeda and its host government, the Taliban regime of Afghanistan.

The attacks of September 11, the American response and the international community's approval of the military action represent a new paradigm in international law relating to the use of force.[6] Previously acts of terrorism were seen as criminal acts, carried out by private, non-governmental entities. In contrast, the

September 11 attacks were regarded as an act of war.[7] This effectively marked a turning point in the long-standing premise of international law that military force was an instrument of relations between states.[8] Terrorism was no longer merely a serious threat to peace and stability to be combated through domestic and international penal mechanisms – use of force was now an avenue for managing the consequences of terrorist strikes. September 11 was a paradigm-changing event that generated a new dimension in international legal and political debate.

Though international discourse on terrorism is abundant and terrorism continues to be the subject of sustained debate, the attacks of September 11 elevated the discourse to another level. The attacks instigated the momentum for the international legal system to seek to co-opt military responses to counter terrorism within the regime of lawful force contained in the UN Charter. Many of the strict requirements of the *Nicaragua Case*[9] which considered the issue of state responsibility in light of international norms on the use of force are now being challenged, infusing Article 51 of the UN Charter with a new focus. In view of the dangers posed by terrorism, broadening state responsibility and imposing severe punishment for breaches seems understandable. However, the issue is whether, once responsibility is triggered by establishing that the state in question knowingly tolerates the responsible parties, encourages them, or fails to do anything about them, should this be followed up with the lethal use of military force?

This chapter aims to examine the legitimate use of force in counteracting state-sponsored terrorism, in the light of the September 11 attacks, by engaging state responsibility. In Part II the chapter sets the parameters of state-sponsored terrorism through an evaluation of the tenets of state responsibility. It will do so by examining ICJ jurisprudence and UN resolutions which have discussed the responsibility of states for terrorist activity. This is an issue that continues to be on uncertain ground. Under customary international law, states are not perpetrators of terrorism because terrorism is a penal offence and states are not subjects of international criminal law.[10] Nonetheless, General Assembly resolutions that repeatedly condemn states undertaking and/or supporting terrorism implicitly acknowledge that states are involved in terrorist activities.[11]

Part III will discuss the enshrined norms on the use of force regime proscribed in the UN Charter. It will argue that the prohibition on the use of force has traditionally been balanced against the 'inherent' right to self-defence as contained in the UN Charter. It will be submitted that the UN Charter regime on the use of force is visibly engaged in a process of change, especially in the light of the September 11 attacks. This chapter evaluates this within the framework of the uncertainty and indeterminacy of the doctrine of state responsibility in providing the necessary linkage between state-sponsored terrorist acts and the use of military force against those states. Can terrorist attacks be co-opted into the understanding of 'armed attack' and thus a basis for the use of military force against the responsible entity? This question is important since the potential for abuse of the option of military force is significantly reduced if states observe the evidentiary thresholds that apply when determining who is responsible for the attack. The recognition that acts of private actors may give rise to an 'armed attack' is anything but revolutionary. However, it is not entirely clear from the practice in the aftermath of September 11 whether the requirement of the attribution of a terrorist act to a specific state actor was, in fact, fully abandoned, or whether the qualification of 'armed attack' still requires a nexus of the terrorist act to a state entity.

State Responsibility

State responsibility in the Cold War era began a gradual evolution as a basis for US and Israeli strikes on terrorist targets (real or perceived) in states accused of sponsoring terrorism. If a state is suspected of supporting or condoning terrorism activity, analysis of the principles governing state responsibility is not only appropriate but the only way in which to apply established principles that will rule out military adventurism and restrict military responses to clear cases.

Physical Control

State responsibility is based upon a state's physical control over harmful events occurring through its explicit or implicit support. In considering responses to terrorism, it must be determined who is in fact responsible for the acts. If a state is suspected, analysis of the principles governing state responsibility is appropriate.

> Customary international law holds that a state is normally responsible for those illegalities which it has originated. A state does not bear responsibility for acts injurious to another state committed by private individuals when the illegal deeds do not proceed from the command, authorization, or culpable negligence of the government. However, a state is responsible vicariously for every act of its own forces, of the members of its government, of private citizens, and of aliens committed on its territory. If the state neglects the duties imposed by vicarious responsibility it incurs original liability for the private acts and is guilty of an international delinquency. No state, however, bears absolute responsibility for international illegalities committed by individuals acting on its territory.[12]

It is beyond dispute that states are directly responsible under international law to control terrorists operating within their borders, as is the fact that states have a responsibility to refrain from actively supporting terrorist organizations.

As early as 1970, the UN General Assembly, in Resolution 2625,[13] made it clear that a state's mere acquiescence in terrorist activity emanating from its soil is a violation of the state's international obligations. Numerous other resolutions from both the UN General Assembly and the UN Security Council leave no doubt that harbouring or supporting terrorist groups violates a state's responsibility under international law.[14]

Abraham D. Sofaer asserts that: 'A corporation or group is responsible for the acts of its authorized agents, and the concept of apparent authority requires that principals exercise reasonable care to prevent any action that could reasonably lead a third person to infer that an agent has actual authority to engage in the conduct at issue. These rules reflect the governing law throughout the world's legal systems.'[15] As Professor Thomas Franck concluded on the basis of an extensive survey: 'the approach to criminal complicity is strikingly similar among all legal systems. The domestic law of all civilized states [has] recognized that persons who aid or abet other persons are guilty of the (or another) offense.'[16] The widespread acceptance of these rules is significant in determining proper international behaviour. Where domestic laws constitute 'general principles of law recognized by civilized nations', they become a source of international law, as defined in Article 38 of the Statute of the ICJ.[17]

> For years states have supplied funds, arms, and sanctuary to known terrorist organizations without being treated as having responsibility for the terrorist actions. In such situations, states claim they have no knowledge of or do not support terrorist actions, and they explain their support for the groups involved on the ground that the groups have other, legitimate purposes.[18]

With the development of the law on state responsibility to encompass terrorism, a claim currently made by states allowing terrorist groups sanctuary within their borders is that they have warned the groups not to commit terrorist acts and that they are prepared to punish or to expel any terrorist that is proved to be guilty of a terrorist act.[19]

A prominent example of liability relating to physical control is the *Corfu Channel Case*.[20] As Lieutenant Commander Michael Franklin Lohr notes:

> This case involved Albanian responsibility for mine explosions flowing from the proof of Albanian knowledge of mine laying in her territorial waters. While the court was careful to state that knowledge could not be imputed simply by reason of the fact that the minefield was discovered in Albanian waters, territorial control was important to the court. First, it created a duty to give warning of mines if their presence was known to the Albanian authorities. Second, exclusive control (over territorial waters) had a critical impact upon the respective burdens of proof.[21]

Extra-territorial Responsibility

It is often said that a state can be responsible only for events occurring within its territory. However, state responsibility may be based upon a state's physical control over harmful events occurring outside its territory. In general terms the test is physical control, not sovereignty.[22] Lieutenant Commander Michael Franklin Lohr notes that: 'Although state responsibility is typically thought of in terms of injury to a state's nationals and redress on behalf of those nationals by a state vis-à-vis another state (indirect injury to the state), there is an emerging consensus that direct injury to the state, that is to say breaches of the state's own sovereignty, fall within the parameters of the concept.'[23] Professor Ian Brownlie, in his treatise *System of the Law of Nations, State Responsibility*, asserts:

> As a matter of essence and policy there is no great difference between ... 'protection of nationals' ... and 'direct injury' to the state. It is absurd to suggest that the interest which a state has in the treatment of its nationals is of a second order.... Moreover, many fact situations cannot be divided up into 'state ... interests' and matters of 'indirect injury'.[24]

Several decisions of arbitral tribunals in the past have granted substantial damages against states for failing to prevent persons within their jurisdictions from conducting hostile activities against other states. In 1872, an international arbitral panel awarded the United States $15,500,000 in a proceeding against Great Britain (the *Alabama Arbitration*) for allowing a Confederate warship to be completed and to leave British territory, thereafter capturing or destroying more than sixty Union vessels.[25]

The *Alabama* claims were a diplomatic dispute between the United States and Great Britain that arose out of the US Civil War. In the instant case, the United States demanded compensation from Britain for the damage wrought by the British-built, Southern-operated commerce raiders, based upon the argument that the British Government, by aiding the creation of a Confederate Navy, had inadequately followed its neutrality laws. Though based on violation of neutrality laws, the arbitral tribunal was acting consonant to recognized customary international law doctrine that holds that a state is normally responsible for those illegalities which it has originated. If the state neglects the duties imposed by vicarious responsibility, it incurs original liability for the private acts and is guilty of an international delinquency.

Some five decades later, in the *Texas Cattle Claims* arbitration, the American-Mexican Claims Commission found Mexico liable on four legal bases for raids into Texas by outlaws or military personnel:

(1) active participation of Mexican officials in the depredations;
(2) permitting the use of Mexican territory as a base for wrongful actions against the US and the citizens thereof, thus encouraging the wrongful acts;
(3) negligence, over a long period of years, to prosecute or otherwise to discourage or prevent the raids; and
(4) failure to cooperate with the Government of the US in the matter of terminating the condition in question.[26]

The Texas Claims Commission was constituted under the terms of the General Claims Convention signed on 8 September 1923, in Washington DC by the United States of America and the United Mexican States. The convention, which took effect on 1 March 1924, was intended to improve relations between the countries by forming a commission to settle claims arising after 4 July 1868, (this related to the American-Mexican War) 'against one government by nationals of the other for losses or damages suffered by such nationals or their properties' and 'for *losses or damages originating from acts of officials or others acting for either government and resulting in injustice*'.[27]

The position the arbitral tribunals is evident in the judgments of the International Court of Justice (ICJ) in the *Corfu Channel* and *Iran Hostage* cases, where the position of the arbitral tribunals was reaffirmed. In the *Corfu Channel Case* as well as the *Iran Hostage Case*, the ICJ found that Albania and Iran, respectively, had a duty under international law to make every reasonable effort to prevent illegal acts against foreign states and had acted unlawfully by knowingly allowing its territory to be used for illegal acts.[28]

Guilt by Association: Attribution of Actions

In the *United States Diplomatic and Consular Staff in Tehran (United States of America v Iran) (Merits)*,[29] the ICJ was presented with the question whether Iran was responsible for the taking of US hostages by private militants, premised on the fact that the Iranian Government sanctioned and perpetuated the hostage crisis.[30] The ICJ was faced with the question of whether the action of the Iranian students in occupying the US embassy and taking embassy staff hostage could be attributed to the Government of Iran. In its opinion, the ICJ divided the events into two phases: the initial takeover by the students and the subsequent lengthy occupation of the embassy. The Court found that during the initial phase the students did not act on behalf of the state; therefore, the state did not bear responsibility for their actions – despite acknowledging that Iranian authorities were obliged to protect the embassy, and had the means to do so, but failed. According to the Court, only after the takeover was complete did the Iranian Government bear responsibility for the actions of the students, because only then did the Ayatollah Khomeini express his approval of the occupation and indicate that the embassy and consular staffs were 'under arrest'. This fundamentally transformed the legal situation and permitted the occupation from that point to be attributed to the state of Iran. This case upheld the position by Professor Brownlie that state responsibility may be based upon the approval and adoption of harmful acts by state organs as agents.[31]

Six years later, the ICJ handed down its judgment in the *Military and Paramilitary Activities in and against Nicaragua*[32] which had presented the question of whether the actions of Nicaragua in supporting rebels in El Salvador constituted an armed attack by Nicaragua sufficient to justify military action by the US in collective self-defence with El Salvador. Nicaragua provided weapons and logistical support to rebels seeking to overthrow the government of El Salvador. The US argued that this support justified mining Nicaraguan waters and taking other military action against Nicaragua. The ICJ soundly rejected the arguments of the US. It said sending 'armed bands' into the territory of another state would be sufficient to constitute an armed attack, but 'the supply of arms and other support to such bands cannot be equated with armed attack', and did not justify the use of military force by the US against Nicaragua.[33]

The ICJ ruled that the US was not responsible for the rebel activities of Nicaraguan Contras, because evidence that the Contras were controlled and dependent on the US was insufficient to establish that the US directed the Contras' each and every act.[34] The ICJ ruled that US support for the Contras infringed on Nicaragua's territorial sovereignty in contravention of international law,[35] but concluded that the evidence did not demonstrate that the US 'actually exercised such a degree of control in all fields as to justify treating the Contras as acting on its behalf'.[36] In order to attribute the actions of the Contras to the US, the ICJ required proof in each instance that operations launched by the Contras 'reflected strategy and tactics wholly devised by the United States'.[37]

Summing up the general tenor of the Nicaragua and Iran cases, Travalio and Altenburg observe:

These authorities strongly suggest that the ability to attack terrorist groups where they live, where they train, where they amass their weapons, and where they plan their attacks is severely limited. The *Nicaragua* and *Iran Hostages* cases indicate that a state must direct and control the activities of the terrorists – or at least expressly sanction and adopt their actions – before their acts will be attributable to that state. Financing, training, and logistical support will not be enough – all of these were provided by the US to the Nicaraguan Contras, yet the ICJ refused to attribute their actions to the US. These same elements of direction and control were key in the Iran Hostages case as well.[38]

'Although scholars were far from unanimous in their view that the support of terrorists could be a basis upon which actions could be imputed to the supporting state,[39] it is clear that there was no consensus in the years following the *Nicaragua* and *Iran Hostages* cases that these cases represented the law as applied to transnational terrorist groups.'[40] Since the *Nicaragua* and *Iran Hostages* decisions, a variety of scholars and other writers have argued that substantial support of terrorists by a state can be sufficient to impute the actions of the terrorists to the supporting state.[41] Among the most prominent is renowned international law scholar Professor Oscar Schachter, who stated: '[W]hen a government provides weapons, technical advice, transportation, aid and encouragement to terrorists on a substantial scale it is not unreasonable to conclude that the armed attack is imputable to that government.'[42]

However, this position is at variance with the ICJ's conclusion in *Nicaragua* that found the acts of the Nicaraguan Contras could not be attributed to the US. It was clear from the evidence that, in many ways, the Contras were a proxy army for the US and could not have existed without the financing and support of the US. The ICJ recognized the extent of US participation, but nonetheless concluded that the acts of the Contras could not be attributed to the US:

> The Court took the view ... that US participation, even if preponderant or decisive, in the financing, organizing, training, supplying and equipping of the Contras, the selection of its military or paramilitary targets, and the planning of the whole of its operation, was still insufficient in itself, on the basis of the evidence in the possession of the Court, for the purpose of attributing to the US the acts committed by the Contras in the course of their military or paramilitary operations in Nicaragua.[43]

The Court held that there was no clear evidence that the US had 'exercised such a degree of control in all fields as to justify treating the Contras as acting on [the US'] behalf.'[44] The Court appeared in both situations to be unwilling to attribute the acts of persons supported by a state to the state itself unless the state exercised effective control over the actors. In essence, the ICJ diluted the notion of attribution and thus responsibility.

The Court found the extent of US support for the Contras to be significant and included financing for food and clothing, military training, arms and tactical assistance. However, the Court concluded that these forms of support were insufficient to hold the US accountable, because the Contras remained autonomous. The Court asserted that it did 'not consider that the assistance given by the US to the Contras warrants the conclusion that these forces are subject to the US to such an extent that any acts they have committed are imputable to that state'.[45]

Unwittingly, the ICJ '… provided states that assist terrorist groups with important support in their attempt to evade responsibility for the terrorist conduct of such groups in other states'.[46]

> The Court's ruling in the litigation had the effect of relieving the US of liability for Contra activities and thereby limiting the effect of the Court's ruling on liability. But the long-run consequences of this ruling will be as pernicious to peaceful relations among states as the Court's rulings limiting the scope of self defense.[47]

In a critical review of the Court's judgment, Abraham D. Sofaer points out that:

> The Court had no basis in established practice or custom to limit so drastically the responsibility of states for the foreseeable consequences of their support of groups engaged in illegal actions, whether the actions are called 'armed resistance' or whether the perpetrators are called terrorists. Established principles of international law and many specific decisions and actions strongly support the principle that a state violates its duties under international law if it supports or even knowingly tolerates within its territory activities constituting aggression against another state.[48]

Despite the Court's misstep, the author contends that Judge Schwebel's strong and well-reasoned dissent addressed critical issues that the majority judgment had blurred. Schwebel noted that the UN Definition of Aggression proscribes not only the 'sending' of 'armed bands, groups, irregulars, or mercenaries' to carry out 'acts of armed force', but also any 'substantial involvement therein'.[49] Schwebel's position finds support in Scott Malzahn's observation that:

> [w]hereas the judgment in the *Tehran Case* was met with general approval and approbation, the *Nicaragua* decision was criticized for its 'painstaking examination' of specific acts. The ICJ's act-by-act approach to *de facto* agency, reflected in Article 8 of the *ILC Draft Articles* requires proof of State authorization of each and every act carried out by private persons before the conduct is attributed to the State.[50]

In *Nicaragua*, the ICJ adopted an 'all-or-nothing' approach to state responsibility. In the absence of sufficient proof to demonstrate that the Contras were *de facto* agents of the US government, the US escaped any responsibility for the Contras' actions.[51] Despite the criticism of the case, one of its most important aspects was that the ICJ suggested that active support by a state constitutes a substantial degree of state control, which would be sufficient to legally charge a state for an 'armed attack' (as used in Article 51 of the UN Charter) committed by international terrorists within its borders.[52]

While state responsibility for terrorist activities actively supported by the state logically follows from the state's complicity in the offence,[53] more problematic is a state's responsibility for acts of terrorism that it failed to prevent. A state is not expected to prevent every act of international terrorism that originates from within its territory.[54] What is expected is that states exercise due diligence in the performance of their international obligations so as to take all reasonable measures under the circumstances to protect the rights and securities of other states.[55]

Professor Richard Lillich, a leading scholar on international terrorism and state responsibility,[56] agrees that customary international law expects states to prevent their territory from being used by terrorists for the preparation or commission of acts of terrorism against aliens within its territory or against the territory of another state.[57] Concurring with Professor Lillich, it is submitted that under international law, states are now under a general duty to carry out prevention of terrorism by exercising measures that are reasonable in the circumstances in order to prevent the occurrence of terrorist attacks.[58] The tolerance by a state of the use of its resources for terrorist activity against foreigners also serves as a basis for liability under state responsibility principles.[59] Indeed, it is rarely asserted that state acquiescence in or tolerance of acts of international terrorism is lawful – states are more inclined to deny that their action or inaction rises to the level of state support or that the alleged act of terror meets the legal definition of terrorism.

The ICJ jurisprudence discussed above and supported by writings of leading scholars leads the author to strongly support the position that Article 2(4) of the UN Charter implicitly prohibits state support of international terrorism by explicitly ordering all member states to 'refrain in their international relations from the threat or use of force against the territorial integrity or political independence of any state, or in any other manner inconsistent with the Purposes of the United Nations'.[60] This implied prohibition was made express in 1970 when the General Assembly approved Resolution 2625,[61] which states:

> Every State has the duty to refrain from organizing, instigating, assisting or participating in acts of civil strife or terrorist acts in another State or acquiescing in organized activities within its territory directed towards the commission of such acts, when the acts referred to in the present paragraph involve a threat or use of force. Also, no State shall organize, assist, foment, finance, incite or tolerate subversive, terrorist or armed activities directed towards the violent overthrow of the regime of another State, or interfere in civil strife in another State.[62]

Unlike Article 2(4) of the UN Charter, which only requires that states refrain from the threat or use of force, the Declaration Concerning Friendly Relations requires positive action on the part of the state so as not to acquiesce in or tolerate terrorist activities originating from within its territory. The Declaration Concerning Friendly Relations, though a General Assembly, resolution carries significant weight. As Scott Malzahn notes:

> [a]lthough passed only once, some commentators regard the Declaration Concerning Friendly Relations as an authoritative interpretation of the Charter of the UN because of the drafting committee's mandate to restate the fundamental principles of international law.[63]

In any case, there is a long-standing General Assembly practice of passing resolutions that condemn both active and passive state support of terrorism,[64] and in recent years, the Security Council has stated that 'all States shall [r]efrain from providing any form of support, active or passive, to entities or persons involved in terrorist acts …'.[65] This position is strongly articulated by the Draft Articles on the Responsibility of States for Internationally Wrongful Acts adopted in November

2001 by the International Law Commission (ILC). Article 8 of these Draft Articles provides: 'The conduct of a person or group of persons shall be considered an act of a state under international law if the person or group of persons is in fact acting on the instructions of, or under the direction or control of that state in carrying out the conduct.'[66]

Use of Force and State-sponsored Terrorism

The problem for the state-centric regime on the use of force is that terrorist groups do not claim to represent or constitute internationally recognized states. The drafters of the UN Charter were concerned with a completely different set of problems – the use of armed force by a state against the sovereignty, territorial integrity or political integrity or political independence of another state. Further, the traditional theories of customary international law were developed in a completely different era, with no concern for the danger presented by a modern well-financed terrorist organization in a world of chemical, biological and nuclear weapons capable of horrific destruction, yet portable by a single individual. A terrorist 'war' does not consist of a massive attack across an international border. Nor does it consist of one isolated incident that occurs and is then past. It is a drawn out, patient, sporadic pattern of attacks.

The first move to address force as a countermeasure against state-sponsored terrorism within the purview of the international system arose from within the statal sphere. In the early 1980s, the US and Israel forcefully pronounced and expressly linked military responses to counter terrorism to international law.[67] The move was clearly signalled amidst increased terrorist attacks against US interests and nationals. In 1983, the US Department of Defense Commission, in commenting upon the devastating attack on the US Marine Headquarters in Beirut, concluded:

> State sponsored terrorism is an important part of the spectrum of warfare and ... [An] adequate response to this increasing threat requires an active national policy which seeks to deter attack or reduce its effectiveness. The Commission further concludes that this policy needs to be supported by political and diplomatic actions and by a wide range of timely military response capabilities.[68]

A year later, then US President Ronald Reagan, signed the National Security Decision Directive which assigned responsibility for developing strategies for countering terrorism and made it clear that, while the US must use all the non-military weapons in its arsenal to the fullest, it must also be prepared to respond within the parameters set by the law of armed conflict. Robert McFarlane, a former Assistant to the President for National Security Affairs, suggested at a Defense Strategy Forum on 25 March 1985, that the directive supported resistance by force to state-sponsored terrorism 'by all legal means'.[69] The Vice-President's Task Force refined this construct and explained that: 'States that practice terrorism or actively support it will not do so without consequence. If there is evidence that a State is mounting or intends to conduct an act of terrorism against this country, the United States will take measures to protect its citizens, property and interests.'[70]

Israel took the lead in practically christening the US policy. On 1 October 1985, Israeli jets bombed the PLO Headquarters in Tunis, asserting that it was being used to launch attacks on Israel and Israelis in other places. The US denounced the bombing but abstained from voting on a Security Council resolution that, among other things, condemned 'vigorously the act of armed aggression perpetrated by Israel against Tunisian territory in flagrant violation of the Charter of the United Nations, international law and norms of conduct'.[71] The US opposed the Israeli action on the basis of policy, not legal, considerations.[72] As Sofaer notes, the US was reluctant to criticize the legality of the act owing to its support of 'the right of a state to strike terrorists within the territory of another state where the terrorists are using that territory as a location from which to launch terrorist attacks and where the state involved has failed to respond effectively to a demand that the attacks be stopped'.[73]

Sofaer's incisive observation is supported by Ambassador Vernon Walters – the US Ambassador to the UN at the time – who stated that the US regarded such an attack as a proper measure of self-defence where it is necessary to prevent attacks launched from that base.[74] The legal/policy binary gained further amplification later in the same year, in December, when several airline passengers were killed by terrorists in simultaneous attacks at the Rome and Vienna airports, including five Americans; many more were wounded.[75] An incensed US moved swiftly to impose drastic sanctions short of force. Significantly, then US President Ronald Reagan announced:

> By providing material support to terrorist groups which attack US citizens, Libya has engaged in armed aggression against the US under established principles of international law, just as if he [Qadhafi] had used its own armed forces ... If these [economic and political] steps do not end Qadhafi's terrorism, I promise you that further steps will be taken.[76]

Libya had effectively been placed on notice. On 5 April 1986, Le Belle discotheque in West Germany, a popular hang-out for off-duty American servicemen, was bombed leaving two Americans dead and 154 people injured.[77] President Reagan responded by bombing military targets in Tripoli and Benghazi on 15 April 1986. In addition, Reagan stated: 'I warned that there should be no place on earth where terrorists can rest and train and practice their skills. I meant it. I said that we would act with others if possible and alone if necessary to ensure that terrorists have no sanctuary anywhere.' Despite the US claim that the Berlin bombing had actually been ordered by the Libyan Government, the US action was widely condemned. The UN General Assembly adopted a resolution condemning the US.[78] A proposed Security Council resolution condemning the US action failed to pass, owing to vetoes by the US, the United Kingdom and France.[79]

'As the threat of transnational terrorism became more apparent, however, the world community became more tolerant of military actions against states that supported terrorism.'[80] There was little objection to the 1993 cruise missile attacks against Iraq for its role in the foiled assassination attempt on former President George Bush Sr. In 1998, when the US bombed terrorist targets in Afghanistan and Sudan, the world reaction to the US attacks against Afghanistan was unquestionably muted. While the criticism of the bombing of the pharmaceutical factory in Sudan was more intense, the protest was largely confined to the quantity of proof presented by the US that chemical weapons were processed at the factory.[81]

In the aftermath of the September 11 attacks, the statements were more strident and unequivocal. On the day of the attacks, President George Bush Jr stated succinctly, 'We will make no distinction between the terrorists who committed these acts and those who harbor them.'[82] On 16 September 2001, Vice-President Cheney stated that 'if you provide sanctuary to terrorists, you face the full wrath of the United States of America'.[83] Earlier, Congress, in its joint resolution on 14 September 2001, had authorized the use of force against those who 'aided' or 'harbored' those who carried out the September 11 attacks, as well as those who committed the attacks.[84]

In a speech before a joint session of Congress on 20 September 2001, President Bush strongly echoed the resolution's stipulations, noting: 'From this day forward, any nation that continues to harbor or support terrorism will be regarded by the US as a hostile regime',[85] and later elaborated in sweeping terms: 'America has a message for the nations of the world: If you harbor terrorists, you are terrorists. If you train or arm a terrorist, you are a terrorist. If you feed a terrorist or fund a terrorist, you're a terrorist, and you will be held accountable by the US and our friends.'[86]

The policy reflected by these statements, to treat those who harbour terrorists no differently than the terrorists themselves, was described by White House spokesman Ari Fleischer as 'a dramatic change in American policy'.[87] 'Yet, despite the breadth of these statements and others, and although they appeared seriously at odds with the decisions in the *Nicaragua* and *Iran Hostages* cases, the world community barely voiced an objection. Instead, nations either said little about this "dramatic change" in US policy or appeared to endorse it.'[88] Professor Ileana M. Porras argues that: 'The world reaction – or more accurately, the lack of a world reaction – to the consistently repeated US position is perhaps the strongest manifestation of evolving customary international law regarding the use of force against terrorism.'[89]

The question that arises especially after post-September 11 is: to what extent may a state lawfully respond with armed force against the state that has sponsored the terrorists deemed responsible for the attack? Under international law, the response of a targeted state is predicated on principles of self-defence, and these are in turn based on what the international community regards as the 'inherent' right to ensure national security and the attendant duty to protect one's citizens from terrorist attacks.[90] The norms of self-defence revolve around survival, and a state's inherent right to protect and defend its sovereignty; this in turn brings into play the UN Charter regime on the use of force vis-à-vis terrorism.

Military Force in the Context of Self-defence

Despite the forceful pronunciations of the US that were backed by actual military responses to counter terrorism, from the international legal perspective, purported defensive responses to state-sponsored terrorism need to be valid under customary and conventional legal requirements. Managing the terrorist threat posed by state sponsors requires identification of the threat, clear establishment of linkage to a state sponsor and, in the event of use of military force, the meeting of the dual legal requirements of self-defence – necessity and proportionality.[91] The problem is that often responses to terrorism are coloured, often negatively, by the reality that states intertwine responses with their own national interest. This reality weakens the substantive international legal bases which support military action, despite frequent justifications that action is supported in customary international law by the inherent right of self-defence and a realistic interpretation of Article 51 of the UN Charter, which takes into account modern weapons capabilities.

Any move to endorse the right of states to attack terrorist organizations located in other states with military force must necessarily be consistent with the requirements of Article 2(4) of the UN Charter. Professor Gregory M. Travalio has suggested that Article 2(4) can only be used if the degree of support by the host state is to such an extent that terrorists are effectively the instruments through which the armed forces of that state are exercised.[92] To use force under circumstances where the host country is merely supporting terrorists indirectly would amount to a breach of Article 2(4), which precludes the use of force against the political independence or territorial integrity of the host country.

However, if terrorism is state-sponsored, other nations can direct their response to terrorist attacks at the state itself (in addition to the terrorist groups). If it can be established that state-sponsored terrorism exists, then the sponsoring state may be in violation of Article 2(4). This article has been interpreted to apply to non-member states as well.[93] That provision was applied in Resolution 748[94] in 1992 to impose economic sanctions on Libya for its connection with terrorist activities and for its refusal to extradite two Libyan nationals alleged to have participated in the 1988 bombing of Pan Am Flight 103 over Lockerbie, Scotland.[95] Resolution 748 stated: 'Every State has the duty to refrain from organizing, instigating, assisting or participating in terrorist acts in another State or acquiescing in organized activities within its territory directed towards the commission of such acts, when such acts involve a threat or use of force.'[96] In addition, the UN has this explication of state-sponsored terrorism affecting regions outside a state:

> Every State has the duty to refrain from organizing or encouraging the organization of irregular forces or armed bands including mercenaries, for incursion into the territory of another State. Every State has the duty to refrain from organizing, instigating, assisting or participating in acts of civil strife or terrorist acts in another State or acquiescing in organized activities within its territory directed towards the commission of such acts, when the acts referred to in the present paragraph involve a threat or use of force.[97]

This has been interpreted to constrain states from the maintenance of terrorist training camps in the techniques of assassination, destruction and sabotage; the direct or indirect collection of funds; the provision of direct financing for training camps and other programmes; the purchase of arms, ammunition and explosives; and preparation of foreign propaganda.[98] When the location of a terrorist camp is known and the territorial state refuses to cooperate within the 'extradite or prosecute' framework laid down by international conventions,[99] domestic law enforcement is completely ineffective in defending a state and its interests abroad. In this situation where states openly engage in, or support, acts of violence and attacks on another state, an appropriate response of the victim state may be the use of armed force.[100]

Although arguably effective and temporarily satisfying, the important concern is whether a policy of armed response is wise in view of its probable violation of international law. If a state concludes that an illegal use of force is too costly a response, the state is left with a limited choice of alternatives for dealing with terrorist incidents. Countries are therefore in search of a permissible and effective response in order to thwart terrorism. That search has led to the use of Article 51 of the UN Charter, the claim of self-defence, as a way of legitimizing the use of armed force. Article 51 permits a victimized state to engage in 'individual or collective self-defence' until recourse has been taken by the Security Council to establish peace.[101] Nothing in the UN Charter restricts the identity of aggressors against whom states may respond, since private agents as well as governments may be the sources of aggression.

Self-defence in the Context of State-sponsored Terrorism   Self-defence was addressed by the drafters of the UN Charter in the context of large-scale attacks by the regular armed forces of one state against the territory of another, not the mere harbouring of a terrorist group[102] or support of the same. However, use of Article 51 of the UN Charter to defend a state's decision to use armed force against terrorists and terrorist havens is not novel.[103] Although the right of self-defence may be described as 'inherent',[104] even the UN Charter does not specify what is intended by the word.[105] This has been interpreted by a number of international law scholars to mean that the right of self-defence is one which antedates and exists independently of the UN Charter.[106]

Even allowing for the view that the right of self-defence antedates the UN Charter and continues to exist, it should be noted that in contrast to international customary law, the UN Charter appears to have added a new requirement to the 'inherent' right – the occurrence of an 'armed attack'. It is unclear whether this new criteria was intended to narrow the existing right of self-defence. Even if this is the intention, it is equally unclear how and to what extent the right is limited. There appears to be no discussion of the phrase 'armed attack' in the records of the United Nations Conference on International Organization (UNCIO).

One explanation might be that the drafters felt that the words themselves were sufficiently clear. Given that the main concern of the UN Charter is the unilateral use of force, the prerequisites of an actual attack by armed forces would severely limit such action. Therefore, the UN Charter may be interpreted as limiting the use of force to only those situations involving the most serious and dangerous forms of threats to international peace.

It is also significant that the drafters chose the word 'attack' over the term "aggression" which is used repeatedly throughout the UN Charter. Even then, under the UN Charter the term 'aggression' is undefined but can be logically presumed to have a wider meaning than 'attack'.[107] The determination of 'aggression' is, however, entrusted to the Security Council based on a case-by-case basis of whether a particular action constitutes unlawful aggression. While arguably the drafters at UNCIO chose this more flexible system because 'the progress of the technique of modern warfare renders very difficult the definition of all cases of aggression',[108] there is no evidence to suggest that such flexibility and subjectivity was to be accorded to the exercise of the right of self-defence. As Professor J.E.S. Fawcett points out:

> It could be said that there is some evidence that the drafters of the *Charter* used the precise and restrictive notion of 'armed attack' in preference to 'aggression' or 'threat to the peace', precisely because they wished to avoid giving too much latitude within the *Charter* system to the recognized right of self-defence ...[109]

Though legality of the use of force under international law, *jus ad bellum*, is instructive in matters relating to state-sponsored terrorism, the nature of terrorism renders this concept rather vague and blurred, since terrorism does not fall easily into traditional principles of international law. Terrorists are not state actors bound by international law, but rather are similar to criminals in that they act outside of the scope of law.[110] This condition presents states with an intractable problem – how to respond legally to groups who are not adhering to legal strictures.

It is arguable that well-organized terrorist groups with the means to reach across international borders and inflict significant damage on a country on an ongoing basis, such as Al-Qaeda, must represent the sort of threat against which self-defence is legitimate if the doctrine is to have any practical contemporary value. There are no obvious examples of UN members claiming that the 1998 missile strikes against Al-Qaeda camps could not be acts of self-defence because the alleged perpetrators of the embassy bombings were a non-state group. State practice would therefore seem to support the hypothesis that an Article 51 'armed attack' may be perpetrated by a non-state group. In any case, the symbiotic relationship of Al-Qaeda in Afghanistan and the Taliban regime meant that at least the Al-Qaeda leadership could not be seen purely as a non-state entity, and that the Taliban shared significant responsibility for Al-Qaeda's actions in the September 11 attack. Nonetheless, depending on the factual circumstances, the definition of the terrorist acts of September 11 as 'armed attacks' may not necessarily imply that the concept actually refers to acts that are attributable to a state.[111]

Resort to Retaliatory Strikes   Frustration with the legal strictures inherent in the concept of self-defence in the face of the ever-increasing threat of terrorism and the inability to root out terrorist groups, have led states such as the US and Israel to resort to retaliatory strikes against terrorist cells located in sovereign states. These states contend that terrorist threats represent a legitimate justification for the use of force abroad. The idea of strategic deterrence of future terrorist attacks is not without controversy, considering that the UN Charter and customary international law authorize the use of force only for self-defence. When the UN Charter was drafted in 1945, the right of self-defence was the only included exception to the prohibition of the use of force, though customary international law had previously accepted reprisal, retaliation and retribution as legitimate responses as well.[112]

Reprisals and retaliatory strikes are illegal under contemporary international law because they are punitive, rather than legitimate, actions of self-defence.[113] It would be difficult to reconcile acts of reprisal with the overriding dictate in the UN Charter that all disputes must be settled by peaceful means. Further, under the UN Charter regarding self-defence, there are three main principles that go into examining the *jus ad bellum* dimensions of a state's response if it has suffered a terrorist attack. These principles dealing with the timeliness of the response and the requirements of necessity and proportionality are difficult to reconcile with retaliatory strikes.

In customary law, conventional law and *opinio juris*, the practice of reprisals through the use of unilateral force has been denounced.[114] A sharp distinction has also been drawn between the use of force in self-defence and its use in reprisals.[115] The legal status of reprisals is stated very succinctly by Professor Ian Brownlie: '[t]he provisions of the Charter relating to the peaceful settlement of disputes and non-resort to the use of force are universally regarded as prohibiting reprisals which involve the use of force.'[116] Since 1953, the use of force by way of reprisals has been strongly condemned by the UN as an illegal use of force under the UN Charter.[117]

Cast against the backdrop of the survey above on the use of force to counter terrorism, the legal response to the September 11 attacks was unusual. The international community broadly qualified the September 11 attacks as 'armed attacks' against the US, justifying the exercise of self-defence with quasi-unanimous statements of support coupled with offers of assistance to the US to facilitate the military action that soon followed.[118] By recognizing the 'inherent right of individual and collective self-defence' in the preambles of Resolution 1368 and Resolution 1373,[119] the doctrine of self-defence clearly underlies the military strikes against the Taliban in 2001. The main question is how the events of September 11 affect the interpretation of the 'armed attack' requirement under the UN Charter. It is this difficult question that the next section of the chapter considers.

Expanding the Definition of Armed Attack

The right of self-defence laid down in Article 51 of the UN Charter, being the only exception to the prohibition of force of practical significance, is the pivotal point upon which disputes concerning the lawfulness of the use of force in inter-state relations usually concentrates. Commenting on the practical implications of Article 51, Professor Ian Brownlie explains that:

> It is believed that the ordinary meaning of the phrase precludes action which is preventive in character ... There is no further clarification of the phrase to be gained from study of the *travaux preparatoires*. However, the discussions at San Francisco assumed that any permission for the unilateral use of force would be exceptional and would be secondary to the general prohibition in Article 2, paragraph 4. There was a presumption against self-help and even action in self-defence within Article 51 was made subject to control by the Security Council. In these circumstances the precision of Article 51 is explicable.[120]

A major question is whether the right of self-defence under Article 51 is limited to cases of 'armed attack' or whether there are other instances in which self-defence may be available. A number of writers argue that an 'armed attack' is the exclusive circumstance in which the use of armed force is sanctioned under Article 51.[121] Furthermore, the ICJ in *Nicaragua* clearly stated that the right of self-defence under Article 51 only accrues in the event of an 'armed attack'.[122] Also, it is a traditional requirement of self-defence that a triggering event justifying a military response has already occurred or at least be imminent.[123]

When a state harbouring[124] terrorists provides active support for the terrorist group, as distinguished from mere tolerance and encouragement, there is a raging debate among international lawyers over whether, and under what circumstances, such support can constitute an 'armed attack', under Article 51 of the UN Charter, against the target state. On this point there is considerable authority for the proposition that under some circumstances active support to terrorist groups can constitute an 'armed attack' against another state. For example, Professor Oscar Schachter has stated that 'when a government provides weapons, technical advice, transportation, aid and encouragement to terrorists on a substantial scale it is not unreasonable to conclude that the armed attack is imputable to that government'.[125]

The *Nicaragua Case* is the most analogous on this issue. In the *Nicaragua Case*, the ICJ rejected the claim of the US that the support of Nicaragua to the rebels in El Salvador justified the use of force by the US against Nicaragua in self-defence under Article 51. The Court said clearly that the provision of weapons or logistical support by one state to the opposition in another state is not an 'armed attack' under Article 51.[126] Consequently, this opinion suggests that even active support by a state to terrorist groups would not be an armed attack under Article 51. *Nicaragua*, however, is far from directly on point and leaves many questions unanswered. For example, what if the support includes not only weapons and logistical support, but includes the provision of training and a secure base of operations? Does it change matters if the terrorists might have access to weapons of mass destruction? Might support to terrorists acting trans-nationally be sufficient to be an armed attack against a target state even though support to an armed opposition located within the target country would not? None of these questions is addressed by *Nicaragua*. Professor Rosalyn Higgins indicates that if the support reaches a sufficient scale, it can constitute an 'armed attack' for the purpose of Article 51.[127] Other commentators support the idea that the level of support to terrorist groups can rise to a level sufficient to become an armed attack under Article 51.[128]

Apart from reference to phrases in Article 2(4) to which it is sought to give a restricted meaning, it can be argued that Articles 2(4) and 51 were not intended to, and do not, restrict the right of member states to use force in self-defence within the meaning of that concept to be found in the customary law. Article 51, it is said, refers merely to 'armed attack' because it was inserted for the particular purpose of clarifying the position of defence treaties which are concerned only with external attack, and being in this way specific, it leaves the broader customary right, which is always implicitly reserved, intact. Professor Derek Bowett's view supports the position that Article 2(4) left the right of self-defence unimpaired and that the right implicitly accepted was not confined to reaction to 'armed attack' within Article 51, but permitted the protection of certain substantive rights:

> Action undertaken for the purpose of, and limited to, the defence of a State's political independence, territorial integrity, the lives and property of its nationals (and even to protect its economic independence) cannot by definition involve a threat or use of force 'against the territorial integrity or political independence' of any other State.[129]

However, a significant number of commentators argue that the right to use force in self-defence under Article 51 is not limited to cases of 'armed attack'.[130] As Professor Travalio observes:

> These commentators generally argue that the intention of the drafters of the *United Nations Charter* was to incorporate into Article 51 all of the rights of self-defence that existed in customary international law at the time of the *Charter*. In addition, the International Court of Justice in the *Nicaragua Case* indicated that the right of self-defence in Article 51 simply recognized a pre-existing right of customary international law.[131]

It has been argued that because the customary right of self-defence includes instances in addition to an 'armed attack', military force may be legally available as an option against terrorists even if an 'armed attack' has not occurred. This view holds that the presence of an 'armed attack' is one of the bases for the exercise of the right of self-defence under Article 51, but not the exclusive basis.[132] Professor Oscar Schachter sums up this position thus:

> On one reading [of Article 51,] this means that self-defence is limited to cases of armed attack. An alternative reading holds that since the article is silent as to the right of self-defence under customary law (which goes beyond cases of armed attack) it should not be construed by implication to eliminate that right ... It is therefore not implausible to interpret article 51 as leaving unimpaired the right of self-defence as it existed prior to the *Charter*.[133]

Richard Erickson, in his monograph on international terrorism and the use of military force, states that 'the traditional view is that State toleration or encouragement is an insufficient State connection' to constitute an 'armed attack' under Article 51 of the UN Charter.[134] This position is shared by a number of other commentators and can be readily supported by arguments distilled from provisions in the UN Charter.[135] Even if the right of self-defence extends beyond the 'armed attack' provision of Article 51, there are, at the very least, serious hurdles that must be overcome before self-defence, as traditionally understood, can be used to justify attacks against terrorists or terrorist facilities located in another state.

A Silent Revolution: Armed Attacks and Non-statal Entities   The terrorist attacks against the World Trade Centre and the Pentagon seemed to create a political will to adapt the concept of self-defence to a new threat – the threat of large-scale terrorist attacks against nations as such. For traditional self-defence scenarios, the restrictive interpretation of Article 51 would still be valid, but in defence of 'open societies' against the new threat, there was a widespread feeling among political decision-makers that preventive military action should no longer be ruled out.[136]

Particularly important was the meeting of the UN Security Council on 8 October 2001. The Council had met to receive information on and discuss the US–UK bombings of targets in Afghanistan which had started the preceding day. In a statement by the President of the Council, it was underlined that the military action had been reported to the Council as measures of self-defence.[137] The Council members were reported to have received the presentation of the US and the UK appreciatively.[138] No member of the Council, the most important body of the international community, objected to the new interpretation of Article 51.[139]

Before September 11, Article 51 of the UN Charter was generally interpreted in a restrictive fashion. Most states (with the exception of the US and Israel) did not recognize a right of self-defence against terrorist networks hiding in territories of other states. Nor did a majority of states recognize the legitimacy of military action intended to prevent future attacks. Self-defence was seen as an action of immediate response to an ongoing armed attack. Preventive or anticipatory self-defence was more or less ruled out. However, the terrorist attacks on September 11 marked a turning point in the international regime on the use of force. The world community moved to embrace certain acts of terrorism as an act of war. This poses new challenges for the historically fixed international rules relating to self-defence, especially since the international community largely assented to the invocation of self-defence as a legal basis for the use of force initiated by the US and the UK against Afghanistan on 7 October 2001.

September 11 ignited heated debate and discourse as to whether the concept of 'armed attack' as contained in Article 51 must originate from a state (government) rather than a non-state actor like Al-Qaeda.[140] In its preamble, Resolution 1368 'recogni[zes] the inherent right of individual or collective self-defence in accordance with the Charter'.[141] The recognition that acts of private actors may give rise to an 'armed attack' is anything but revolutionary. The term 'armed attack' was traditionally applied to states, but nothing in the UN Charter indicates that 'armed attacks' can only emanate from states. The main question is whether a terrorist act must be in some form attributable to another state in order to qualify as an 'armed attack' for the purposes of the UN Charter.

It is not entirely clear from the practice in the aftermath of September 11 whether the requirement of the attribution of a terrorist act to a specific state actor was, in fact, fully abandoned. The North Atlantic Treaty Organization (NATO), for instance, introduced an interesting new formula when determining whether the September 11 attacks amounted to 'armed attacks'. It did not expressly inquire whether the attacks were 'attributable' to the Taliban or Afghanistan, but instead asked whether 'the attack against the United States on September 11 was directed from abroad' and could therefore 'be regarded as an action covered by Article 5 of the Washington Treaty'.[142]

It may be of greater consequence to admit openly that the requirement of attribution does not play a role in the definition of 'armed attack'. A similar argument can be made with regard to 'armed attacks' under Article 51. One may argue that the criterion of the attribution of an 'armed attack' is only relevant in the context of the question towards whom the forcible response may be directed, but not in the context of the definition of an 'armed attack'. Carsten Stahn postulates that 'the main criteria to determine whether a terrorist attack falls within the scope of application of Article 51 should not be attributability, but whether the attack presents an external link to the state victim of the attack'.[143]

Reviewing the relationship between Articles 2(4) and 51 vis-à-vis other coercive uses of force, Professor Myres McDougal states:

> Article 2(4) refers to both the threat and use of force and commits the Members to refrain from 'threat or use of force against the territorial integrity or political independence of any

state, or in any other manner inconsistent with the Purposes of the United Nations'; the customary right of defence, as limited by the requirements of necessity and proportionality, can scarcely be regarded as inconsistent with the purposes of the United Nations, and a decent respect for balance and effectiveness would suggest that a conception of impermissible coercion, which includes threats of force, should be countered with an equally comprehensive and adequate conception of permissible or defensive coercion[.][144]

In an exposition of the significance of Professor McDougal's statement, Lieutenant Colonel James Perry notes that:

In Professor McDougal's interpretation is the recognition of the right to counter the imminent threat of unlawful coercion as well as an actual attack. This comprehensive conception of permissible or defensive coercion, honouring appropriate response to threats of an imminent nature, is merely reflective of the customary international law. It is precisely this anticipatory element of lawful self-defence that is critical to an effective policy to counter state-sponsored terrorism…[145]

The premise of this contention is that self-defence is an inherent right whose contours have been shaped by custom and subject to customary interpretation. Thus, although the drafters of Article 51 may not have anticipated its use in protecting states from the effects of terrorist violence, international law recognizes the need for flexible application if the constitutive nature of the UN Charter is to have any meaning.

Nonetheless, even though the language of Article 51 may be thought to lend itself to an expansive interpretation, so that the manner in which a state protects itself from suffering a further terrorist attack must be flexible, this would permit any state to employ force against those who they believe to be responsible for the attack when a terrorist attack occurs or is imminent.[146] Though self-defence was addressed by the drafters of the UN Charter in the context of large-scale attacks by the regular armed forces of one state against (the territory of) another, not the mere harbouring of a terrorist group, it can be argued that, given the radically different contemporary realities compared to 1949, Article 51 needs to be interpreted more broadly.

Considering that the preferred *modus operandi* of terrorist organizations is a drawn out, patient, sporadic pattern of attacks, it is very difficult to know when or where the next incident will occur. This state of affairs was simply not contemplated at the time the UN Charter was drafted. As observed by Professor Travalio:

Reasonable arguments can be made that the definition of 'armed attack' should be interpreted to include the purposeful harbouring of international terrorists. The potential destructive capacity of weapons of mass destruction, the modest means required to deliver them, and the substantial financial resources of some terrorist organizations, combine to make the threat posed by some terrorist organizations much greater than that posed by the militaries of many states.[147]

The UN was founded on the unfulfilled promise that the UN Security Council would protect international peace and security and in return, states would forgo self-help in favour of collective-help. The reality is that the UN Charter system is not strongly coherent or controlling. It is arguable that in the face of the reality of the alleged weaknesses of the UN system in guaranteeing peace and security, the right of self-defence under Article 51 ought to be read to include all of the rights of self-defence that existed in customary international law at the time it was drafted.[148] Indeed, the customary right of self-defence has included instances in which military force might be legally appropriate as self-defence, even when no 'armed attack' has occurred.[149]

Conclusion

As a matter of public international law, terrorism presents several problems: the identification of terrorists is often difficult; the inconsistent international legal system fails to deter terrorist operations; and the complicated cross-border nature of terrorist networks makes it difficult to effectively diminish the threat. In the face of these problems, states that are targeted by terrorists essentially have two options in responding. If the terrorists are located within the target state's borders, they may be captured and prosecuted under domestic criminal laws. However, as is frequently the case, if terrorists are located outside the target state, military strikes against them may be undertaken. However, this frequently involves incursions into neutral sovereign states. Though it is clear that effective deterrence demands that terrorists do not have safe havens and that terrorists must fear that they will ultimately pay a price for their criminal mayhem, there is no indication that the world community is prepared to accept the use of force against sovereign territories in pursuit of modern terrorists, since fundamental principles of the international system will be breached.

There is no doubt from the discussion above that the distinction between 'armed attacks' and 'terrorist acts' has become blurred in the aftermath of the acts that took place on September 11, possibly because of the enormous consequences of this event. By 'recognizing the inherent right of individual or collective self-defence in accordance with the Charter' a preambular paragraph of Resolution 1368 appeared to imply that the terrorist acts in New York, Washington and Pennsylvania represented an 'armed attack' within the meaning of Article 51 of the UN Charter.[150] A similar preambular paragraph was also included in Resolution 1373.[151] Even more explicit was the statement that an 'armed attack' occurred, made by NATO on 12 September 2001, which states that if it were deemed that the attack on the US was from abroad, it would fall within the ambit of Article 5 of the Washington Treaty, which in turn states: 'an armed attack against one or more of the Allies in Europe or North America shall be considered an attack against them all.'[152]

The significance of September 11 lies in the apparent official recognition by states that acts of terrorism carried out by independent private actors fit, albeit somewhat uneasily, within the parameters of Article 51. However, the events of September 11 have another more profound impact on the law of self-defence – they affect the system itself. Stahn has postulated that the effects of September 11 are likely to be a strengthening of Article 51 as a 'Grundnorm governing the unilateral use of force by states against armed violence'.[153] The corollary of this is a broadened concept of 'armed attack' with a relaxation of the nexus concerning the act of terrorism to state actors. Stahn postulates that the relaxation in the nexus will lead to a long-run increase in the invocation and extension of the scope of Article 51.[154] Another ramification of September 11 is 'a growing focus on the use of force in response to violence on Article 51. The lowered threshold for attributing terrorist acts to non-State actors will push States to rely on Article 51 to justify military means, rather than invoke a right to self-defence under customary law or the existence of a State of necessity'.[155]

In principle, the growing centralization of the system around Article 51 is a desirable development. An expansion of Article 51 is preferable to the creation of unwritten exceptions under the UN Charter because it does not further erode the prohibition of the use of force under Article 2(4), but simply opens a broader spectrum of justifications for what continues to be unlawful conduct under Article 2(4). A broadening of the 'law of justification' is much less detrimental to the regulatory framework of the UN Charter than a limitation of its prohibitory character. In addition, Article 51 presents the decisive advantage of containing inherent limits to self-defence, leaving less room for abuse than an (unlimited) exception to Article 2(4). In the enthusiastic words of Stahn:

> On a more general level, the broadening of the notion of armed attack to include acts of terrorism by non-state actors such as al-Qaeda may ... be viewed as a recognition of the adaptability of the system from within. It avoids the perpetuation of the Kosovo dilemma, namely, the emergence of categories of uses of force that may be said to be 'illegal but justifiable' while further isolating the 'Glennonists' of international law, who call into question the viability of the *Charter* rules on the use of force. Moreover, many of the dangers of a broad definition of the notion of 'armed attack' may be attenuated by a reasonable application of the principles of necessity and proportionality, which are the cornerstones of the permissibility of the use of force in self-defence.[156]

Whatever the particular circumstances, policymakers and lawyers must keep in mind that there are significant potential dangers in expanding the category of 'armed attack' in Article 51 beyond its obvious meaning of a direct attack by the military of one state against the territory, property or population of another. It does seem to stretch the common understanding of the term to suggest that a state has committed an 'armed attack' against another by tolerating persons on its soil who are, in one view, nothing more than criminals. Too loose a definition of 'armed attack' invites future abuse and undermines the predictability of international law regarding the use of force. Moreover, while the right of self-defence, even against armed attack, is subject to limitations of proportionality and necessity, it is generally accepted that self-defence against an armed attack includes both a right to repel the attack and, in limited cases, to take the war to the aggressor state to prevent a recurrence.

The terrorist threat posed by biological, chemical or nuclear attacks is chilling, but intervention to prevent the sinister marriage of international terrorism and weapons of mass destruction presents serious questions of legitimacy. It is not necessarily in the interest of the international community to make the category of 'armed attack' under Article 51 so broad and potentially open-ended that nations harbouring groups committing violent acts in other states will be considered to have made armed attacks on the target state. Further, the scope of a nation's permissible military response is almost certainly greater in the event of an 'armed attack' by another state than in other situations in which a more limited military response might be justified, and a broad definition of 'armed attack', including occasions where states are simply harbouring terrorists, would too readily justify the robust use of military force.

Notes

1   See Spencer Crona and Neal Richardson (1996), 'Justice for War Criminals of Invisible Armies: A New Legal and Military Approach to Terrorism', 21 *Oklahoma City University Law Review* 349, 355.
2   Ibid., 350–4.
3   For example, *Convention on Offences and Certain Other Acts Committed On Board Aircraft* (Tokyo Convention), opened for signature 14 September 1963, 704 U.N.T.S. 219; *Convention for the Suppression of Unlawful Seizure of Aircraft* (Hague Convention), opened for signature 16 December 1970, 860 U.N.T.S. 105; *Convention for the Suppression of Unlawful Acts Against the Safety of Civil Aviation* (Montreal Convention), opened for signature 23 September 1971, 974 U.N.T.S. 177; *Protocol for the Suppression of Unlawful Acts of Violence at Airports Serving Civil Aviation*, ICAO Doc. 9518; reprinted in 27 I.L.M. 627 among others.
4   See Bradley Larschan (1986), 'Legal Aspects to the Control of Transnational Terrorism; An Overview', 13 *Ohio Northern University Law Review* 117, 140–4.
5   Ibid., 134.
6   Davis Brown (2003), 'Use of Force Against Terrorism after September 11th: State Responsibility, Self-Defense and Other Responses', 11 *Cardozo Journal of International & Comparative Law* 1, 2.
7   Ibid.
8   Ibid.
9   *Nicaragua v United States of America (Merits)* [1986] I.C.J. Rep 14.
10   Krzysztof Skubiszewski (1989), 'Definition of Terrorism', 19 *Israel Yearbook of Human Rights* 39, 45.
11   See, e.g., G.A. Res 31/102, U.N. GAOR, 31st sess, 99th plen mtg, U.N. Doc A/RES/31/102 (1976); G.A. Res 34/145, U.N. GAOR, 34th sess, 105th plen mtg, U.N. Doc A/RES/34/145 (1979); G.A. Res 38/130, U.N. GAOR, 38th sess, 101st mtg, U.N. Doc A/RES/38/130 (1983); G.A. Res 44/29, U.N. GAOR, 44th sess, 72nd plen mtg, U.N. Doc A/RES/44/29 (1989); G.A. Res 46/51, U.N. GAOR, 46th sess, 67th plen mtg, U.N. Doc A/Res/46/51 (1991); G.A. Res 51/210, U.N. GAOR, 51st sess, 88th plen mtg, U.N. Doc A/RES/51/210 (1996); G.A. Res 53/108, U.N. GAOR, 53rd sess, 83rd plen mtg, Agenda Item 155, U.N. Doc A/RES/53/108 (1999); G.A. Res 56/160, U.N. GAOR, 56th sess, 88th plen mtg, Agenda Item 119b, U.N. Doc A/RES/56/160 (2001) (*'General Assembly Resolutions'*).
12   I. L. Oppenheim (8th ed. 1955) H. Lauterpacht), *International Law*, London; New York: Longmans & Green, 337–38, 365.
13   G.A. Res No 2625, U.N. Doc No A/8018 (1970).
14   Ibid., G. A. Res. 40/61, U.N. Doc No A/RES/40/61 (1985); S. C. Res. 748, U.N. Doc No S/RES/748 (1992).
15   Abraham D. Sofaer (1989), 'The Sixth Annual Waldemar A. Solf Lecture in International Law: Terrorism, the Law, and the National Defense', 126 *Military Law Review* 89, 99.
16   Thomas Franck and Oskar Niedermeyer (1989), 'Accommodating Terrorism: An Offense against the Law of Nations', *Tel Aviv University Law Review*.

17   International Status of South West Africa Case, 1950 I.C.J. 146, 148 (Sep. Op. McNair, J.) (Advisory Opinion). Principles recognized by civilized nations have been relied on by the ICJ in formulating international law in several cases.

18   Sofaer, 'The Sixth Annual Waldemar A. Solf Lecture', 100-101.

19   See, e.g., statement of President Assad of Syria, in *Time*, 3 April 1989, 30.

20   *Corfu Channel Case* (UK v Albania) 1949 I.C.J. 4 (Judgment, 9 April 1949).

21   Michael Lohr (1985), 'Legal Analysis of US Military Responses to State-Sponsored International Terrorism', 34 *Naval Law Review* 1, 9-10.

22   Ian Brownlie (1983), *System of the Law of Nations, State Responsibility*, Oxford [Oxfordshire]; New York: Clarendon Press, 165.

23   Michael Lohr (1985), 'Legal Analysis of US Military Responses to State-Sponsored International Terrorism', 34 *Naval Law Review* 1, 7.

24   Brownlie, *System of the Law of Nations*, Part I, 236.

25   *Moore's Digest of International Law* (1970), New York: AMS Press, 999.

26   *American Mexican Claims Commission, Report to the U.S. Secretary of State*, reprinted in Marjorie M. Whiteman (1967), *Whiteman Digest of International Law*, Washington DC: U.S. Dept. of State; U.S. Govt. Printing Office, Vol. 8, 748, 753.

27   Benson Latin American Collection, Rare Books and Manuscripts, Inventory, Collection Relating to the General Claims Commission, United States and Mexico, Extract, 12 August 2004 online at http://www.lib.utexas.edu/benson/Mex_Archives/ Claims_Commission.html.

28   *Corfu Channel Case* (UK v. Albania.) 1949 I.C.J. 4, 22 (Judgment on the Merits); Case Concerning United States Diplomatic and Consular Staff in Tehran (U.S. v. Iran), 1980 I.C.J. 32–33, 36.

29   [1980] I.C.J. Rep 3 (*'Tehran Hostages'*).

30   Ibid., 74.

31   For example, following the occupation of the US Embassy in Iran by militant students, expressions of approval came 'from numerous Iranian authorities, including religious, judicial, executive, police and broadcasting authorities'. The International Court of Justice found that the action of these responsible Iranian authorities transformed the students' occupation of the embassy and detention of the hostages into acts of the Iranian state. Brownlie, *System of the Law of Nations, State Responsibility*, 1571.

32   *Nicaragua v United States of America (Merits)* [1986] I.C..J Rep 14.

33   Ibid., 126–127.

34   Ibid., 109.

35   Ibid., 108.

36   Ibid., 109.

37   Ibid.

38   Greg Travalio and John Altenburg (2003), 'Terrorism, State Responsibility, and the Use of Military Force', 4 *Chicago Journal of International Law* 97, 104.

39   Gregory M. Travalio (2000), 'Terrorism, International Law, and The Use of Military Force', 18 *Wisconsin International Law Journal* 145, 157-59 and authorities cited therein.

40   Travalio and Altenburg, 106.

41   See, for example, Alberto Coll (1987), 'The Legal and Moral Adequacy of Military Responses to Terrorism', 81 *American Society of International Law Proceedings* 297; John Murphy (1989), *State Support of International Terrorism: Legal, Political and Economic Dimensions*, Boulder, Colo.: Westview Press; London: Mansell Pub., 99–109.

42   Oscar Schachter (1993), 'The Lawful Use of Force by a State Against Terrorists in Another Country', in Henry H. Han (ed.) *Terrorism and Political Violence: Limits and*

Possibilities of Legal Control, New York: Oceana Publications, 243, 249 (one state cannot be invaded by another state in response to terrorism unless responsibility for the terrorist attack can be imputed to the invaded state).

43   *Nicaragua Case,* 64.
44   Ibid., 62.
45   Ibid., 65.
46   Sofaer, 'The Sixth Annual Waldemar A. Solf Lecture', 101.
47   Ibid.
48   Ibid., 102.
49   *Nicaragua,* 343–44 (Dissenting Opinion of Judge Schwebel Jr).
50   Scott M. Malzahn (2002), 'State Sponsorship and Support of International Terrorism: Customary Norms of State Responsibility', 26 *Hastings International and Comparative Law Review* 83, 100–1. For a detailed exposition of this assertion, see Keith Highet (1987), 'Evidence, the Court, and the Nicaragua Case', 81 *American Journal of International Law* 1, 40–1; see also Francis Boyle (1987), 'Determining US Responsibility for Contra Activities in International Law', in Harold Maier (ed.), 'Appraisals of the ICJ's Decision: *Nicaragua v United States (Merits)*', 81 *American Journal of International Law* 77, 86.
51   Mark Gibney, Katarina Tomaševski and Jens Vensted-Hansen (1999), 'Transnational State Responsibility for Violations of Human Rights', 12 *Harvard Human Rights Journal* 267, 287.
52   See Travalio, 'Terrorism, and International Law and the Use of Military Force', 155.
53   See Richard Lillich and John Paxman (1976), 'State Responsibility for Injuries to Aliens Occasioned by Terrorist Activities', 26 *American University Law Review* 217, 236–7.
54   Oppenheim, 549.
55   Ibid.
56   The writings of widely respected scholars, so long as they reflect the actual status of the law rather than personal recommendations, are a subsidiary source of international law: *Statute of the ICJ* art. 38(1).
57   Lillich and Paxman, 245, 261. See also Oppenheim, 400–1.
58   Lillich and Paxman, ibid., 245–6.
59   Ibid., 257, 274.
60   *UN Charter*, art. 2(4).
61   *Declaration on Principles of International Law Concerning Friendly Relations and Co-operation among States in Accordance with the Charter of the United Nations,* G.A. Res 2625, U.N. GAOR, 25th sess, 1883rd plen mtg, Supp 28, 121–3, U.N. Doc A/8082 (1970) ('*Declaration Concerning Friendly Relations*').
62   Ibid., 123.
63   Malzahn, 88.
64   See *General Assembly Resolutions.*
65   S.C. Res 1373, U.N. SCOR, 56th sess, 4385th mtg, U.N. Doc S/RES/1373 (2001). See also S.C. Res 1269, U.N. SCOR, 54th sess, 4053rd mtg, U.N. Doc S/RES/1269 (1999); S.C. Res 1377, U.N. SCOR, 56th sess, 4413rd mtg, Annex, U.N. Doc S/RES/1377 (2001).
66   *Draft Articles on Responsibility.*
67   See the discussion in Part IV, Chapter 3.
68   US Department of Defense, *Report of Department of Defence Commission on Beirut International Airport Terrorist Act, October 23, 1983,* 1 October 2003, 129 online at http://www.ibiblio.org/hyperwar/AMH/XX/MidEast/Lebanon-1982-1984/DOD-Report/.
69   Robert McFarlane (1985), 'Terrorism and the Future of Free Society', speech delivered

at the Defense Strategy Forum, National Strategic Information Centre, Washington DC (15 March).

70 The Center for Research on Population and Security, *Vice President's Task Force on Combating Terrorism, Public Report 2* (February 1986) 7, 1 October 2003 online at http://www.population-security.org/bush_and_terror_pdf.

71 U.N. S.C. Res. 573, reprinted in Office of the Historian, U.S. Dep't of State, 1985 *Am. Foreign Policy Current Doc.* 517.

72 Sofaer, 'The Sixth Annual Waldemar A. Solf Lecture', 108.

73 Ibid.

74 Statement before the UN Security Council on October 4, 1985, reprinted in Office of the Historian, U.S. Dep't of State, 1985 *Am. Foreign Policy Current Doc.* 581.

75 See Gregory Francis Intoccia (1987), 'American Bombing of Libya: An International Legal Analysis', 19 *Case Western Reserve Journal of International Law* 177, 182. (Immediately after these attacks, in which several civilians were killed, the Libyan leader Muammar Qadhafi hailed the killers as 'heroes').

76 Weekly Compilation of Presidential Documents 17–18 (7 January 1986).

77 *New York Times*, 6 April 1986, A1, Col. 6.

78 G.A. Res. No 41/38, U.N. Doc No A/RES/41/38 (1986).

79 Sean D. Murphy (2002), 'Terrorism and the Concept of "Armed Attack" in Article 51 of the U.N. Charter', 43 *Harvard International Law Journal* 41, 47.

80 Travalio and Altenburg, 106.

81 If it had been clear that chemical weapons were, in fact, being processed at the factory, it seems likely that the world community would have accepted the US action. Neither the Security Council nor the General Assembly took any formal action with regard to either attack.

82 In his address to the nation immediately following the terrorist attacks on September 11, President Bush stated that America would 'make no distinction between the terrorists who committed these acts and those who harbor them'. President Bush's Remarks, *Washington Post*, 12 September 2001, A2.

83 Louise Fenner, '*Cheney: Terrorists, Those Who Harbor Them, Face "Full Wrath" of U.S.*', (16 September 2001, interview on NBC 'Meet the Press'), available at http://www.usembassy.it/file2001_09/alia/a1091402.htm (last visited 28 April 2005).

84 Congress Authorizes President to Use All Necessary Force, 15 September 2001 online at http:// usinfo.state.gov/topical/pol/terror/01091706.htm.

85 Address to a Joint Session of Congress and the American People, President Declares 'Freedom at War With Fear' 20 September 2001 online at http://whitehouse.gov/news/releases/2001/09/20010920-8.html.

86 Remarks by President to Troops, President Shares Thanksgiving Meal with Troops, 21 November 2000, online at http://www.whitehouse.gov/news/releases/2001/11/20011121-3.html. See also the statement by the United States Ambassador to the United Nations on 12 September 2001: 'There should be no doubt: we will deal with those who support and harbor terrorists as we deal with the terrorists themselves.' UN Press Release, Ambassador Cunningham Statement to UN General Assembly, 12 September 2001, online at http://usinfo.state.gov/topical/pol/terror/01091304.htm.

87 Wendy S. Ross (2001), 'No Discussions, No Negotiations with Taliban, White House Says', (21 September) online http://usinfo.state.gov/topical/pol/terror/01092111.htm. See also another statement by Ari Fleischer in which he said: 'I think you need to look at it exactly as the President described it, which is that anybody who harbors terrorism will be the target of our operations and the target of our actions.' Excerpt: 'Afghan People Not Synonymous with Taliban', 25 September 2001, online at http://usinfo.state.gov/topical/pol/terror/01092521.htm.

88 Travalio and Altenburg, 109.

89   Ibid.
90   See generally US Department of State, 'UN Secretary-General Affirms US Rights to Self-Defence', 8 October 2001, online at http://usinfo.state.gov/topical/pol/terror/01100903.htm.
91   See Carsten Stahn (2003), 'Security Council Resolutions 1368 (2001) and 1373 (2001): What They Say and What They Do Not Say', *European Journal of International Law* 13–14, online at http://www.ejil.org/forum_WTC/ny-stahn.html; Byers, Michael, 'Iraq and the Bush Doctrine of Pre-emptive Self-Defence', Crimes of War Project, Expert Analysis, 1 June 2004, online at http://www.crimesofwar.org/expert/bush-byers.html (visited 20 October 2004).
92   Travalio, 'Terrorism, International Law and the Use of Military Force', 171–2 (citations omitted).
93   See also Hermann Mosler (1974), 'The International Society as a Legal Community', 140 *Recueil des Cours* 283.
94   U.N. SCOR, 3063rd mtg, 47th sess, 52, U.N. Doc S/RES/748 (1992).
95   See Paul Lewis (1992), 'Security Council Votes to Prohibit Arms Exports and Flights to Libya', *New York Times*, A1 (1 April).
96   Resolution 748, 52.
97   Resolution 2625, 123.
98   See Ruwantissa Abeyratne (1995), 'The Effects of Unlawful Interference with International Civil Aviation on World Peace and the Social Order', 22 *Transportation Law Journal* 449, 466.
99   See, e.g., *Convention for the Prevention of Unlawful Seizure of Aircraft*, art. 4; *Convention on the Prevention and Punishment of Crimes Against Internationally Protected Persons, Including Diplomatic Agents*, art. 3; *Convention for the Suppression of Unlawful Acts against the Safety of Civil Aviation*, art. 5; *Convention for the Suppression of Unlawful Acts Against the Safety of Maritime Navigation*, art. 6.
100   As John Cohan notes, one might analyse the existence of state-sponsored terrorism along the lines of a four-part continuum ranging from active to passive support:

> (a) The State actively sponsors, controls or directs the terrorist activities.
> (b) The State encourages the activities by providing training, equipment, money and/or transportation.
> (c) The State tolerates the terrorists operating as such within its borders by making no effort to arrest or oust them, although it does not actively support them. By not ejecting or arresting the terrorists, the State is 'enabling' them to carry on their activities.
> (d) The State, due to political factors or inherent weakness of leaders, is simply unable to deal effectively with the terrorists; therefore there is inaction.

John Cohan (2002), 'Formulation of A State's Response to Terrorism and State-Sponsored Terrorism', 14 *Pace International Law Review* 77, 90–1. See also Travalio, 150.
101   See *UN Charter* art. 51, which states that:

> Nothing in the present *Charter* shall impair the inherent right of individual or collective self-defence if an armed attack occurs against a Member of the United Nations, until the Security Council has taken measures necessary to maintain international peace and security. Measures taken by Members in the exercise of this right of self-defence shall be immediately reported to the Security Council and shall not in any way affect the authority and responsibility of the Security Council under the present *Charter* to take at any time such action as it deems necessary in order to maintain or restore international peace and security.

102   See Travalio, 'Terrorism, International Law and the Use of Military Force', 156.
103   The Israelis used it in defence of its raid on Entebbe, as did the US in attempting to justify its bombing of Libya. Such claims did not win a favourable response from the international community. See, e.g., John Murphy (1978), *Legal Aspects of International Terrorism*, Lexington, Mass.: Lexington Books, 556; Francis Boyle (1986), 'Preserving the Rule of Law in the War against International Terrorism', 8 *Whittier Law Review* 735, 736–8.
104   It is clear that the word was intentionally used because the initial draft of Article 51 did not contain the term 'inherent'. Ibid (Murphy).
105   M. Baker (1987), 'Terrorism and the Inherent Right of Self-Defence (A Call to Amend Article 51 of the United Nations Charter', 10 *Houston Journal of International Law* 25, 31.
106   Yehuda Blum (1986), 'The Legality of State Response to Acts of Terrorism', in Benjamin Netanyahu (ed.), *Terrorism: How the West Can Win*, New York: Farrar, Straus, Giroux, 137. Professor Derek Bowett writes:

> It is ... fallacious to assume that members have only those rights which the *Charter* accords to them; on the contrary they have those rights which general international law accords them except and in so far as they have surrendered them under the *Charter*.

Derek Bowett (1958), *Self-Defence in International Law*, New York, NY: Praeger, 185. See also Arthur Goodhart (1951), 'The North Atlantic Treaty of 1949', 79 *Recueil des Cours* 187, 192, where the author states that the 'members of the United Nations when exercising their inherent powers do so not by grant but by already existing rights'. It was also the view of one of the committees at San Francisco that inherent meant that the 'use of arms in legitimate self-defence remains admitted and unimpaired': UNCIO Docs (1945), Vol. VI, 459.

107   See *Definition of Aggression*, G.A. Res 3314, U.N. GAOR, 29th Sess, 2319th plen mtg, Annex, Supp No 31, 142, U.N. Doc A/Res/3314 (1974) which attempts to give guidance to the Security Council in dealing with this matter. Note, however, that the annex and arts 2, 4 and 6 of the *Definition of Aggression* clearly indicate that the Security Council is not limited by the *Definition* and further, that the *Definition* is not intended as a modification or amendment of the *Charter*.
108   UNCIO Docs (1945), Vol. XII, 505.
109   J. E. S. Fawcett (1961), 'Intervention in International Law, A Study of Some Recent Cases', 103 *Recueil Des Cours* 361.
110   Wallace Warriner (1988), 'The Unilateral Use of Coercion under International Law: A Legal Analysis of the United States Raid on Libya on April 14, 1986', 37 *Naval Law Review* 49, 76–7.
111   For example, in *Nicaragua*, the ICJ gave a restrictive view of attribution when it found that there was 'no clear evidence of the US having actually exercised such a degree of control in all fields as to justify treating the Contras as acting on its behalf'. *Nicaragua* [1986] I.C.J. Rep 14, [109].
112   'Reprisal' allows a state to commit an act that is otherwise illegal to counter the illegal act of another state. 'Retaliation' is the infliction upon the delinquent state of the same injury that it has caused the victim. 'Retribution' is a criminal law concept, implying vengeance, that is sometimes used loosely in the international law context as a synonym for 'retaliation'. See generally Malcolm Shaw (4th ed., 1997), *International Law*, Cambridge: Cambridge University Press, 777–91.
113   See Bowett, 13.
114   Warriner, 77.
115   See, e.g., Oppenheim, 419, fn 12.

116   Ian Brownlie (1963), *International Law and the Use of Force by States*, Oxford: Clarendon Press, 281 (citation omitted).

117   The UN condemned Israel when it used force against Palestinians in Tunisia in retaliation for repeated terrorist attacks in 1985. It had the same response to Britain when it attacked Yemen for similar reasons in 1964. Though some in the international community would argue that reprisal action is inherent to maintaining security, most states condemn the practice. Bowett, 13–14; Warriner, 63–4.

118   See Jack Beard (2002), 'Military Action against Terrorists under International Law· America's New War On Terror: The Case for Self-Defence under International Law', 25 *Harvard Journal of Law and Public Policy* 559, 571.

119   See Resolution 1368, preamble; and Resolution 1373, preamble.

120   Brownlie, 275 (citation omitted).

121   See, e.g., Yoram Dinstein (3rd ed, 2001), *War, Aggression, and Self-Defence*, New York: Cambridge University Press, 168. Dinstein argues that as the choice of words in art. 51 is deliberately restrictive, the right of self-defence is limited to armed attack. See also Phillip Jessup (1948), *A Modern Law of Nations: An Introduction*, New York: Macmillan, 166.

122   The ICJ stipulated in *Nicaragua* that the exercise of the right of self-defence by a state under art 51 'is subject to the State concerned having been the victim of an armed attack'. *Nicaragua* [1986] I.C.J. Rep 14 [103].

123   See generally Hilaire McCoubrey and Nigel White (1992), *International Law and Armed Conflict*, 91–2.

124   Harbouring entails providing sanctuary and training to international terrorists as well as conditions that support their ability to engage in terrorist activities: see, e.g., S.C. Res 1193, U.N. SCOR, 53rd sess, 3921st mtg, 3, U.N. Doc S/RES/1193 (1998); S.C. Res 1214, U.N. SCOR, 53rd sess, 3952nd mtg, 4, U.N. Doc S/RES/1214 (1998).

125   Oscar Schachter (1993), 'The Lawful Use of Force by a State against Terrorists in Another Country', in Henry Han (ed.), *Terrorism and Political Violence: Limits and Possibilities of Legal Control*, 250. See also Alberto Coll (1987), 'The Legal and Moral Adequacy of Military Responses to Terrorism', 81 *American Society of International Law Proceedings* 297, 298.

126   *Nicaragua Case*, 228.

127   Rosalyn Higgins (1994), *Problems and Process: International Law and How We Use It*, Oxford: Clarendon Press; New York: Oxford University Press, 250.

128   See, e.g., John Murphy (1989), *State Support of International Terrorism: Legal, Political and Economic Dimensions*, 120; Sage Knauft (1996), 'Proposed Guidelines for Measuring the Propriety of Armed State Responses to Terrorist Attacks', 19 *Hastings International and Comparative Law Review* 763, 765; Jeffrie McCredie (1987), 'The April 14, 1986 Bombing of Libya: Act of Self-Defense or Reprisal', 19 *Case Western Reserve Journal of International Law* 215, 219.

129   Bowett, 185–6 (citation omitted).

130   See, e.g., Myres McDougal and Florentino Feliciano (1961), *Law and Minimum World Public Order: The Legal Regulation of International Coercion*, New Haven: Yale University Press, 234–41.

131   Travalio, 159–60 (citations omitted).

132   See James Terry (1986), 'Countering State-Sponsored Terrorism: A Law-Policy Analysis', 36 *Naval Law Review* 159, 170; Oscar Schachter (1984), 'The Right of States to Use Armed Force', 82 *Michigan Law Review* 1620, 1633–4.

133   Schachter, ibid.

134   Richard Erickson (1989), *Legitimate Use of Force against State Sponsored Terrorism*, Maxwell Air Force Base, Ala.: Air University Press, 134.

135 Louis Henkin (1989), 'The Use of Force: Law and US Policy' in Louis Henkin et al (eds), *Right v Might: International Law and the Use of Force*, New York: Council on Foreign Relations, 44–6.

136 Through a process of state proclamation between 12 September 2001 and 10 October 2003 – which included UN Security Council resolutions, NATO declarations, supportive statements by the European Union, and a declaration by the Organisation of Islamic States – the traditional rule of self-defence appeared to have been extended. See 'The Patriot Resource History: September 11, 2001', 1 October 2003, online at http://www.patriotresource.com/wtc.html; 'The September 11 Web Archive', 1 October 2003, online at http://september11.archive.org which exhibit a collection of statements by various states and organizations in the aftermath of the September 11 attacks condemning the acts, pledging support and calling on the international community to confront terrorism, while trumpeting America's right to self-defence.

137 See UN Charter art. 51, which requires that actions in self-defence should be so reported.

138 Richard Ryan (2001), 'Press Statement on Terrorist Threats by Security Council President', Press Release, (8 October; U.N. Doc S/PRST/2002/26.

139 'Security Council, Moving to Support Global Efforts, Seeks Reports From All Countries on Steps Taken against Terrorism', U.N. SCOR, 4618th and 4619th mtgs, U.N. Doc SC/7524 (2002).

140 See, e.g., Byers, 406–12; Stahn, 49–50.

141 See Resolution 1368, 1. However, it is instructive that the operative part of the resolution describes the attacks as 'terrorist attacks' (not armed attacks) that 'represent a threat to international peace and security'. Thus, Resolution 1368 is ambiguous on the issue of whether the right of self-defence applies in relation to any parties as a consequence of the September 11 attacks.

142 See NATO (2001), 'Statement of the North Atlantic Council', Press Release 124, (12 September) online at http://www.nato.int/docu/pr/2001/p01-124e.htm.

143 Carsten Stahn (2003), '"Nicaragua is Dead, Long Live Nicaragua"' – The Right to Self-defence under Art. 51 UN Charter and International Terrorism' (Paper presented at the Impressum Conference, 'Terrorism as a Challenge for National and International Law', Max Planck Institute for Comparative Public Law and International Law, Heidelberg (24–25 February) 27 online at http://edoc.mpil.de/conference-on-terrorism/present/stahn.pdf at 1 October 2003.

144 Myres McDougal (1963), 'The Soviet-Cuban Quarantine and Self-Defense', 57 *American Journal of International Law* 597, 600 (citation and emphasis omitted).

145 Terry, 171. US Secretary of State Shultz emphasized this point when he said:

> The UN Charter is not a suicide pact. The law is a weapon on our side and it is up to us to use it to its maximum extent … There should be no confusion about the status of nations that sponsor terrorism against Americans and American property.

> George Shultz (1986), 'Low Intensity Warfare: The Challenge of Ambiguity', (January) US Department of State Current Policy No 783, 3.

146 Abraham D. Sofaer (1989), 'Terrorism, the Law and the National Defence', 126 *Military Law Review* 89, 95.

147 Travalio, 'Terrorism, International Law and the Use of Military Force', 155 (citations omitted).

148 Ibid., 156.

149 Ibid., 160.

150 Resolution 1368.

151 Resolution 1373.

152 Statement of the North Atlantic Council. Neither the Security Council Resolutions nor the NATO statement attempted to establish a link between the terrorist acts and a particular state. However, these texts do not provide a clear indication whether they intend to refer to a wide concept of 'armed attack' which would also comprise acts which are not attributable to a state. The issue of whether the acts in question could be regarded as state acts depends on factual elements which are still controversial.

153 Carsten Stahn (2003), 'Terrorist Acts as "Armed Attack": The Right to Self-Defence, Article 51(1/2) of the UN Charter, and International Terrorism', 27 *Fletcher Forum of World Affairs* 35, 37.

154 Ibid., (citation omitted).

155 Ibid.

156 Ibid., 38 (citations omitted).

Chapter 6

The War on Terror: Rattling International Law with Raw Power?

Introduction

The early 1990s marked the end of the Cold War, which paralyzed the United Nations from its inception. The event was a cause for celebration and hope. Following the historic Security Council Summit Meeting of January 1992, the then Secretary-General of the United Nations, Boutros Boutros-Ghali, spoke of a growing conviction 'among nations large and small, that an opportunity has been regained to achieve the great objectives of the UN Charter – a United Nations capable of maintaining international peace and security, of securing justice and human rights and of promoting, in the words of the Charter, "social progress and better standards of life in larger freedom"'.[1] The spirit of this bold and idealistic statement had been echoed two years earlier by former President George H. W. Bush Sr's statement to the United Nations General Assembly as United States and coalition forces were gathering to push Saddam Hussein's Iraqi army out of Kuwait:

> We have a vision of a new partnership of nations that transcends the Cold War. A partnership based on consultation, cooperation, and collective action, especially through international and regional organizations. A partnership united by principle and the rule of law ... A partnership whose goals are to increase democracy, increase prosperity, increase the peace, and reduce arms.[2]

Over a decade after 'Operation Desert Storm' and in the aftermath of the terrorist attacks of September 11, a newly assertive United States has placed considerable strain on the existing international legal rules governing the use of force by reserving a right to use unilateral force and of course demonstrating that practically. Reacting to the legalities and justifications surrounding 'Operation Iraqi Freedom', Professors Richard Falk and David Kreiger observe:

> There are two main ways to ruin the UN: to ignore its relevance in war/peace situations, or to turn it into a rubber stamp for geopolitical operations of dubious status under international law or the UN Charter. Before September 11, Bush pursued the former approach; since then – by calling on the UN to provide the world's remaining superpower with its blessings for an unwarranted war – the latter.[3]

The crusade against terror is not a sole US enterprise; many of its fears are shared by a large majority of the international community. The crusade should, however, not be allowed to numb states and the broader international community to the need of international rule of law and the utility of international law as central pillars of the international community. 'The attempt by the Bush administration to introduce a new principle of international law permitting "pre-emptive strike" by a nation against another, solely at its own discretion, represents a quantum, and highly dangerous, innovation. Were such a principle to prevail, we would have reversed decades of advances, modest but hard won, toward peace-making and returned to an era of dominance through might.'[4]

Besides the contentious notion of pre-emptive military action, loosening the standards of state responsibility poses another dangerous avenue. There is no doubt that the events of September 11 have made it necessary to redefine the different roles of domestic law and international law in the combating of internationalized violence. However, the implicit danger in expanding the concept of self-defence by loosening the indicia of state responsibility may result in the militarization of crime. While military force has its place in combating terrorism, in the long term, this strategy is likely to result in a might is right scenario.

A Step Back in Time

Modern forms of terrorism began in earnest in the 1960s with the world emerging from colonialism and state-sponsored racism.[5] From Asia to Africa and the Middle East, many states sought freedom from foreign control and/or domination. In the face of vastly superior, well-equipped and financed imperial armies, nationalist and anti-colonialist organizations resorted to terror violence, attacking civilian targets to instil a sense of terror in the white community and white-dominated governments that ruled by force. With few members, limited firepower and comparatively few organizational resources, these groups opted to rely on dramatic, often spectacular, bloody acts of violence to attract attention to themselves and their cause. In this era '..."terrorism" was used to describe the violence perpetrated by indigenous nationalist, anticolonialist organizations that arose throughout Asia, Africa, and the Middle East in opposition to continued European rule'.[6]

Many countries owe their independence at least in part to nationalist movements that used terrorism. Various disenfranchised or exiled nationalist minorities also embraced terrorism as a means to draw attention to their plight and generate international support for their cause. This *modus operandi* did work and occasionally paid handsome dividends.[7]

Abraham D. Sofaer observes that '[n]o international consensus then existed that these terrorist acts, including the killing of civilians, were unlawful. Politically motivated violence had a favoured position in international affairs, including international law. The United Nations General Assembly debates on terrorism in 1972 illustrate this point.'[8] In the aftermath of the killings by Japanese terrorists sympathetic to the Palestinian cause at Lod Airport, Israel, and the murders of members of the Israeli Olympic team in Munich by PLO terrorists of the Black September organization, Secretary-General Waldheim called on the Assembly to place on its 1972–1973 agenda an item entitled: 'Measures to prevent terrorism and other forms of violence which endanger or take innocent human lives or jeopardize fundamental freedoms.' The item ran into a storm of protest.

'During the debates that followed that and later proposals, it became clear that many states regarded acts of terror as lawful when undertaken by persons deprived of basic human rights, dignity, freedom, or independence from foreign occupation.'[9] These ideological and geopolitical differences between states regarding the permissibility of violence in various political contexts ensured that no broad generic approach would be taken and obscured the fact that numerous states and organizations resort to clearly impermissible violence when convenient to or desirable for their objectives.

The growing lethality and regularity of terrorist acts, however, transformed the matter as ideological motivations increasingly replaced revolutionary goals. This convinced the international community of the need to reach agreement that certain acts were criminal in all circumstances and should confer jurisdiction on all states to prosecute them, or alternatively an obligation to extradite persons charged with such acts to other states for prosecution.

In order to mobilize consensus, the international community adopted a piecemeal approach to combating terrorism, choosing to target very specific acts of terrorism, occurring in specific situations, circumstances or places and generally providing for extradition and prosecution regimes. The first terrorism conventions related to aviation security and followed a spate of hijackings in the 1970s. They covered hostage taking, internationally protected persons (including diplomats), and nuclear material. In the 1980s, the focus was on maritime terrorism, following the hijacking of the *Achille Lauro*. It was not until December 1985 that the UN General Assembly finally condemned 'unequivocally ... as criminal, all acts, methods and practices of terrorism'.[10]

Even that resolution, however, reaffirmed each people's inalienable right to self-determination and the legitimacy of struggles against colonial and racist regimes and other forms of alien domination. Many state representatives affirmed the right to engage in all necessary actions in these struggles. Subsequently, three further conventions, on plastic explosives, terrorist bombings and terrorist financing, were negotiated in the 1990s, wrapping up efforts under the aegis of the UN to address and combat terrorism in the 20th century.[11]

The law enforcement approach initially predominated counter-terrorism responses.[12] In the mid-1980s, growing inadequacy of the domestic legal enforcement framework in the face of state-sponsored terrorism led states (notably Israel and the United States) to suggest that terrorist acts might be approached from a conflict management perspective, rather than exclusively from a law enforcement viewpoint. The belief was that only the use of armed force will result in the degree of decisive action that will minimize the likelihood that offenders will go unpunished, based on the argument that terrorists must be seen, not as criminals, but as persons jeopardizing national security.[13]

With the end of the Cold War, acts generally described as 'terrorism' proliferated in frequency and severity. The rise of globalization and religious extremism on one hand, and the increasing accessibility and availability of weapons and technology on the other, enabled well-financed and organized terrorist organizations to transform themselves into global outfits with greater reach and lethality.[14] Globalization and technology were quickly enhancing the capabilities of the outfits. With less confrontation and more cooperation between states in the post-Cold War era, terrorism soon gained the recognition that Cold War ideological and political squabbles prevented it from gaining – a pernicious and underestimated threat to international peace and security.

There is no doubt that terrorism is an evil that states should combat aggressively. Terrorism aims at killing the innocent and the unarmed. It has no ethics or conscience. Nonetheless, it should not be forgotten that countries have many tools they can use in their fight against terrorism including covert actions and a variety of economic sanctions against a state or group that supports terrorists.[15]

The author is inclined to concur with Joseph Thomas' observation that the rise and threat posed by international terrorism is the third world war which is upon us in all its ferocity. It may be a war without end, but it should be fought with courage.[16] However, it is Thomas' belief that: 'This war calls for merciless punitive action, not thoughtless murders',[17] which the author takes issue with.

Massive military force, however selectively and carefully carried out, will always lead to mistakes, and the mistakes will inevitably be counted in numerous unnecessary deaths of innocent civilians. Professor Christopher Blakesley cautions: 'Care must be taken to ensure that international and domestic action taken to obtain justice and to prosecute perpetrators does not fall into the same trap that ensnared those who committed the crimes. If we allow ourselves to descend to simple vengeance, we are lost.'[18]

Terrorists are elusive and more so when states turn their back on their international responsibilities and obligations and grant them save havens and support. However, these failings do not justify a resort to vigilante justice. Unilateral solutions fuelled by nationalistic agendas are bound to tear the fabric of restraint that is central to the international regime on the use of force. It is all too easy to reach the simple solution of eliminating the enemy, but much harder to practically implement without the use of raw military power and thus a move to centralize power as a medium of international relations. Such a move ensures that, inevitably, international rule of law becomes part of the casualty toll.[19]

Changing Gear Without Engaging International Law

The devastating consequences of the attacks of September 11, 2001 led President George Bush Jr to declare a 'war' on terrorism. The first stage of this war was a full-scale military operation in Afghanistan, which destroyed the Taliban and Al-Qaeda as fighting forces, and replaced the Taliban regime with an internationally approved transition government. But the United States was soon squandering the legal and political capital when it turned its focus on Iraq. 'Operation Iraqi Freedom' generally lacked the support of the UN and most sovereign states, including some key traditional US allies.

The rapid fizzling of international support for 'Operation Iraqi Freedom', despite the abundance of the same when the United States launched 'Operation Enduring Freedom' against Afghanistan, was premised on what was viewed as a lack of appreciation by the United States of the complications to the international system that this engendered. This was more so considering that the United States had flagged that it was embarking on a new and dramatically different policy in dealing with terrorism than it has followed for many years.[20]

In his first State of the Union address after the September 11 terrorist attacks, President Bush's bellicose remarks regarding the 'axis of evil' raised international concerns that the war on terrorism might spread in terms of geography and nature. The international community (including United States allies) '… reacted with alarm and repudiation, fearing that the president's rhetoric signalled a unilateral escalation of global tension. They also objected to the overall mood of the address, and in particular, the pugnacious way in which President Bush promised to deal with those who threatened American security.'[21]

One-by-one foreign leaders scolded the United States for its defiant, go-it-alone attitude.[22] Sensing the Bush administration's heightened interest in Iraq, the EU, China, Russia and Germany warned the United States not to attack Iraq without first working through international diplomatic channels.[23] The appeals by the international community, however, fell on deaf ears. This was not surprising considering that President Bush's address to the UN General Assembly on 12 September 2002, a year after the September 11 bombings, had set the terms of the debate.[24] In that address, '[r]emarkably, Bush succeeded both in flashing his multilateralist credentials and in portending the death of multilateralism if the UN failed to follow the American lead'.[25]

It was not lost on the international community that the Bush administration was increasingly gravitating towards unilateralism and a nationalistic agenda evidenced by the administration's rejection of several international agreements, resulting in feverish charges, especially from allies abroad, that the United States was behaving unilaterally.[26]

> The administration's critics argued that American unilateralism endangered the global cooperation that is the only means through which common problems can be solved and common interests advanced. The uncompromising rhetoric used by the president and other [US] government leaders in describing how the United States would confront Iraq – with or without allied support – provided more ammunition for those who denounced the Bush administration's perceived unilateralism.[27]

The belligerence in the rhetoric of the Bush administration (especially in light of the United States' military might) painted a troubling picture of not allowing its agenda to be deterred or diluted by the strictures of international law or the preferences of the international community. If allies agree with the United States' position, they should join the crusade; if not, the implication is that they are soft on terrorism and – of course for states outside the close circle – sympathizers.

Marginalizing the UN and International Law?

It is abundantly clear that the push for a state-centric determination on the use of lethal military force to counter terrorism is exerting tremendous stress on international cooperation and goodwill and contributing to mounting anti-American sentiment. It is significant that in a break with the past, a justification under law was not part of the Bush administration's public position when it began discussing an invasion of Iraq.[28] Professor Mary Ellen O'Connell observes that: 'This is one of the rare occasions since the adoption of the UN Charter that the United States has been so disinterested in international law as to not provide an explanation as to how a major use of armed force would comply with the law.'[29] Professor O'Connell then sums up the matter thus:

> The significance of this is not that the United States has always acted consistently with international law and now suddenly it is not. The United States has plainly violated international law on the use of force in the past. The difference is that now the prevailing view sees no need to offer explanations. The United States need not show how it has acted consistently with the principles of the community. The United States is above the law. That is a significant departure from the past that may well have serious negative consequences for future legal restraints on the use of force.[30]

In the invasion of Iraq, US planners gave little indication that they were concerned with the law of self-defence.

> In the past the United States has sought to characterize its uses of force as within the international rule of law – even if that meant manipulating facts as in the cases of Vietnam and Grenada. The United States has officially argued its uses of force were lawful. The invasion of Iraq, however, presents a significant new development…[in which it seems] some United States foreign policy planners apparently believe that the United States has a privileged, exceptional position in international relations and that puts it above international law.[31]

The stance that no multilateral organization authorization or other justification under law to invade Iraq was necessary will have profound consequences if permitted to be the guiding principle of the United States in its crusade against terror. The most powerful country on earth cannot afford to be solely preoccupied with self-preservation.[32]

Undoubtedly, the United States enjoys a position of preponderant military, economic and political might as well as privilege in the international community. 'America is no mere international citizen. It is the dominant power in the world, more dominant than any since Rome. Accordingly America is in a position to reshape norms, alter expectations and create new realities.'[33] But this surely does not entail tearing apart the international framework and unravelling many decades of hard-won battles to discipline sovereign excesses. If this be so, Professor Mary Ellen O'Connell cautions that:

> Allowing the United States to move to a position above the law will have repercussions for the law. Those repercussions will unlikely be the ones the United States wants. The United States wants an orderly world under the rule of law for everyone, but some also want the United States to have a right to pick and choose the rules it obeys. This is not how law works. Law is based on a psychological element of belief and commitment. When these are absent, there can be no law. If the United States breaks this fiction and declares itself above the law, it will help break down the commitment to law generally in the international community.[34]

Resort to force, even when lawful, requires great care. Mistakes or excessive collateral damage can undermine its effectiveness. 'While the United States may act unilaterally in its self-defence, it must be prepared to defend its actions or to admit and pay for its mistakes.'[35] But such mistakes (likely to be colossal as Iraq demonstrates) will result in undermining rather than furthering the crusade against terrorism. Opponents of an independent right for states to determine the use of military force outside the dictates of the UN Charter as a countermeasure against terrorism criticize the proposition as an imprudent expansion of the legitimate use of force with limitless potential for misuse. These opponents echo the fears expressed by the International Court of Justice over fifty years ago in the *Corfu Channel case*:

> [The ICJ] can only regard the alleged right of intervention as the manifestation of a policy of force such as has in the past given rise to most serious abuses and such as cannot find a place in international law. It is still less admissible in the particular form it would take here – it would be reserved for the most powerful states.[36]

UN Secretary-General Kofi Annan echoed this position in 1999 when he commented that 'enforcement actions without Security Council authorization threaten the very core of the international security system founded on the Charter of the United Nations. Only the Charter provides a universally accepted legal basis for the use of force.'[37] It may be prudent for self-defence not to expand so rapidly that it erases the preclusion of unilateral recourse to armed force. After all, as Professor Schachter observes: '[t]he absence of binding judicial or other third-party determinations relating to the use of force adds to the apprehension that a more permissive rule of self-defence will open the way to further disregard of the limits on force.'[38] As Professors Byers and Chesterman observe:

> a select group of states (such as Western liberal democracies, or perhaps the United States alone) agreeing on criteria [for intervention] amongst themselves – would seriously undermine the current system of international law: It would also greatly undermine the position of the United Nations as an effective organization in the field of peace and security, after the decade in which, despite some obvious failures, it achieved more than in the previous half-century.[39]

'The Bush Doctrine, perceiving the failure of deterrence to inhibit terrorists and "rogue" states that possess the will and the means to wreak catastrophic destruction, avers that the terrorist threat has become an overriding threat to national survival that trumps existing international law. The United States feels it cannot afford to let terrorists have any safe harbour from which to craft a future catastrophic attack on America.'[40] The United States is forceful in averring that '... [t]he war on terror will not be won on the defensive'.[41] What the United States seems to be ignoring or giving scant attention to is the fact that '... the Article 2(4) prohibition is not a one-sided provision that hampers only the United States policy; it applies to all members of the United Nations. Accordingly, an erosion of the prohibition on the use of force enables not only the United States, but also all other states to use force more freely.'[42] United States policymakers, perhaps considering other states too weak to exploit the new principles it seeks to write into the rule book for the use of force, may be willing to tolerate this situation.

Though the military actions in Afghanistan and Iraq have, from a technical point of view, 'been fought and won, a battle still rages over the legitimacy of the United

States' actions under international law. As the world hegemon, the actions of the United States receive a great deal of attention.'[43] The United States chose not to act within the parameters of international law when it invaded Iraq without proper authority leaving the international community angry and frustrated. It did not help that the action occurred in the shadow of lowered world opinion of the United States due to its unilateral moves regarding the environment and missile defence.[44] The invasion of Iraq served only to reinforce the fears that the international community had of a hyper-power determined to have its way whether through law or simply raw power.

The anger of the international community was not based on any support for the Saddam regime, which the international community was well aware supported terror in one form or another. Rather it was premised on the United States' determination to invade Iraq based on faulty and dodgy intelligence, which served to undermine the United States' claim of a right to act unilaterally against Saddam's regime on behalf of the interests of the international community.

In essence the United States seemed fixated with the need to get rid of the murderous regime – not a bad mindset, but disturbing when it sought to wrap up its political agenda together with the interests of the international community. The spill-over effect is that it opened the door to other countries to justify violating the law in the same manner – by tying the interests of the international community together with national foreign policy goals. The move by the United States thus unwittingly establishes a dangerous precedent.

The Future

The events of September 11 establish that terrorism poses one of the most serious threats to international order and global human rights in the 21st century. Terrorism also represents a grave crime under international law. The war on terror has the UN Charter regime on the use of force enrolled in an era of change. Within the United Nations regime – the system of collective security – self-defence is subject to restrictions (in other words is finite). The 'Bush Doctrine' and similar doctrines or justifications are running against the grain of Article 2(4). Considering that an amendment to the UN Charter is near impossible, a change in customary law might be a way.

Professor Michael Bothe points out: '[a] usual procedure to modify customary law is to break it and to accompany the breach by a new legal claim.'[45] The case for a change of the restrictive Charter-based concept of self-defence is made by the National Security Strategy:

> Given the goals of rogue states and terrorists, the United States can no longer solely rely on a reactive posture. The inability to deter a potential attacker, the immediacy of today's threats, and the magnitude of potential harm that could be caused by our adversaries' choice of weapons, do not permit that option. We cannot let our enemies strike first.[46]

The argument that a state cannot wait to absorb a potentially lethal attack before acting is not new. Indeed, the traditional approach has always had the drawback of depriving a potential victim of the possibility to choose the most advantageous moment to fight a danger which may be extreme. It has been used by Israel to justify a number of incursions into the territory of its neighbours, and has been rejected by the Security Council.[47] The prohibition of the use of force, including the prohibition of anticipatory self-defence, has developed in international practice and doctrine despite the awareness of this drawback. 'Does President Bush's National Security Strategy constitute a step in this direction?'[48] Any new rule to be created would have to give an adequate answer to many thorny questions. Professor Bothe raises some of these questions thus:

> How to define and limit a possibly expanded right of self-defence? How serious must the threat be? Is possession of weapons of mass destruction enough? Who is threatened and who may attack? What about the possession of nuclear arms by India, Pakistan, North Korea and Israel? What precisely distinguishes them (if there is a difference), in legal terms, from Iraq? What does 'harbouring' terrorists mean? There must be knowledge. But if there is, what kind of effort is a state required to make in order not to be considered as harbouring terrorists?[49]

Satisfactory answers to these questions are not at hand. All too easily, a standard of reasonableness boils down to subjectivity and speculation. The National Security Strategy seems to recognize the dilemma, in particular the risk of abuse, by noting that nations should not use pre-emption as a pretext for aggression.[50] This observation, however, is followed by a somewhat enigmatic postulate: '... in an age where the enemies of civilization openly and actively seek the world's most destructive technologies, the United States cannot remain idle while dangers gather.'[51]

The prickly issue is whether this seems to imply a differentiation between (other) 'nations' and the United States? And thus seeks to create a different yardstick for the world's sole superpower. An essential argument for maintaining the restrictive concept is the problem of vagueness and the possibility of abuse, since this is the greatest vulnerability of the prohibition of the use of force. The impossibility of placing any legal limit on the exception means that the validity of the prohibition of the use of force itself will be in jeopardy.

The attempt to create a rule which is unable to give a workable definition of permissible force might end in the abolition of the prohibition of the use of force altogether, as previously occurred. This would mean destroying one of the most important and salutary cultural and political achievements of the 20th century. That danger is all the more real as the rule prohibiting the use of force is particularly vulnerable for another reason as well. This rule was not really developed by state practice. There has never been a consistent practice of abstention from the use of force. What changed after World War I was the reaction of relevant actors against the use of force.

If we want to maintain international law as a restraint on the use of military force, we should very carefully watch any attempt on the part of opinion leaders to argue that military force is anything other than an evil that has to be avoided. The lessons of history are telling. If we revert to such broad concepts, such as the just war concept, to justify military force, we are stepping on a slippery slope, one which would make us slide back into the 19th century when war was not illegal.

It is important that states remember that, despite the weaknesses and perceived failings of the UN in dealing with terrorism, the UN is not sitting on its hands. Even before the September 11 attacks, when the UN General Assembly adopted the Millennium Declaration, it urged among other things a concerted action against international terrorism by states, as well as their accession to all relevant international conventions.[52] About a year later, on 28 September 2001, acting under Chapter VII of the UN Charter, the Security Council adopted Resolution 1373, reaffirming its unequivocal condemnation of the September 11 attacks.[53] The resolution also established the Counter-Terrorism Committee to monitor the implementation of Resolution 1373 by all states and spearhead attempts to increase the capability of states to fight terrorism. Shortly thereafter, at the behest of the Secretary-General, in October 2001 the Policy Working Group on the United Nations and Terrorism was established. Its purpose has been to identify the longer-term implications and broad policy dimensions of terrorism for the United Nations and to formulate recommendations on the steps that the United Nations system might take to address the issue.

It may well be that the international community is committed to reshaping the paradigm on the use of force to counter terrorism and will one day accept some instances of pre-emptive use of force. This, it is submitted, is a much safer approach to the interpretation and development of *jus ad bellum* than loosening any real restraint by boiling it down to a rule of reason – a self-destructive mechanism for the prohibition of the use of force. While there are serious doubts about the wisdom of the traditional rule which strictly limits anticipatory self-defence, practicable substantive legal restraints on the use of pre-emptive force are not readily available. Loosening these limits without setting out workable limits is dangerous.

Conclusion

The 'War on Terror' is a noble crusade that seeks to counter the rise of international terrorism fuelled by a combination of resurgent religious extremism, well-financed and coordinated terrorist organizations, and the availability of cheap weapons technology. However, the pugnacity demonstrated by the Bush administration in facing the threat is a source of concern. In profound foresight, in 1999, Hubert Vedrine, then Foreign Minister of France, coined a new term describing the United States as a 'hyper-puissance', or 'hyper-power'.[54] The term was not an expression of awe but rather a fear of the capacity of the United States to resort to unilateralism in view of its dominant military and economic power. Perhaps the prophesy is coming true, with events subsequent to the September 11 attacks painting a disturbing picture.

Despite the horror of September 11, the 'Bush Doctrine', if taken to its logical conclusion, is too all-encompassing to conform to even an expansive reading of the UN Charter. No doubt the September 11 terrorist attacks reinforced the proposition that the UN Charter system is ill-equipped to deal with contemporary security threats. However, part of the problem is a result of the Cold War and the obstructionist politics that accompanied it.[55] Despite instances of resort to military action to counter terrorism in the Cold War, the actions were often shrouded in a jumble of half-truths not helped by a confusing mish-mash of legal justifications. The end result is that the illusion of self-defence was (and still is) used and misused, preventing the evolution of any meaningful state practice and *opinio juris*, thus retarding the development of meaningful international discourse.

> Antiterrorism efforts must ultimately be judged by whether they prevent attacks. Any conceivable deterrent effect of criminal prosecutions of low-level conspirators is lessened by the fact that they take years to complete and may take place after additional attacks. Law enforcement activity cannot be expected to shut down terrorist organizations operating in hostile and uncooperative states...[56]

It is a reality that criminal prosecutions are generally ineffective in deterring fundamentalist terrorist groups able to recruit individuals willing to sacrifice their lives in suicide bombings. These terrorists are crazed killers, as prepared for sacrifice as good soldiers.[57] However, in the face of the ever-present reality that 'Al Qaeda and similar organizations limit the damage any individual can inflict by functioning in loose-knit cells',[58] the fight against terrorism cannot be won purely by force or by causing the other side an unacceptable rate of casualties. Professor Christopher Blakesley cautions:

> International and domestic law equip us to extricate ourselves from the 'infernal dialect' of violence; they provide the means whereby we may avoid accepting or participating in the oppression or the slaughter of innocents, even by our own acquiescence. It is error of the highest order to accept the ideologue's argument that, because some nations or rebel groups participate in oppression or other terror-violence, it is inevitable and therefore necessary to combat it with like conduct. It is practical and necessary to alter this vision. To commit evil acts because of perceived or even actual evil acts perpetrated by the object of our acts is to accept the evil as ours and to become evil. Self-defence under the rule of law does not include the use of innocents as tools. We must re-establish the vision of a world made up of human beings controlled by the rule of law and morality, not by raw power.[59]

The current climate dictates that there is a need '... to realign the existing rules on the use of force to match the altered international security environment and yet maintain meaningful limits on the use of force'.[60] Viable solutions can be reached but only by states maintaining the centrality of the UN even in the face of unconventional threats.

The UN is well aware that it will remain relevant only if it explores and develops new avenues for dealing with the threat of international terrorism. Obviously measures from another era that simply impose a limit on the use of force that frustrates a nation's ability to defend itself will result in the UN being marginalized, as states will fall back on the expansive right of self-preservation, and inevitably place their own survival above adherence to an international law system that cannot guarantee their security and the safety of their citizens. The signs from the UN are good; patience and support for its efforts are what is needed.

Notes

1   *Report of the Secretary General on the Work of the Organization*, U.N. GAOR, 47th Sess, U.N. Doc A/47/277, S/24111 (1992) para 3.
2   President George H. W. Bush (1990), '"The UN: World Parliament of Peace", Address to the United Nations General Assembly', (1 October), in (1990) 1 *US Dep't. St. Dispatch* 151, 152.
3   Richard Falk and David Kreiger (2002), 'Subverting the UN', *The Nation*, 2002 WL 2210961 (4 November).
4   See generally David Krieger (2003), 'The Bush Administration's Assault on International Law' in Richard Falk and David Krieger (eds.) *The Iraq Crisis and International Law*.
5   Abraham D. Sofaer (2002), 'Judicial Responses to Terror: Issues, Problems and Prospects', *American Society of International Law Proceedings* 250, 255.
6   Bruce Hoffmann (2004), 'Terrorism', Microsoft Encarta Online Encyclopaedia 2004, 20 May 2004 online at http://encarta.msn.com.
7   For example, Dr Bruce Hoffmann notes that: 'The murder of 11 Israeli athletes at the 1972 Olympic Games provides one of the most notorious examples of terrorists' ability to bring their cause to world attention.' He goes on to observe that:

> The PLO effectively exploited the publicity generated by the Munich hostage taking. In 1974 PLO leader Yasir Arafat received an invitation to address the UN General Assembly and the UN subsequently granted special observer status to the PLO. Within a decade, the PLO, an entity not attached to any state, had formal diplomatic relations with more countries (86) than did Israel (72) – the actual, established nation-state. The PLO would likely never have attained such recognition without the attention that its international terrorist campaign focused on the plight of Palestinians in refugee camps.

Hoffmann, 'Terrorism', ibid.
8   Sofaer, 'Judicial Responses to Terror', 255.
9   Ibid.
10 G.A. Res 40/61, 40th sess, 108th plen mtg, [1], [6], U.N. Doc A/RES/40/61 (1985).
11 Over the last 30 years, the international community has negotiated 12 conventions covering terrorism.
12 This approach considers terrorist events as purely criminal acts to be addressed by the domestic criminal justice system and its components. It *ensures due process* and is a more precise instrument for meting out *individualized justice*.
13 Emanuel Gross (2001), 'Thwarting Terrorist Acts by Attacking the Perpetrators or Their Commanders as an Act of Self-Defense: Human Rights Versus the State's Duty to Protect Its Citizens', 15 *Temple International and Comparative Law Journal* 195, 202; see also Abraham D. Sofaer (1989), 'The Sixth Annual Waldemar A. Solf Lecture in International Law: Terrorism, the Law, and the National Defence', 126 *Military Law Review* 89, 89–90.
14 In relation to the rise of terrorism, see Peter Chalk (1996), *West European Terrorism and Counter-Terrorism: The Evolving Dynamic*, New York: St. Martin's Press, specifically Chapters 2 and 4.
15 These sanctions include freezing assets, denying credit or investment funds to countries supporting terrorists, and working with multilateral banks to block loans. Sofaer, 'Judicial Responses to Terror', 251.
16 Quoted from Ravindra V. Parasnis (2001), 'Third World War', *The Rediff Special*, (12 September) online at http://www.rediff.com/news/2001/sep/12spec.htm.
17 Ibid.

18 Christopher L. Blakesley (2003), 'Ruminations on Terrorism and Anti-Terrorism Law and Literature', *University of Miami Law Review* 1041, 1145–1146.
19 Ibid., 1139-40.
20 Sofaer,' Judicial Responses to Terror', 254.
21 Allison Ehlert (2003), 'Iraq at the Apex of Evil', 21 *Berkeley Journal of International Law* 731, 736 See also Massimo Calabresi (2002), 'The Axis of Evil: Is It For Real?; What Bush is Really Saying when He Talks Tough about Rogue States', *Time*, 30 (11 February) (stating that: 'As a phrase, "axis of evil" is misleading. There is no alliance among the three countries Bush chose to label.'); Anna Quindlen (2002), 'The Axis of Re-election', *Newsweek*, 64 (4 March) (remarking that 'the choice of that word to describe the three nations the president singled out seemed peculiar, even bizarre. Bad as they may be, there's little to link them.'); Elisabeth Bumiller (2002), 'Axis of Debate: Hawkish Words', *New York Times*, Week in Review (3 February); Suzanne Daley (2002), 'Many in Europe Voice Worry US Will Not Consult Them', *New York Times*, A12 (31 January).
22 See, e.g., Steven Erlanger (2002), 'Germany Joins Europe's Cry That the US Won't Consult', *New York Times*, A18 (13 February); Dave Clark (2002), 'France's Vedrine Attacks "Simplistic" US Foreign Policy', *Agence France-Presse* (6 February) available at LEXIS, News Library; Ian Black, John Hooper and Oliver Burkeman (2002), 'Bush Warned Over "Axis of Evil": European Leaders Insist Diplomacy is the Way to Deal with Three Nations Singled Out by America', *The Guardian* (London) 13 (5 February 2002).
23 Ian Black, John Hooper, and Oliver Burkeman (2002), 'Bush Warned Over "Axis of Evil": European Leaders Insist Diplomacy is the Way to Deal with Three Nations Singled out by America', *The Guardian* (London), 13 (5 February); Steven Erlanger (2002), 'Russian Aide Warns US Not to Extend War to Iraq', *New York Times*, A10 (4 February 2002); Martin Fletcher (2002), 'Stay out of Iraq, Patten tells America', *The Times* (London) (20 February) available at LEXIS, News Library; Roland Watson (2002), 'President Jiang tells Bush not to Bully Iraq', *The Times* (London) (22 February) available at LEXIS, News Library.
24 Address to the United Nations General Assembly in New York City, 38 *Weekly Compilation of Presidential Documents* 1529 (12 September 2002).
25 Ehlert, 'Iraq at the Apex of Evil', 755.
26 Ibid., 765.
27 Ibid.
28 One of the most complete accounts of what invasion planners had in mind as of Spring 2002 is found in Thom Shanker and David E. Sanger (2002), 'US Envisions Blueprint on Iraq Including Big Invasion Next Year', *New York Times*, 1 (28 April).
29 Mary Ellen O'Connell (2002), 'American Exceptionalism and the International law of Defence', 31 *Denver Journal of International Law and Policy* 43, 44.
30 Ibid.
31 Ibid., 54.
32 George Soros (2003), 'Bush's Inflated Sense of Supremacy', *Financial Times*, 13 (13 March).
33 Charled Krauthammer, quoted in Detlev F. Vagts (2001), 'Hegemonic International Law', 95 *American Journal of International Law* 843.
34 O'Connell, 'American Exceptionalism', 57.
35 Sofaer, 'Judicial Responses to Terror', 259.
36 See *Corfu Channel* (UK v Albania), 1949 I.C.J. 4, 34 (9 April).
37 *Report of the Secretary General on the Work of the Organization*, U.N. GAOR, 54th Sess, Supp No 1, para 66, U.N. Doc A/54/1 (1999).
38 Oscar Schachter (1991), *International Law in Theory and Practice*, 145 (*Developments in International Law Series*, Vol. 13).

39 See Michael Byers and Simon Chesterman ((2003), 'Changing the Rules about Rules? Unilateral Humanitarian Intervention and the Future of International Law', in Holzgrefe and Keohane (eds.) *Humanitarian Intervention: Ethical, Legal and Political Dilemmas,* 202.

40 Patrick McLain (2003), 'Settling the Score with Saddam: Resolution 1441 and the Parallel Justifications for the Use of Force Against Iraq', 13 *Duke Journal of Comparative and International Law* 233, 280.

41 President George W. Bush (2002), Graduation Address at the US Military Academy (1 June), online at htttp://www.whitehouse.gov/news/releases/2002/06/print/20020601-3.html.

42 McLain, 'Settling the Score with Saddam', 285–286. See also Christine Gray (2000), *International Law and the Use of* Force, 23 ('the language of states in their interpretation and application of the UN Charter could operate as a precedent and later be invoked against them').

43 Jason Pedigo (2004), 'Rogue States, Weapons of Mass Destruction, And Terrorism: Was Security Council Approval Necessary for the Invasion of Iraq', 32 *Georgia Journal of International and Comparative Law* 199, 201.

44 Michel Martin (2002), 'A Greedy Bully', ABC News (8 September) online at http://abcnews.go.com/sections/nightline/DailyNews/foreign_journalists020908.html.

45 Michael Bothe (2003), 'Terrorism and the Legality of Pre-Emptive Force', 14 *European Journal of International Law* 227, 233.

46 President George W. Bush (2002), 'The National Security Strategy of the United States of America', 15 (17 September) online at http://www.whitehouse.gov/nsc/nss.pdf (last visited 2 August 2003); *A.P Newswires*, 20 September 2002, available at *Westlaw.*

47 See, for instance, S.C. Res 487 of 19 June 1981 relating to the Israeli attack against the nuclear reactor in Baghdad.

48 Bothe, 233.

49 Ibid., 234.

50 National Security Strategy.

51 Ibid.

52 United Nations Millennium Declaration, G.A. Res 55/2. 8 September 2000, para 9. The full text is available online at http://www.un.org/millennium/declaration/ares552e.htm (visited 20 April 2004).

53 U.N. SCOR, 56th Sess, 4370th mtg, U.N. Doc S/RES/1368 (2001).

54 'To Paris, US Looks Like a "Hyperpower" ', *International Herald Tribune*, 5 February 1999, 5.

55 Pedigo, 'Rogue States', 226. See also Thomas M. Franck (2001), 'When If Ever May States Deploy Military Force without Prior Security Council Authorization?', 5 *Washington University Journal of Law and Policy* 53.

56 Sofaer, 'Judicial Responses to Terror', 258.

57 Ibid., 259.

58 Ibid.

59 Blakesley, 'Ruminations on Terrorism', 1080.

60 McLain, 'Settling the Score with Saddam', 291.

Select Bibliography

Books

Avneri, A. (1970), *The War of Attrition*, Jerusalem, Madim Books.
Bassiouni, M.C. (1974), *International Extradition and World Public Order*, Leyden: Sijthoff ; Dobbs Ferry, N.Y. : Oceana.
Bassiouni, M.C. (ed.) (1988), *Legal Responses to International Terrorism: US Procedural Aspects XV*, Dordrecht; Boston: Norwell, MA: M. Nijhoff.
Bobbitt, P. (2002), *The Shield of Achilles: War, Peace and the Course of History*, New York: Knopf.
Booth, K. and Dunne, T. (2002), *Worlds in Collision: Terror and the Future of Global Order*, London: Palgrave Macmillan.
Brownlie, I. (1963), *International Law and the Use of Force by States*, Oxford: Clarendon Press.
Brownlie, I. (1983), *System of the Law of Nations, State Responsibility*, Oxford [Oxfordshire]; New York: Clarendon Press.
Cassesse, A. (1986), *International Law in a Divided World*, Oxford: Clarendon Press; New York: Oxford University Press.
Colbert, E. (1948), *Retaliation in International Law*, New York: King's Crown Press.
Crelinsten, R. and Schmid, A.P. (1992) (eds), *Western Responses to Terrorism: A Twenty-Five Year Balance Sheet*, Aldershot, UK; Brookfield, VT: Ashgate.
Erickson, R. (1989), *Legitimate Use of Force Against State Sponsored Terrorism*, Maxwell Air Force Base, Ala.: Air University Press.
Falk, R. and Krieger, D. (eds), *The Iraq Crisis and International Law*, Santa Barbara: Nuclear Age Peace Foundation.
Ferencz, B. (1975), *Defining International Aggression, The Search for World Peace: A Documentary History and Analysis*, Dobbs Ferry, NY: Oceana Publications, Vol. I.
Goodrich, L.M., Hambro, E. and Simons, A.P. (1969), *Charter of the United Nations*, New York: Columbia University Press.
Gray, C. (2000), *International Law and the Use of Force*, Oxford; New York: Oxford University Press.
Haggen-Macher, P. (1983), *Grotius et al Doctrine de la Guerre Juste*, Paris: Presses Universitaires de France.
Hall, W.E. (1880), *A Treatise on International Law*, Oxford: Clarendon Press.
Hannum, H. (1996), *Autonomy, Sovereignty, and Self-determination: The Accommodation of Conflicting Rights*, Philadelphia, PA: University of Pennsylvania Press.

Henderson, H. (2001), *Global Terrorism: The Complete Reference Guide*, New York: Checkmark Books.

Henkin, L. (1991), 'The Use of Force: Law and US Policy', in *Right v Might: International Law and the Use of Force*, New York: Council on Foreign Relations.

Higgins, R. and Flory, M. (eds) (1997), *Terrorism and International Law*, London; New York: Routledge.

Hindmarsh, A. (1933), *Force in Peace: Force Short of War in International Relations*, Cambridge, Mass.: Harvard University Press.

Hoffman, B. (1998), *Inside Terrorism*, New York: Columbia University Press.

Hyde, C. (2nd ed., 1945), *International Law: Chiefly as Interpreted and Applied by the United States*, Boston: Little, Brown.

Kalshoven, F. (1971), *Belligerent Reprisals*, Leyden: Sijthoff.

Kegley Jr., C.W. (1990), *International Terrorism: Characteristics, Causes, Controls*, New York, NY: St. Martin's.

Kegley Jr., W.R. (ed.) (1990), *International Terrorism*, New York, NY: St. Martin's.

Lauterpacht, H. (ed.) (1952), *Oppenheim's International Law: Disputes, War and Neutrality*, London: Longmans, Vol. II.

Long, D. (1990), *The Anatomy of Terrorism*, New York: Free Press; Toronto: Collier Macmillan Canada; New York: Maxwell Macmillan International.

Maogoto, J. (2004), *War Crimes and Realpolitik: International Justice from World War I into the 21st Century*, Boulder: Lynne Rienner Publishers.

McDougal, M.S. and Feliciano, F.P. (1961), *Law and Minimum World Public Order: The Legal Regulation of International Coercion*, New Haven: Yale University Press.

Montgomery, J.F. (1947), *Hungary, the Unwilling Satellite*, New York: Devin-Adair Co.

Moore, J. (1906), *A Digest of International Law as Embodied in Diplomatic Discussions, Treaties and other International Agreements, International Awards, the Decisions of Municipal Courts, and the Writings of Jurists*, Washington DC: Government Printing Office.

Murphy, J. (1978), *Legal Aspects of International Terrorism*, Lexington, Mass.: Lexington Books.

Murphy, J. (1989), *State Support of International Terrorism: Legal, Political and Economic Dimensions*, Boulder, Colo.: Westview Press; London: Mansell Pub.

Netanyahu, B. (ed.) (1986), *Terrorism: How the West Can Win*, New York: Farrar, Straus, Giroux.

Nicolson, H. (1961), *The Congress of Vienna: A Study in Allied Unity; 1812–1822*, London: Constable.

Oppenheim, L. (1st ed., 1905), *International Law: A Treatise (Peace)*, London: Longmans & Green.

Phillimore, R. (1879-89), *Commentaries Upon International Law*, London: Butterworths.

Russell, R.B. (1958), *A History of the UN Charter; The Role of the United States, 1940–1945*, Washington, Brookings Institution.

Schindler, D. and Toman, J. (eds) (3rd revised ed.) (1988), *The Laws of Armed Conflicts: A Collection of Conventions, Resolutions, and other Documents*, Dordrecht, Netherlands: Nijhoff; Geneva: Henry Dunant Institute; Norwell, MA,

Boston, London, Publication for The International School of Peace, Ginn and Company.

Scott, J.B. (ed.) (1908), *Texts of the Peace Conferences at The Hague, 1899 and 1907*.

Scott, J.B. (ed.) (1917), *The Reports to The Hague Conferences of 1899 and 1907*, Oxford: Clarendon Press.

Shaw, M.N. (4th ed., 1997), *International Law*, Cambridge: Cambridge University Press.

Sorenson, M. *Manual of Public International Law*, London, Melbourne [etc.]: Macmillan; New York: St. Martin's.

Stern, J. (1999), *The Ultimate Terrorists*, Cambridge, Mass.: Harvard University Press.

Stone, J. (1958), *Aggression and World Order; A Critique of United Nations Theories of Aggression*, Berkeley, University of California Press.

Sunga, L.S. (1997), *The Emerging System of International Criminal Law: Developments in Codification and Implementation*, The Hague; Boston: Kluwer Law International.

Twiss, T. (1861), *The Law of Nations Considered as Independent Political Communities. On the Right and Duties of Nations in Time of Peace*, Oxford: The University Press.

Watson, A. (1992), *The Evolution of International Society: A Comparative Historical Analysis*, London: Routledge.

Webster, C.K. (2nd ed., 1934), *The Congress of Vienna, 1814–1815*, London: H.M. Stationery Office.

Westlake, J. (1904-07), *International Law*, Cambridge: The University Press.

Wilson, H.A. (1988), *International Law and the Use of Force by National Liberation Movements*, Oxford [Oxfordshire]: Clarendon Press; New York: Oxford University Press.

Articles

Baker, Mark (1987), 'Terrorism and the Inherent Right of Self-Defence (A Call to Amend Article 51 of the United Nations Charter)', 10 *Houston Journal of International Law* 25.

Bassiouni, M. Cherif (2002), 'Legal Control of International Terrorism: A Policy-Oriented Assessment', 43 *Harvard International Law Journal* 83.

Beard, Jack (2002), 'Military Action Against Terrorists under International Law: America's New War on Terror: The Case for Self-Defence under International Law', 25 *Harvard Journal of Law and Public Policy* 559.

Beres, Louis R. (1992), 'The Permissibility of State-Sponsored Assassination during Peace and War', 5 *Temple International and Comparative Law Journal* 231.

Beres, Louis Rene (1994), 'On International Law and Nuclear Terrorism', 24 *Georgia Journal of International and Comparative Law* 1.

Beres, Louis Beres (1995), 'The Meaning of Terrorism: Jurisprudential and Definitional Clarifications', 28 *Vanderbilt Journal of Transnational Law* 239.

Bisharat, George E. (2003), 'Tyranny with Justice: Alternatives to War in the Confrontation with Iraq', 7 *Journal of Gender, Race and Justice* 1.

Blakesley, Christopher L. (1987), 'Jurisdiction as Legal Protection against Terrorism', 19 *Connecticut Law Review* 895.

Bonafede, Michael C. (2002), 'Here, There and Everywhere: Assessing the Proportionality Doctrine and the US Uses of Force in Response to Terrorism after the September 11 Attacks', 88 *Cornell Law Review* 155.

Bowett, Derek (1972), 'Reprisals Involving Recourse to Armed Force', 66 *American Journal of International Law* 1.

Boyle, Francis (1986), 'Preserving the Rule of Law in the War against International Terrorism', 8 *Whittier Law Review* 735.

Brown, Bartram (2000), 'Humanitarian Intervention at a Crossroads', 41 *William and Mary Law Review* 1683.

Burris, Christopher C. (1997), 'Re-Examining the Prisoner of War Status of PLO Fedayeen', 22 *North Carolina Journal of International Law and Commercial Regulation* 943.

Byers, Michael (2002), 'Terrorism, the Use of Force and International Law after 11 September', 51 *International and Comparative Law Quarterly* 401.

Campbell, Leah (2000), 'Defending against Terrorism: A Legal Analysis of the Decision to Strike Sudan and Afghanistan', 74 *Tulane Law Review* 1067.

Carpenter, Allegra (1995), 'The International Criminal Court and the Crime of Aggression', 64(2) *Nordic Journal of International Law-Acta Scandinavica Juris Gentium* 223.

Coll, Alberto R. (1987), 'The Legal and Moral Adequacy of Military Responses to Terrorism', 81 *American Society of International Law Proceedings* 297.

Crona, Spencer and Richardson, Neal (1996), 'Justice for War Criminals of Invisible Armies: A New Legal and Military Approach to Terrorism', 21 *Oklahoma City University Law Review* 349.

Eisner, Douglas (1993), 'Humanitarian Intervention in the Post-Cold War Era', 11 *Boston University International Law Journal* 195.

Falk, Richard (1969), 'The Beirut Raid and the International Law of Retaliation', 63 *American Journal of International Law* 415.

Falk, Richard (1985), 'The Decline of Normative Restraint in International Relations', 10 *Yale Journal of International Law* 265.

Franck, Thomas M. (2001), 'The Institute for Global Legal Studies Inaugural Colloquium: The UN and the Protection of Human Rights: When If Ever May States Deploy Military Force without Prior Security Council Authorization?' 5 *Washington University Journal of Law and Policy* 57.

Glennon, Michael J., (2002), 'The Fog of Law: Inherence, Self-defence and Incoherence in Article 51 of the United Nations Charter', 25 *Harvard Journal of Law and Public Policy* 539.

Gross, Emmanuel (2001), 'Thwarting Terrorist Acts By Attacking The Perpetrators or Their Commanders as an Act of Self-Defense: Human Rights Versus The State's Duty To Protect Its Citizens', 15 *Temple International and Comparative Law Journal* 195.

Intoccia, Gregory Francis (1987), 'American Bombing of Libya: An International Legal Analysis', 19 *Case Western Reserve Journal of International Law* 177.

Kash, Douglas (1993), 'Abductions of Terrorists in International Airspace and on the High Seas', 8 *Florida Journal of International Law* 65.

Kelly, Michael J. (2003), 'Time Warp to 1945 – Resurrection of the Reprisal and Anticipatory Self-defence Doctrines in International Law', 13 *Journal of Transnational Law Policy* 1.

Levitt, Geoffrey (1989), 'The International Legal Response to Terrorism: A Reevaluation', 60 *University of Colorado Law Review* 533.

Lillich, Richard and Paxman, John (1976), 'State Responsibility for Injuries to Aliens Occasioned by Terrorist Activities', 26 *American University Law Review* 217.

Lohr, Michael F. (1985), 'Legal Analysis of US Military Responses to State-Sponsored International Terrorism', 34 *Naval Law Review* 1.

Luigi, Condorelli (1989), 'The Imputability to States of Acts of International Terrorism', 19 *Israel Yearbook on Human Rights* 233.

Mallison Jr., W.T. and Mallison, S.V. (1973), 'The Concept of Public Purpose Terror in International Law: Doctrines and Sanctions to Reduce the Destruction of Human and Material Values', 18 *Howard Law Journal* 412.

Malzahn, Scott (2002), 'State Sponsorship and Support of International Terrorism: Customary Norms of State Responsibility', 26 *Hastings International and Comparative Law Review* 83.

Manning, Shirlyce (December 1995-January 1996), 'The United States' Response to International Air Safety', 61 *Journal of Air Law and Commerce* 505.

Maogoto, Jackson (2002), 'Aggression: Supreme International Offence Still in Search of Definition', 6 *Southern Cross University Law Review* 278.

Maogoto, Jackson (2003), 'Rushing to Break the Law? The Bush Doctrine of Pre-Emptive Strikes and the UN Charter on the Use of Force', 7 *University of Western Sydney Law Review* 1.

Maogoto, Jackson (2004), 'New Frontiers, Old Problems: The War on Terror and the Notion of Anticipating the Enemy', 51 *Netherlands International Law Review* 1.

McLain, Patrick (2003), 'Settling the Score with Saddam: Resolution 1441 and the Parallel Justifications for the Use of Force against Iraq', 13 *Duke Journal of Comparative and International Law* 233.

Murphy, John (1989), 'Defining International Terrorism: A Way Out of the Quagmire', 19 *Israel Yearbook on Human Rights* 13.

Murphy, John F. (1980), 'Terrorism: Documents of International and Local Control', 74 *American Journal of International Law* 711.

Paust, Jordan J. (1986), 'Responding Lawfully to International Terrorism: The Use of Force Abroad', 8 *Whittier Law Review* 711.

Porras, Ileana M. (1994), 'On Terrorism: Reflections on Violence and the Outlaw', 12 *Utah Law Review* 119.

Posteraro, Christopher Clarke (2002), 'Intervention in Iraq: Towards A Doctrine of Anticipatory Counter-Terrorism, Counter-Proliferation Intervention', 15 *Florida Journal of International Law* 151, 155.

Raimo, Tyler (1999), 'Winning at the Expense of Law: The Ramifications of Expanding Counter-Terrorism Law Enforcement Jurisdiction Overseas', 14 *American University International Law Review* 1473.

Reisman, W. Michael (1999), 'International Legal Responses to Terrorism', 22 *Houston Journal of International Law* 3.

Roberts, Guy B. (1987), 'Self-Help in Combating State-Sponsored Terrorism: Self-Defence and Peacetime Reprisals', 19 *Case Western Reserve Journal of International Law* 243.

Rowles, James P. (1987), 'Military Responses to Terrorism: Substantive and Procedural Constraints in International Law', 81 *American Society of International Law Proceedings* 287.

Rowles, James P. (1987), 'The Legal and Moral Adequacy of Military Responses to Terrorism: Substantive and Procedural Constraints in International Law', *American Society of International Law, Proceedings of the 81st Annual Meeting* 307.

Schachter, Oscar (1984), 'The Right of States to Use Armed Force', 82 *Michigan Law Review* 1620.

Schachter, Oscar (1989), 'The Extra-Territorial Use of Force against Terrorist Bases', 11 *Houston Journal of International Law* 309.

Scheideman, Sara N. (2000), 'Standards of Proof in Forcible Responses to Terrorism', 50 *Syracuse Law Review* 249.

Seymour, Philip A. (1990), 'The Legitimacy of Peacetime Reprisal as a Tool against State-Sponsored Terrorism', 39 *Naval Law Review* 221.

Sofaer, Abraham D. (1986), 'Terrorism and the Law', 64 *Foreign Affairs* 901.

Stahn, Carsten (2003), 'International Law Under Fire; Terrorist Acts as "Armed Attacks": The Right to Self-Defense, Article 51(1/2) of the UN Charter, and International Terrorism', 27 *Fletcher Forum of World Affairs* 35.

Terry, James (1986), 'Countering State-Sponsored Terrorism: A Law-Policy Analysis', 36 *Naval Law Review* 159.

Travalio, Gregory M. (2000), 'Terrorism, International Law, and the Use of Military Force', 18 *Wisconsin International Law Journal* 145.

Travalio, Greg and Altenburg, John (2003), 'Terrorism, State Responsibility, and the Use of Military Force', 4 *Chicago Journal of International Law* 97.

Waldock, Claud H.M. (1952), 'The Regulation of the Use of Force by Individual States in International Law', 2 *Recueil Des Cours* 451.

Warriner, Wallace (1988), 'The Unilateral Use of Coercion under International Law: A Legal Analysis of the United States Raid on Libya on April 14, 1986', 37 *Naval Law Review* 49.

Wolfenson, Andrew (1989-90), 'The U.S. Courts and the Treatment of Suspects Abducted Abroad Under International Law', 13 *Fordham International Law Journal* 705.

Yonah, Alexander (1999), 'Terrorism in the Twenty-First Century: Threats and Responses', 12 *DePaul Business Law Journal* 59.

Yoo, John (2003), 'International Law and the War in Iraq', 97 *American Journal of International Law* 563.

International Instruments

Convention for the Prevention and Punishment of Terrorism, 16 November 1937, art. 19 League of Nations O.J. 23 (1938).

Convention for the Suppression of Unlawful Acts against the Safety of Civil Aviation, opened for signature 23 September 1971, 974 U.N.T.S. 177.

Convention for the Suppression of Unlawful Seizure of Aircraft, opened for signature 16 December 1970, 860 U.N.T.S. 105.

Convention on Offences and Certain Other Acts Committed On Board Aircraft, opened for signature 14 September 1963, 704 U.N.T.S. 219.

Convention on the Prevention and Punishment of Crimes against Internationally Protected Persons, Including Diplomatic Agents, opened for signature 14 December 1973, 1035 U.N.T.S. 167.

Convention on the Safety of United Nations and Associated Personnel, G.A. Res 59, U.N. GAOR, 49th Sess, U.N. Doc A/49/59 (1994).

Convention to Prevent and Punish Acts of Terrorism Taking the Form of Crimes Against Persons and Related Extortion that are of International Significance, O.A.S. Doc A/6/Doc 88 rev 1, corr1 (2 February 1971) reprinted in 10 I.L.M. 255.

Covenant of the League of Nations, 2 Bevans 43.

Declaration on Principles of International Law Concerning Friendly Relations and Co-operation among States in accordance with the Charter of the United Nations, G.A. Res 2625, 25 U.N. GAOR Supp. (No 28), U.N. Doc A/8028 (1970).

Definition of Aggression, G.A. Res 3314, U.N. GAOR, 29th Sess, 2319th plen mtg, Annex, Supp No 31, U.N. Doc A/RES/3314 (1974).

General Treaty for the Renunciation of War, signed at Paris 27 August 1928, 94 L.N.T.S. 47; United States Statutes at Large Vol. 46, Part 2.

Geneva Convention Relative to the Protection of Civilian Persons in Time of War, opened for signature 12 August 1949, 75 U.N.T.S. 287.

International Convention for the Suppression of Terrorist Bombings, 9 January 1998, 37 I.L.M. 251.

Protocol Additional to the Geneva Conventions of 12 August 1949, and relating to the Protection of Victims of Non-International Armed Conflicts, Geneva, 10 June 1977.

Protocol for the Suppression of Unlawful Acts of Violence at Airports Serving Civil Aviation, ICAO Doc. 9518; reprinted in 27 I.L.M. 627.

Treaty of Peace between the Allied and Associated Powers and Germany, concluded at Versailles, 28 June 1919.

Index